MW00984305

I Have

Everything

I Need

2 people, 2 years, 20 countries:
Trading leisure and enlightenment

for sunburns, scars, and blisters.

Written and Illustrated
by Bridget McGee Houchins

Edited by Stephen Courtney

Copyright © 2019 by Bridget McGee Houchins.

All rights reserved. No part of this publication may be reproduced, distributed or transmitted in any form or by any means, including photocopying, recording, or other electronic or mechanical methods, without the prior written permission of the author, except in the case of brief quotations embodied in critical reviews and certain other noncommercial uses permitted by copyright law. For permission requests, write to the author at the web-address: www.roamsandwrites.com

Some names have been changed to protect the privacy of individuals.

Artwork and Illustrations: Bridget McGee Houchins

Book Layout: ©BookDesignTemplates.com

Copyeditor: Stephen Courtney

ISBN (paperback): 978-1-7332217-0-2

ISBN (ebook): 978-1-7332217-1-9

Dedicated to everyone who supported us, cheered us on, gave us a couch to sleep on, or fed our dogs and cat during these years of adventures. As well as to the many friends, family, acquaintances, inspirational strangers, and pets who have passed on during our travels or the writing of this book.

Contents

Introduction: There Once Was a Girl from San Diego

I was up with the sunrise, loading the last of the things I needed into my brand-new teal Osprey hiking backpack: snacks, a sweatshirt, Chapstick, hair-ties, Swiffer pads, a compact yellow vacuum, toilet cleaner, dusting cloths, and a telescoping tub scrubber, to name a few. I threw my backpack over my shoulder and headed out the door. I am ready to train for hiking the Pacific Crest Trail.

It was February 2015 in Oakland, California, and sure, one might train for a 2,650 mile long-distance backpacking trip from the Mexican border to the Canadian border with the help of a personal trainer or by actually backpacking; but with limited free time and money, I had decided to be somewhat resourceful and attempted to turn work into working out.

Two weeks prior, I had lost my job as a personal assistant, and, after first partying a week of unemployment away in celebration of my twenty-ninth birthday, I decided to try supplementing my income by cleaning houses. Housecleaning meant hauling a large luggage bag in and out of my car, onto public transportation, through miles of downtown San Francisco city blocks, and through puddles of steaming sidewalk pee, just to work my butt off scrubbing the shower pubes of wealthy people's million-dollar condos. After only one day of tripping over the cleaning company's standard luggage bag, I was ready to toss it off the Bay Bridge.

If only I could carry my vacuum and cleaning supplies on my back instead of in a rolling bag three times my size, I thought. I went home and ripped my fresh new hiking backpack out of its plastic wrapping. *I shall backpack my way through puddles of steaming pee to sweat in rich people's houses!* I decided. I already looked like a nerd, now I just looked like a homeless nerd who smelled strongly of grapefruit scented all-purpose cleaning spray. This way, even on the days where I was too swamped with school to make the gym or go on a practice hike, my day would still end with sore muscles, blistered feet, and broken fingernails.

Although I was good at planning and my boyfriend of five years, Tim, was good at saving, the limited money we had to put away meant half-assing much of our gear and preparations for our two years of travel. Tim's teenage years and young adulthood included a lot of "urban backpacking," one might say. He was no stranger to carrying a backpack and living on the cheap for years at a time. He'd left San Diego at the age of eighteen to ride freight trains across the country, hide goat heads for the police to find in busted squats, and throw punk shows in sewers; eventually "settling down" to collect unwanted dogs and drive box trucks.

I had grown up doing quite a bit of fishing, camping, and day hikes, so of course - like any other pretty little princess - I would often be found rolling in dirt and pocketing lizards. My childhood hobbies included thinking about dogs, constantly making art, and attempting to get the other little girls into *Star Wars*. As a seven-year-old, I once spent multiple weeks digging through our apartment building's dumpsters, foraging for the materials to build a pirate ship in the neighboring canyon. And no, my parents were not happy about that. Although neither Tim or I had ever thru-hiked a long distance trail, we both felt such a thing wouldn't be too far out of our comfort zones.

My story started in San Diego County. Well before my time, my great-great-grandparents left Ireland to immigrate to the United States. After starting their family in Pennsylvania, their children eventually moved, deciding to permanently settle down in El Cajon, California, which is where I write the pages you are reading. El Cajon is a suburb of San Diego County, east of the city. When my grandpa grew up here, it was rural, but during my lifetime it had become known for things such as meth, racists, homelessness, and being a generally ugly and boring place. Today, it is one of the top two cities in the country for Christian Iraqi immigrants, as well as having taken in many Syrian refugees and people from other Middle Eastern countries. If you walked down dusty ol' Main Street today, you would see cafés sporting Trump flags sandwiched between Middle Eastern markets.

I never thought I would find myself back in El Cajon as an adult, but it has its benefits. Friends who live in San Diego's city center may get to walk or bike to the best bars and restaurants, but for us they are only a fifteen-minute drive away. We also don't have to worry as much about things such as lack of parking, car break-ins, street sweeping, slumlord rent hikes, pet rent, and so on. We have a great situation living in an illegal pool house we rent from friends. Instead of hearing car alarms, we hear hawks cawing and coyotes yipping. I definitely don't want to be here forever, but for now it is a weird version of home again. Like living in a new place, with constant echoes of a past life coming back like déjà vu. The Vons down the street is where I sometimes get my groceries, but thirteen years ago it was where I would take my friend Sam to steal bottles of Captain Morgan. Sam and I would run the same drill with the 7-Eleven I pass to go to my bank. The 7-Eleven next to my veterinarian's office is the one James got a job at years after his picture hung on the wall to warn employees he was a known beer thief.

I love it when people new to San Diego use their recently acquired knowledge of the city to warn me about El Cajon. "Yeah, don't go there," they all say. "San Diego has better weather than any place on earth," they claim. I just laugh.

"You must have never spent a summer east of the beach," I respond. I grew up all too familiar with hundred-degree summers, driving thirty minutes to the beach just to arrive to overcast skies and a cold breeze. When I turned sixteen and got my driver's license, I lived so far east I would have to wait for the ice to melt on my truck's windshield before I could drive the winding back roads to school during winter. I guess it's not too strange people don't know these kinds of things about San Diego. I once had a roommate who swore not one place in the state of California got "real snow." You think she would have seen a topographical map of the United States at some point in her upbringing. The house we shared for a year was also roughly only three hours from the Sierra mountain range, which contains two of the ten tallest mountains in the country.

My parents divorced in their twenties, when I was one year old, deciding to split me 50-50 from then until I was almost a teenager. I spent two weeks with one parent, then two weeks with the other, back and forth for my entire childhood. I once had a counselor tell me that because I was bounced back and forth, never really having a childhood home due to my parents moving around San Diego quite a bit as well, would result in me never wanting to settle down as an adult. She told me I would never be able to stay put for the rest of my life. I think she was completely wrong, but my childhood definitely made drifting around feel normal to me.

I liked my childhood. I was one of the kids who got two birthdays and two Christmases. One of the few drawbacks was that my friends never knew which phone number to reach me at. Most of my friends whose parents also weren't together only lived with one of them full-time while the other got visitation.

I grew up climbing trees outside of apartment buildings, riding my bike down alleys until the sun set, having lizards as pets, and feeding skunks cat treats from my dad's bedroom window. Some weekends my dad would wake me before sunrise so we could eat breakfast while fishing for trout beside the lake. I would still be in my pajamas, curled in a blanket with a donut in one hand and a child's fishing rod in the other. I camped a lot as a Girl Scout, as well as with my dad when we would go on fishing trips in the Eastern Sierra.

I went to a more urban middle school where I was a complete dork. I knew a lot of the popular kids because we went to Elementary school together, yet we went our separate ways as we aged. I was painfully shy and never talked to anyone I didn't know. There was no way I would ever be popular. My clothes weren't cool, I hated the hottest pop music. I wasn't outwardly witty or funny, and boys didn't talk to me. I couldn't even keep up good grades. Puberty gave me acne and turned my dark brown hair thick and frizzy. I was short, yet also grew so fast my jeans always fit me like high-waters. It didn't help I had a lanky twig body with size eight feet.

I wished the kids into punk and skateboarding would take notice of me, so I decorated my binder with the CD inserts of all of my favorite bands. 90's Offspring, Green Day, and Blink 182. I used white-out to turn my backpack straps checkered like the Ska kids, because I thought it was cool. I figured since I was already an outcast, I might as well look like one too. I started wearing neon pants, skate brand shirts, and Vans shoes. As a child I wore No Fear shirts with Gecko shorts, so it really didn't feel much different. My look had helped me gain a few new friends. People now had something to talk to me about. I did also get called a poser once or twice, and popular girls would loudly say I was ugly while talking to each other. I really didn't care. I now had some sort of visual personality, and it felt good.

My mom moved even further east, giving me new options of where I could go to high school. I could go to the high school right next door to my middle school, with my newer friends as well as the girls I had been friends with almost all my life. With them came the popular kids who thought I was a nerd, as well as three new classes of Sophomores, Juniors, and Seniors to also think of me as a nerd. This high school would be exactly like my middle school. Another option would be to go to a brand-new high school and be part of the first graduating class. I would know nobody, no one would know me. The first year would be just us Freshman, followed by us as Sophomores with a new class of Freshman, and so on. I made my choice to move east to the tract homes and attended the newly opened school nicknamed "horse shit high."

This new school was my chance to show up as whoever I wanted to be, with no one to tell me differently. Well, except for my parents. I spent the entire summer looking into new punk bands and spending the little money I had on CDs at Taang records on the beach, and Blue Meanie records in El Cajon. I cut my hair short, got a studded belt and choker, and switched from Vans to Converse high tops. I still looked like a nerd. I wore flared blue jeans with plain tank tops. I was nervous on my first day. I was still extremely quiet. If no one had approached me I would probably go all four years not making any friends. But after my first class of the day had let out, a tall spikey haired punk boy greeted me in the hallway.

"My name is Lewis. I'm getting all of the punk kids to meet on the stage for lunch. You should come."

"Okay," I said. Then he walked off. *Me? He thinks I'm a punk kid*, I thought. It really couldn't have gone any better. Some of the kids I met on the stage left our school after a year or so, some migrated to other friend groups not long after, and others quickly became my best friends - some which still are today. Our punk kid group evolved and took shape over the next four years with me being the only punk girl for most of it. Quickly the nerdiness faded away and I became a full-blown street punk. I had spiky hair with bleached bangs, winged eyeliner, sewn up skinny jeans, band shirts, Creepers, and wore ripped tights with leopard print mini skirts. We shared mix-tapes and mix-CDs, and I got into all of the best punk music. I went to shows or beach bonfires in town as often as I could get a ride. One time I took city buses for three hours to see Conflict play at a venue on the beach. Their roadies had to sneak me into their show because the age limit was sixteen and up and I was only fifteen. Getting out of the suburb meant you could buy a new CD and bring it back for the entire group to share.

Besides the punks, the other subgroups in our lunch spot at school were the goths, "skate punks," a non-racist skinhead or two, and a few people with unrelated interests who were drawn to us, such as Cancer-Stick Nick the openly gay communist. The "skate punks" wore Dickies with band shirts and skate shoes. They were into skateboarding and more mainstream bands like Social Distortion or Pennywise, and didn't really go to shows. Most of the goths were nerdy dudes who wore trench coats and played Magic the Gathering. Except for Tracy who was more of your classic batcave goth chick. She instantly became one of my close friends.

Every Friday after school, people from our group of friends would meet up and walk a mile and a half down the dusty highway past horse ranches to the shopping center on the other side of the hill. We called this shopping center "Rancho," and behind it, "The Forest." The only reason why the huge hill behind the shopping center wasn't littered with tract homes was because in its hundreds of acres of trees and shrubs lived an endangered hummingbird, making the area a refuge and therefore illegal to build on. This was the case with our other hidden hangout spots around the suburb as well, with names such as: The Other Forest, Punk Rock, James' Rock, Fuck Rock (which was not named by us, but by some middle schoolers years before), and The Plateau. There was also the Space Pad. A UFO group in El Cajon called The Unarius Academy of Sciences bought land out in the boonies to build a literal space pad to make things more convenient for extraterrestrial visitors. It became a teenage drinking spot.

The Rancho shopping center consisted of a movie theater, Target, grocery store, coffee shop, fast food chains, and a mom and pop candy store that for some reason let us keep our backpacks in their back room until closing time. This Friday night migration tripled the size of our friend group, combining it with the punk kids from the other two nearby high schools. It wasn't just the punks who hung out at Rancho, but every type of high school kid in the area. Preppy couples would flirt and go on dates to the theater, the Christian Iraqi kids, called Chaldeans, would wear button down shirts and slacks and get dropped off in limousines owned by one of their family member's businesses. Runaways would prop open the movie theater back doors so they could sleep under the theater curtains at night. Not only was this the hang out for all of our time spent in high school, but until we were all about twenty-one and started slowly moving away. Until Rancho was no more. Heroin infiltrating heavily was another factor in the end of an era.

The stories of "The Rancho Rats" could have a book of their own. Maybe titled Unbelievable Stories of Teenage Mischief, featuring the people who don't want to be reminded of what they've done. The local cops hated us. Justin would carry receipts of recent purchases in his pocket to stop from being detained for loitering, which never helped him. Sam threw an empty forty bottle at a curb to smash it, which ended up bouncing backward and smashing his entire back car window instead. Justin poured gasoline on a Target shopping cart in the parking lot just to light it and watch it melt. We spent weekends in Eddie's van, whose mascot was a dead pigeon in a Carl's Junior hamburger box who remained in the van for at least a few months. He put it in the microwave during a party at Nick's house when his parents were out of town, and that was the end of the pigeon. There was the time Josh flew around the shopping center in circles on his skateboard fully naked, while a group of high school guys tried to chase him down yelling insults and threatening to beat him up. He ducked behind a bush and threw his clothes back on, popping back out to join us just as the mob rounded the corner looking for him.

"Where did he go?? Where did the faggot go?!" they demanded.

Josh enthusiastically responded, "I don't know, he just kept going!" and they ran on looking for him, not realizing they had just talked to the person they were looking for. For a bunch of homophobic dudes, it was pretty hilarious that they could only recognize him by his genitals.

We got used to being accused of everything inside and outside of school, being constantly told to empty our pockets, and the wonderful greeting of "security to the liquor aisle" over the loudspeaker any time one of us walked into the grocery store to buy snacks. A good 85% of the time we weren't even up to any trouble. There was even a time when three of us were threatened a citizen's arrest because Eddie turned on a water spigot. I was still a sweet and quiet kid. I never got into drugs. Not even weed. Not even cigarettes. My image and the people I hung out with meant I was deemed a bad kid by default, which was also the same for some of my friends.

I technically moved out at seventeen. I moved into the house my high school boyfriend lived at with his dad and sister, after my mom's condo came close to burning down in a wildfire and was uninhabitable for a few weeks. At nineteen we broke up, and I found myself with no real place to go. My parents' houses didn't always have space for me, so I spent the next two years living where I could stay for free, between my parent's houses, another boyfriend's house, and the hall closet of a cigarette-smoke-filled punk house apartment. I worked part-time jobs on and off and attempted to go to Community College full-time, when I wasn't dropping or failing classes.

Around this period of time, we ventured deeper and deeper into the forest, using a secret creek crossing we knew the cops would never pass. We realized if we put our change together for Stone Arrogant Bastard we would get a better buzz than if we bought Mickey's forties or a jug of Carlo Rossi. We would drink next to illegal campfires in the nature preserve with cops having no idea how to get to us. Justin and Dan would pull crawdads out of the creek and let them fight, which would make Julie cry.

At twenty-one we started drinking in Rancho somewhat legally. A pizza shop across the street from the movie theater had all draft beers on sale for two dollars every Thursday. And for some strange fucking idea they embraced our group with open arms. The small corner of the front patio near the parking lot would be jam-packed with up to thirty of us, stacking up empty pint glasses in towers across the table. People would be standing in the parking lot, leaning over the railing to chat and chain smoke. Justin would blare music out of a portable speaker. A bunch of us would buy pints for close friends who were underage. This was the beginning of me and my best friend Dionna's relationship, who I had met watching crawdad fights in the forest and chatting between clouds of smoke in the apartment.

My boyfriend at the time was from the Bay Area, and planned on moving back and transferring to San Francisco State University. He told me I would like San Francisco, and I believed him. I wanted to move. To see more. So I applied for a school in San Francisco as well, without ever having been to the Bay Area, and made my own way up with help from my parents. I got a room with no door and no windows between Oakland and Berkeley for the summer until I was able to move to the Outer Sunset in San Francisco. A few of my Rancho Rat friends, Stephan and

James, ended up moving to San Francisco's Outer Sunset as well. Stephan before me, and James not long after. I made some new friends, but none of them were like my friends back home. In fact, my boyfriend wasn't like them either.

Two years living back and forth between San Francisco and the East Bay left me feeling like I was still stuck in a rut. I felt like I needed more. I didn't have the money or knowledge of how to travel by myself. I adopted a fifteen pound, five-year-old mutt who I named Knox, whose name I stole from the singer of The Vibrators. Almost once a month Knox and I would drive through the night back to San Diego to couch surf at my old friends' new punk houses. I ran out of money for school and maxed out the amount of loans they would give me as a dependent, and on top of that I was robbed at gunpoint outside of a friend's house. Once more I was left feeling I had no place to go. I packed up my things and left, making couch surfing San Diego my home until I could afford to get a house with friends.

It was the Summer of 2009, which ended up being one of the best and worst years of my life. I lived with friends for a bit then stayed with my mom while I could, even though I had no bedroom at her house so my things remained in boxes. I was sitting on her couch by myself when I got the call that one of my brothers had committed suicide. It was not long after he had followed my footsteps by moving to San Francisco. I had become unstable in ways I didn't know were possible. I was twenty-three and I was at an all-time low. I continued to hang out at the punk bar so I wasn't by myself. I used the fact that I had nothing to my advantage by hopping into vans and leaving town for punk festivals and shows around the West Coast. I spent a weekend waking up in an old Rancho Rat friend's bed to roosters crowing through the screen-less windows while a well-known European punk band did coke next to the fire pit in the backyard all night long. That December Tim and I started dating, then early the next year I found a decent job and moved into an apartment with Dionna. After a year at our apartment, Knox and I left to live out of a backpack on a docked sailboat for a few months to save money then moved to Oakland with Tim.

Tim had a similar upbringing as me, which was refreshing. Not a lot had to be explained to each other. We both grew up in East County, and had even attended the same middle school, although Tim attended five years prior to me. We went to a lot of the same punk shows when I was a young teenager and he was just out of high school. We had mutual friends both new and from when we were teenagers. Our paths after high school were what differed the most. While I attempted the college kid thing, Tim left home the minute he turned eighteen. Squatting in San Diego after working and living with friends, then leaving to do the same thing across the country until his mid-twenties. I loved hearing his stories and sometimes wished I chose a similar path instead of slowly working my youth away for a degree I never completed, stuck in two different four-year relationships that didn't last. At the same time I was thankful for what I had, the opportunities I was given, and the friends I became closer with along the way.

Tim and I both wanted to travel more. Neither of us had been out of the country except for Mexico. When we first started hanging out, he was freshly out of a relationship and thought since he had nothing going for him he would get a plane ticket to Europe and spend the next few years traveling around and living there for free like he did when he was younger. One of my goals was to go to Europe, but to spend months there instead of a few weeks. At the very beginning of us dating we had made the decision, we were going to save for Europe.

Tim and I moved into a punk house in Oakland that threw shows in the backyard. Part of the reason we moved was for a change of scenery, the other being cheaper rent than San Diego, meaning we could hopefully afford to save money. Before moving, we saved up two month's rent to put up front, allowing us to travel for one month and spend the other finding jobs. Tim took me on a trip from Roseville to Portland and back, traveling for free. When we came back Tim got a job delivering for a shady furniture business until he found something better, and my unfinished progress toward a photography degree helped me get a part-time job as a pet photographer.

We moved to a better house in Oakland with a badass punk mother and daughter, and stayed in Oakland for a total of four years, gaining a second dog and a dog-like cat. During this time I went through various part-time jobs, sometimes working multiple at a time while going back to school full-time online. We were still barely able to save. It took almost the entire time we lived in Oakland to save the money we needed. After many changes to our plans, we decided we would do five months hiking the Pacific Crest trail, one month traveling the United States, and four months in Europe. In between these trips we would do odd jobs and travel around in a van we turned into a camper.

Tim and I nerded out on new terms such as "hiker trash" and "ultralight gear" during the planning stages of our trip. Tim was already convinced I was developing "packorexia." You'd think with our research and background knowledge we would be smart about our first real weekend backpacking in the woods of Big Sur, but of course we came equipped with important necessities such as a three-liter bag of wine. You know, a box of wine minus the box – since we were now ultralight. Tim decided to stash some fancy jewelry in his pack as well, an engagement ring he popped out at the end of a night drinking un-boxed wine in moonlit hot springs, ten miles into the steep forest trail.

Besides eventually planning a DIY wedding, our next step was to put our belongings in storage and explore as much as we could via foot, van, thumb, bus, train, plane, bike, and boat for the next two years. It was ten years since I had graduated high school, and I had finally completed my Bachelor's degree in Photography. My degree went right into storage with everything else.

When sharing our plans with friends and family we were flooded with questions, congratulations, advice, and sometimes jealousy. Many imagined us giving up the daily grind of work and school to enjoy a lavish life of relaxing in the sunshine on the Pacific Crest Trail, sipping sangria outside of quaint Spanish cafés, and zipping through small villages on air-conditioned high-speed European trains. Many of them were unfamiliar of the ways of cheap traveling. We were taking on thousands of dollars in debt, giving over our beloved pets to sitters, couch surfing, living out of a van, and doing odd jobs in between trips – not for your typical travel magazine's definition of traveling. Instead of drinking martinis on resort balconies or sipping hot chocolate under blankets next to campfires, we would be using bandanas as towels for six months at a time, limping through mountain lion territory tens of miles from civilization, accidentally smuggling pot candy across nineteen borders, sleeping on strangers' floors, sleeping in abandoned castle moats, befriending stray cats in neighborhoods that had banned police, popping blisters with sewing needles, giving ourselves haircuts in public restrooms, and watching metal bands in an underground cave once ravaged by the plague. Even if I could have afforded a luxury vacation, it would have been a shame to travel any other way.

From the years 2015 to 2017 we would attempt to hike from Mexico to Canada, road trip and hitchhike the United States three times, sail Southern California and Santa Catalina island, and explore nineteen European countries in four months. Including riding flea market bikes from Vienna to Budapest. This book contains all true stories from these trips. However, if you are a cop or work for Greyhound, Vons, or 7-Eleven: this is completely fiction. None of it is real. Names of people, venues, and squats may or may not have been changed. Please do not attempt any of the stupid things I have done.

Pacific Crest Trail: A Really Long Walk

'You'll hate the trail by the end. You may flat out despise it. Then you'll get home and it will occupy your thoughts for the rest of your life. You'll spend every spare second figuring out how to get it back." - Redditor SheriffEZPonder

t was getting late and time we head back to our tent in the manzanita grove to get some sleep. I had gone to the local bar in the only available "going out" clothes I had: a black puffy jacket over a shiny grey workout shirt and running pants, with neon pink trail-runners. One of the few outfit options of the narrow thru-hiker uniform, a set of clothing which made other hikers stand out from the locals in trail towns. It definitely wasn't my normal daily outfit consisting of black skinny jeans, slip-on Vans, a band T-shirt, and a sweatshirt with patches.

We walked out of the small forest town's main road and into the darkness, past patches of melting snow. The manzanita grove was just on the other side of a small thrift store parking lot, where I could see a medium sized brown box sitting next to the parking lot's dumpster. I peeked inside and pulled out a few pieces of antique ceramics to get to some blue knitted cloth at the bottom. "A blanket!" I said, as I pulled it out and sniffed to gauge its cleanliness. This blanket was a luxury. Like tap water. Like real clothes. It seemed clean enough, so I brought it back to the tent.

I slept soundly, and woke up earlier than I wanted, but later than I needed to. I packed my things and tried not to think about Devil's Slide. All of the hikers were talking about how much they were dreading the climb. The manzanita grove was in the back of a small bakery whose owner was a Pacific Crest Trail alumni, and now offered the backyard of his business to hikers passing through Idyllwild. Coincidentally, this was also the town Tim and I would end up having our wedding two years later. I went inside the back door and paid for two orders of biscuits and gravy with coffee, while Tim tried to pull off taking his morning poop in the only single bathroom available to both hikers and customers. I sat down to sip my coffee and charge my phone while noticing two little girls trying to force open the door to the bathroom Tim was occupying, without even considering to knock. Eventually they gave up and sat down. Tim came out and ate his breakfast, then we walked the two and a half miles uphill through town to the trailhead for Devil's Slide. Within the next forty-eight hours we would summit Mount San Jacinto and reach the bottom of the desert floor which it towers over. This decent would be the beginning of the end of our hike on the PCT.

"Why try to hike over two thousand miles?" was a question I was asked often. Why not hike for a few weeks through the best parts of the trail? Why choose to leave everything to walk the backwoods for months on end, giving up necessary things like available drinking water? Why would I sell my car in favor of hitchhiking my way to a warm shower once a week, if I was lucky? Some people thru-hike to find themselves or a form of spirituality, some hike because they were inspired by a book or movie, some want to prove to themselves and others they can accomplish something physically difficult. I guess I like to hike just to get lost in the wilderness. I'm not strong, I don't hike fast. I'm not competitive nor do I necessarily like exercising. I love to walk and explore, and I love to live in nature. I wished I could wander trails and camp simplistically for months straight, so why not see if I could hike across the country instead? It was a once in a lifetime opportunity

I was excited to have, even though I had no idea how well I would do.

Besides "why?" we also got a lot of "how?" which was sometimes harder to answer. Even after offering an explanation, some people still couldn't understand how thru-hiking differed from camping or scaling your town's local two-mile mountain peak. One of my most asked questions was "how can you carry five months' worth of food?" Can you imagine what five months, or even one month's worth of food looks like scattered out on a floor? Now, I don't know much about pack animals, but I assume even they would have a hard time carrying five months' worth of food for two people. Fortunately for hikers, the Pacific Crest Trail passes through multiple small towns every few days to a week. There you can re-up your food supply or send yourself hard to find items through the mail to be held at post offices.

Sending hikers letters or goodies through the mail was another thing friends and family kept asking to do for us, but was nearly impossible to explain why it probably wouldn't work. I begged Tim to get us a resupply falcon, but unfortunately he couldn't come through with finding and training a wild bird to deliver us goods in the backwoods. Instead we were left wandering through woods a few miles an hour with no address. "But aren't you sending yourself food?" they would ask. We had to send ourselves boxes general delivery to little post offices along the way. Thousands of other hikers were doing the same thing, which meant we had to plan the exact time frame when we would be picking it up. We had to factor in how long the post office would hold a package, and then when we arrived tell them how many packages we had, and in what way they were distinguishable from all of the other packages (our packages had spray painted neon orange polka dots). Now, I assume you can attempt to time, send, and hold a postcard general delivery, but the post office would probably *hate* you. Or just hate *us* when we ask for them to find it. Receiving postcards on trail would have been awesome, but most likely would have been sent back or become lost in the abyss.

Let's make this even more complicated! When a hiker receives a package, they have to consume whatever is in it instantly or get rid of it. Unless it is something specifically necessary for their upcoming miles on trail that are needed in order to survive or hike comfortably. It is very unlikely they would be willing or able to fit anything more into the entire life they carry on their backs. Like if someone sent us a bottle of wine... I would have loved that, but we most likely would have been about to walk twenty miles right after opening the package. That would mean carrying an absurd amount more weight and trash than normal, walking pretty drunk (which would be brutal in the desert), or handing it off to some lovely non-hiker townsfolk. The most awesome thing people can do for long distance hikers is to meet them places with cold beverages or fresh food that doesn't need added water to become edible. Sending gifts to hikers sounds lovely, but it just isn't practical.

"You better have armed yourselves," people would tell me. I brought a small knife, and a whistle. Those things can fend off pretty much anything you'd find on the trail.

Except for maybe the mosquitos. In all seriousness though, walking to work or walking around certain big cities of California could easily be more dangerous than walking the Pacific Crest Trail. The thing I was most afraid of was snow, but with the drought at the time we wouldn't have been seeing much of that. Rattlesnakes are pretty dangerous, but I couldn't imagine trying to shoot one while passing through a state park. A bit excessive as well as illegal.

"What about an axe?" I mean, hikers aren't exactly trying to build a log cabin out there. Hacking down Joshua trees in the desert to build a fire is another example of excessive and illegal. Campfires are for camping, which can be done in town at campgrounds. On trail a sleeping bag will do, and believe it or not will be more satisfying.

Campo to Scissors Crossing: Handing Over the Most Disgusting Dirty Socks You Have Ever Produced to a Nice Woman at the Front Desk

Let's backtrack to April 16th, 2015. I arrived at the border of Mexico in Campo, California wearing my one and only outfit and a twenty-four-pound backpack filled with the few items I would live off of for hopefully the next five months. My backpack included twenty miles worth of water, which I carried for two days through what started out as a rural residential landscape yet quickly turned into scorching desert hills within the first five miles of leaving the border. Before even leaving the Southern terminus, I had to beg Dionna, who dropped us off at the trailhead, to drive me to the nearest gas station bathroom. Having an upset stomach five minutes in wasn't the sendoff I was hoping for. Immediately within taking our first few steps, Tim and I introduced ourselves to three other members of our class of North Bound 2015 thru-hikers. Two of them were from Korea and we watched them get lost three times within the first two and a half miles of trail.

By our second day on the trail Tim and I both ended up running out of water while scaling one of the hardest desert hills, having to tuck under a small shady bush until the sun went down enough for us to safely hike the last few miles of the day. I hiked fast, especially since I could see the sun setting over Lake Morena, our destination and first water source. To make things more uncomfortable I was scared I was losing a toenail. It terrified me since I had barely left the border yet was hobbling already.

"I feel like my toe is losing a tooth," I said to Tim. I powered through, ignoring my toe, ignoring my dry mouth. I could see the lake reflecting the sunset below us. As we got closer I yelled to Tim with excitement, "Look, I can see it, campfires!" The trail winded downhill to the campground, where I filled my water at a spigot and chugged as much as I could drink. I took a quick soapless shower before setting up the tent in a camping spot with all the other hikers. I inspected what I thought was a loose toenail which turned out to be just an awkward under-the-nail blister, pushing one of my small toenails up at an angle.

Meeting other hikers the next morning made us feel a bit better about ourselves. Most of the people who were doing better than us had recently completed the Appalachian Trail, a few other people also ran out of water where we did, and one guy we ended up becoming friends with even fell off a cliff (thankfully he made it out perfectly okay without help). These eventful two days of hiking were only the beginning of a 2,650-mile goal: from the border of Mexico to Canada on the Pacific Crest Trail.

We left Lake Morena, following the sandy trail through fields of high desert brush and then up into the hills toward Mount Laguna. As we climbed the hills, the heat became a bit too much, so I stripped down into just a sports bra and bike shorts with a brown canvas Indiana Jones style hat to shade my face. I attempted holding a trekking pole in one hand and a flimsy blue umbrella in the other to help shade the rest of me. Day hikers would pass in the opposite direction, always doing a double-take at my choice of hiking clothes, or lack thereof. Most hiker outfits went one of two ways: monochrome or neutral-colored workout clothes consisting of lightweight shorts or pants with a moisture wicking top or sun shirt, or the safari hiker look, as I called it. The safari look was a tan uniform of lightweight material protecting the hiker's skin from top to bottom. Tan pants, tan long sleeve button-up, with a big tan hat. Often the hat also had an attached wall of material draping down to protect the neck. It looked like they were either going on a safari or about to harvest honey from a beehive. With the sun being so relentless, looking at the hikers clothed from top to bottom made me uncomfortable. In reality their outfits were extremely breathable and lightweight. They didn't have to worry about plastering themselves in sunscreen or being attacked by bugs (which weren't an issue yet on this portion of trail).

I slathered my pale, tattooed body in sunscreen just so I could feel as much of the slight breeze as possible. Passing hikers first looked at my face while saying hello, then quickly glanced down to the tattoos across my chest and abdomen, before quickly looking away out of awkwardness or embarrassment on their part. Of course it's weird to get gawked at, but it was worth it to be comfortable.

While ascending Mount Laguna we walked the trail cliffside past boulders overlooking the desert floor. The trail veered up the mountain with manzanita growing on all sides. Most large patches of shade were occupied by another hiker or two, stopping for a break from the sun. We stopped for a break ourselves, under a large tree covering small boulders which were perfect to stretch out and nap on.

As we packed our things away to resume hiking, a small truck pulled up on the dirt road the tree sat against. A man and woman jumped out and handed us each an ice cold can of beer. Our first taste of trail magic.

Trail angels are ordinary people who help thru-hikers for nothing in exchange. They help by offering rides, places to stay, or bringing in trail magic to passing hikers. This could be in the form of coolers of beer and soda, water, or fresh food. We didn't expect it to happen so soon, but it definitely felt like magic. A cold beer on a hot day of hiking where you are already rationing water couldn't get any better. We thanked our angels, then pressed on. We set up camp in a grassy area under trees with a few other hikers we had previously seen basking in the shade, chatting with them as we all made dinner and set up our tents.

The next morning we only had a few miles to go before reaching the small town of Mount Laguna. We weren't sure if we wanted to leave the rest of the day open to camping and visiting the hiker store and market in town, or to press on further down the trail, getting in a full day's mileage. We decided to play it by ear. The pine trees became more prevalent as we headed up the mountain. We left the high desert behind for pinecones and forest.

When we reached the top, we walked into Burnt Rancheria campground, which was still closed to visitors for the season but offered a walk-in group campsite to hikers. Some of the hikers we had seen the day before were relaxing in the campsite, and we were told more were at the hiker store for pack shakedowns.

We continued on to the market, eager for cold drinks and snacks. Climbing the last leg of Mount Laguna didn't take long, yet I was worn out from the sun and craved luxuries like beer and candy. With our most primal needs taken care of, Tim and I then went to the hiker store to see what was going on, and if there were any items we needed to buy. Out front of the store groups of hikers were drinking beer and passing joints for the stoner holiday of April 20th, surrounding a tarp with backpack contents scattered across it. Volunteers were helping hikers sort through their belongings, giving advice on what to keep and what to ditch in order to save weight. This is what is called a pack shakedown. We introduced ourselves to the group and chatted for a few hours in the sunshine, opening our cans of beer as well. We felt too blissful to keep on hiking. Almost everyone else was staying in Burnt Rancheria for the night, and we were having such a good time we decided we would as well. Tim and I went back to set up camp and take showers, bringing in our socks and underwear to quickly scrub before the shower timer stopped. Another trail angel, a hiker from a previous year, plopped a handle of liquor on the table for the hikers to drink. We all stayed up well past hiker midnight (sundown) to chat around the bonfire.

When researching hiking the Pacific Crest Trail online, a lot of advice came from know-it-all bro dudes with large egos and aggressive online personas. Because of this I was convinced I would hate everyone on trail. I would have nothing in common with them, they would be rude, and I would constantly need to defend myself, my hike, my gear, and whatever else. Some people, solo women and people of color specifically, definitely do have issues with this on trail, but thankfully my experience was much more pleasant than I was expecting. Tim and I had decided before starting our hike that we would not be actively searching for trail angel houses or social activities with other hikers. We were going to do our own thing away from the herd and keep to ourselves. Our night in Mount Laguna completely changed that. My eyes were open to the community aspect of thru-hiking and it was a feeling I was grateful to experience. No matter who we were, we were all there together, experiencing something no one else would understand. We were in another dimension to ordinary life.

That night there were no egos, no talk of who had the best gear. All of us were hairy, dirty, sunburned, and sore. We were all nobodies on a brand new journey as hiker trash, pounding beer and cracking jokes under the moonlight.

We woke a few hours after sunrise to another trail angel making coffee and pancakes in the bed of his truck on a two-burner camp stove. I felt spoiled, but I couldn't resist freshly cooked breakfast. We scarfed down a plate of food then got back to hiking, stopping to nap in the shade a few hours later. Even with a late start and a long nap, we still hiked a few miles over our ten mile goal, completing our longest day on trail so far. It was hard to hike on without becoming distracted by the breathtaking desert views below the mountainside we gradually descended. Views of desert and valleys continually lay below us until we reached a boulder field as the sun was setting. There were limited tent sites in the boulder field. It was an awkward place to camp and since we got there late, the best spots were taken. We squeezed our two person tent between boulders, putting our shoes and backpacks in every corner of the tent to hold it down. The ruthless wind was whipping through the boulders so hard, the tent was flapping and shaking non-stop overhead as we tried to fall asleep. I half expected it to catch the tent and carry us both away.

The next day had us following more of the ridgelines until we reached our next water source, which we camped at overlooking the desert below. We introduced ourselves to two men setting up camp in the same area, one of which already had a trail name.

"My name is Illegal." he said.

"How'd you get that name?" we asked.

"Did you see the border patrol helicopter circling yesterday?"

"Yes, we did."

"Well they were looking for someone who supposedly matched my description and stopped me for questioning. I had to convince them I was a hiker. As if someone had crossed the border and was on the run, but just so happened to be on the PCT wearing trail runners and a backpack full of ultralight gear." Illegal shook his head. "Funny thing is, I'm not even Mexican - my ancestors were from Nepal. So that's how I was given my trail name."

Tim and I filtered water, made dinner, popped blisters, and then crawled into our tent exhausted, just as the sun was setting. It was easy to fall asleep so early since my body longed for rest. I could have slept for days on end. Nights were spent tossing and turning, my hips aching from the hard ground intruding up against my inflatable sleeping pad, and my leg muscles cramping endlessly. We took off first thing in the morning and arrived early to Scissors Crossing after hammering out nine miles in four hours. We were in the desert, with green cacti blooming bright colored flowers around us and horny toads greeting us trailside. Eleven and a half miles from Scissors Crossing was Julian, California. A tiny gold rush style old town on the outskirts of San Diego county. If you meet a native San Diegan, odds are they spent at least a few days of their childhood visiting Julian for sledding, eating apple pie, and drinking hot cider. I was excited to experience Julian as a trail town, and it was perfect timing since a huge rainstorm was on its way.

Tim held his class of 2015 thru-hiker bandana out to passing cars. One side said "Hiker to Town" while the other said "Hiker to Trail." The most convenient, pocket-sized hitchhiking sign. A couple pulled over and loaded us into the back of their truck's camper shell. We tried our hardest to avoid sitting on the bed in the back because we were so dirty, but there was no getting around it. We were dropped on Julian's small main strip, and wandered up and down the street trying to find a vacant hotel. We stopped into a restaurant to stuff our faces while searching online for a hotel deal. Everything in Julian was expensive. Over one hundred dollars a night. The clouds grew dark and started dumping rain while we sat in the restaurant. We didn't really have any option that was cheap and dry. The old Julian Gold Rush hotel had a discount sign for hikers, so we thought an expensive room for one night wouldn't hurt.

Julian Gold Rush Hotel was founded during the town's gold rush in 1887, originally as a restaurant and bakery. It is the oldest hotel that has been continuously in operation in all of Southern California. Its original owners were a former slave named Albert Robinson and his wife Margaret Tull Robinson. The hotel was an iconic part of Julian, hosting dances and dinners, and was frequented by many notable people passing through the town. Margaret sold the hotel in 1921, six years after Albert's death. The current owners have tried to keep the hotel in the time period and style the Robinson's meant for it to be. Of course rumors say it's haunted.

I had never stayed in Julian before. Especially in a Victorian bed and breakfast on the main strip. Our presence was in stark contrast to the bed and breakfast's lobby. We were wet from rain and hadn't showered in days. There was a layer of dirt and grime and dried sweat and sunscreen on every inch of our things. We stood at the lobby front counter surrounded by pristine antique furniture and decorative wallpaper. The lights were low and a fireplace warmed the room as raindrops fell outside the window. The front desk woman welcomed us, and showed us to a hiker registry and hiker box, which I was surprised they had in such a fancy place.

Hiker boxes were free boxes for thru-hikers. If you had gear or food you were sick of carrying you could ditch it in the box for another hiker to take. Sometimes you could use things and put it back, such as soaps or lotions. Locals would also sometimes fill the boxes with bandaids, food, clothes, books, and whatever else. Sometimes day hikers or tourists would also take from the boxes and write in the registries, which was disheartening. I peeked inside and pulled out a *Yogi's PCT Handbook*, which I was too cheap to buy for myself. I was excited to get new tips, and just browsing it in general helped to break through the bit of dread I had about going back to the trail and give me some inspiration. While reading Yogi's tips, I already started to miss the trail. It was a weird feeling. Tim took some dark green high school football pants he probably wouldn't fit into. He needed something else he could wear while doing laundry and it was his only option.

We were shown to our room where Tim and I fell back and melted into the bed. It was luxurious. I ripped the duct tape from my blistered toes then took the hottest shower I could stand, *almost* freeing my fingernails and the heels of my feet from dirt stains. My feet looked like hell. I put on my puffy jacket and running pants I had barely worn, then tucked into bed with a cold beer by my side and continued reading my Yogi's guide.

Tim showered and put on his jacket and ridiculous hiker box football pants. I couldn't stop laughing. He was embarrassed but walked back out to the lobby to deliver our dirty laundry, which they did for us for a small fee. Imagine if we had a time machine and could tell our past selves tales of the future: someday as an adult, you will be in flip flops and ill fitting child's clothing, in an extravagant historic hotel, handing over the most disgusting dirty socks you have ever produced to a nice woman at the front desk. Not only the most disgusting dirty socks, but ones you have worn inside and out for days on end while walking through the desert.

Even while in the cozy hotel bed my body ached through the night like I had never felt, often waking to painful cramping in my calves and feet. This was just my life now: always being sore. My muscles beaten to death until they could become stronger and learn to cope.

Already by this point on trail a lot of the other hikers had seemed to have come and gone. Familiar faces were lingering and being replaced by new ones. Tim and I both had a lot of anxiety about hiking. We felt we weren't doing good enough. We were slow at under fifteen miles a day. We had been checking the weather and already decided on taking a zero day (day of no hiking) or two to avoid the continuing forecasted storm. We doubted ourselves and what we were doing, and whether we would make it to Canada. After a night of talking it out and getting some tips from the Yogi's guide, we decided it wasn't about Canada. It was about hiking the Pacific Crest Trail for five months to smell flowers, sleep in the dirt, climb mountains, and see how far we could get. Thinking in the long term was terrifying. Seventy-seven miles down, just under twenty six hundred to go. Thinking about the smaller picture felt more comfortable - seventy-seven down, thirty to go to Warner Springs. The entire trail was still our goal in the long run, but our focus needed to be on each day, each week, each resupply point or water source. We needed to enjoy ourselves day by day and the rest would fall into place if it was meant to be. "Don't think of Canada as your goal. If you want to go to Canada, get on a plane and fly there." - Yogi.

The next morning we went down to breakfast freshly showered and dressed in clean hiker clothes still covered in dirt stains. The dining room was also filled with antique furniture, a lit fireplace, and fine china or whatever. I buttered my toast, not knowing which of the many utensils to use. It was so fancy and quaint, and we were still so out of place. It felt good though, so I didn't care. We grabbed our things after eating and checked out of the hotel, once more we were out in the rain with nowhere to go. We wanted to take the next two days off to avoid the storm, but staying in the bed and breakfast for all that time would have been much too expensive. My aunt Mary lived about twenty-five miles away on twenty acres of land in Ramona, California. Tim and I tucked into a pie shop for more food and coffee, then gave her a call to ask if we could stay to avoid the storm. A few hours later my brother Patrick arrived in Julian to give us a ride to Mary's.

Mary and Mike's land wasn't too different from some of the Southern California sections of the Pacific Crest Trail. A trail wound through their property through oak trees, manzanita, large boulders, and a natural pond filled will bullfrogs. Coyotes and bobcats made their way past the house multiple times a day. In the brush hid rattlesnakes and tarantulas. Mary gave us food and wine which we enjoyed under blankets next to the fireplace while rain poured outside. It was a nice break but we definitely felt guilty avoiding the trail. Immediately once the rain stopped, the relentless sun and heat was back. Mary dropped us back at Scissors Crossing where we could ascend back into the hills.

Scissors Crossing to Idyllwild: Return of the Menace Ball

One week had passed since we started in Campo, and we were already developing leg muscles we had never seen before. Once more, we were going up and down too many mountains to count. We were finally used to rationing water, although it wasn't exactly fun. After resuming from Scissors Crossing it was hot with no shade by midday. Tim and I found a bush to half crawl under just for a break from the sunshine. We were having a miserable day on trail because of the sun, or "menace ball" as we started calling it, but mentally we were in good spirits. Even though it felt like we were exercising in a sauna, I kept daydreaming about past sections of trail I loved and what future sections would be like. After a while though, you get too exhausted to care about what's around you. You just have to focus on successfully dragging your carcass to the next stopping point.

Eight miles in we came across a large flat area big enough for quite a few people to camp, and there were a few of the hikers we had previously met, as well as some new faces. It was becoming late in the day so we figured we might as well join them in setting up camp, even though our mileage for the day was low. We sat down to chat and introduced ourselves to the group. Blue was a hiker from India, he was fast and had the best lightweight gear, but was hiking low miles due to an injury he had developed. Panther was a big guy from Hawaii, he made his way on trail slowly, spending time snapping pictures and developing friendships. Lori and Red were two women from Washington, taking their time hiking their way back north where they were planning to then get married. Jon was the oldest man we had seen on trail so far, he was a determined hiker but seemed to also be suffering from injury. Tim and I instantly felt at home with this group of slower trail outcasts. The majority of the other hikers were either hard bodied accomplished athletes or fit nineteen year olds with a lot of money. It was like we had found our Island of Misfit Toys, strengthening the feeling of trail community once more.

This was the first night on trail I didn't sleep in all of my clothes. We didn't even put the rainfly on the tent. A warm breeze blew over us as we fell asleep under the stars. In the morning we all got up and made our way back onto the trail, yo-yoing past each other all day long. In one and a half days we would be walking into Warner Springs. It was hot again, as we reached a water cache by mid-day. There was shade near the cache, so we decided to cook our dinner early then nap, letting the hottest part of the day pass by, choosing to hike into the cool of the evening instead. In the evening we found a small tentsite on the top of a mountain with views of the desert floor all around us. We could see the mountains in the distance we had passed through, and some that were still to come.

First thing the next morning we came across the one hundred mile marker written out in rocks across the trail. Our first accomplishment! As we continued toward Warner Springs, we descended from the mountains and walked for hours through flat fields. It was such an odd feeling, our first long stretch of flat ground. We could walk faster, watching grasshoppers bounce out of the weeds we brushed against. It finally looked like the movie *Wild*, which was so funny to me. It came on while we were at my aunt Mary's in Ramona and the whole time I was thinking *where is all this flat trail?!* She did start the trail hundreds of miles past where we were, so maybe there was more flat ground up ahead. I had no idea.

We walked down trail and soon enough found Eagle Rock, which is just like it sounds. A huge boulder shaped like an Eagle with its wings spread open. We stopped to snack in the Eagle's shade, then kept going. By evening we had made it to the Warner Springs Resource Center, marking two more achievements: the completion of the Pacific Crest Trail section A and our first fifteen mile day.

The center was crowded with hikers, since "the herd" of the hiking season was now catching up to us. Hundreds of hikers had recently attended the Kickoff event in Lake Morena, and were now passing us slow pokes. Instead of seeing one or two other thru-hikers a day we were now seeing multiple groups. This also meant limited tent sites and cached water, and more toilet paper and trash on trail due to inconsiderate assholes not cleaning up after themselves. Not only did I not care that they were passing us, I actually wished they would pass faster. From the Southern Terminus to Idyllwild is the section of the trail that makes 40% of Northbound hikers quit the PCT, so the only thing we could do was to keep on hiking and hope the feelings of failure affected some of the mass of *Wild* fans instead of us.

Just to make things clear - I have no negative feelings toward the book *Wild*, in fact I thought it was good. I guarantee you it's better than this book. The annoyance for a lot of the class of 2015 hikers was that people were hiking specifically to create their own inspirational story and spiritual journey, which is cool for them, but something the rest of us couldn't escape. The inspirational quotes about nature that plastered the internet were not helpful or truthful, they were suffocating and annoying. Nature is definitely mystical and beautiful, but it also wants you dead. It is not a magic cure for depression, and it can easily drive you crazy. Many people leave trail because of the mental exhaustion. Now add mileage goals, money, injury, weather, water crossings, poisonous plants, venomous animals, drunk assholes, rationing food and water, and counting calories. It's work. Having the PCT become famous the year we hiked just seemed to make it harder for people to understand what we were doing and why we were doing it. And a lot of the people who were hiking just because they were fans of the book or movie did not do enough research to keep themselves safe and responsible on trail. On top of that we also had to deal with the other side of the *Wild* crowd, the loudmouth haters who constantly had to voice their opinion about how horrible *Wild* was because Cheryl was a "nasty slut." Those people may have actually been worse.

We set up camp with our misfit hiker gang and were excited for veggie burgers, soda, and showers, yet we had missed the hot food. We ate cold soaked ramen pad thai then crawled into our tent, hopeful for breakfast in the morning. We woke to hikers packing up to leave, but we weren't ready to join them. We wanted coffee, fresh food, and showers, and we had to wait until mid-day for my mom to meet us with our first resupply package. Because of this we had to either take an unexpected zero day or leave later in the evening.

I hobbled into the center for coffee and to enquire about showers. The staff was incredibly busy and frazzled due to some city workers arriving unexpectedly to ask questions. I sipped my coffee outside, waiting for things to calm down, when the news came. The city workers were there to shut down Warner Springs Resource Center for helping hikers. A school across the street had called the city to complain after seeing so many dirty, hairy men in short shorts. For now, we were all allowed to stay and camp, shower, and use the center, but they were not allowed to continue barbecuing for hikers since they did not have permits for serving food. It was a sad day watching such an important resource get close to being stripped from the trail. Tim and I got our showers in, then asked my mom to take us into town once she arrived so we could get some real food.

My mom arrived at the resource center and we were excited to jump in her car and head to the only nearby restaurant. We inhaled our food, shoving handfuls of French fries in our mouths while taking a breather here and there to fill my mom in about the trail. She gave us our package and brought us back to the resource center. We ripped the package open and sorted through the Ziploc bags seeing what candy, snacks, and dinners we had for the next upcoming days. We said goodbye to my mom and went back to our tent with the other hikers, trying to make our decision to take off or relax with them. It was already late in the day, and we had a few beers we had bought from the store in town to drink before setting off. The other hikers were starting to pop open beers as well. We decided to stay and chat and leave the next morning.

It grew dark and we joined a small group of hikers who were passing around a bottle of whiskey in a neighboring field. By this time everyone had been drinking for a few hours, so some were getting a bit sloppy.

"I can't take any days off, I just can't." a petite young blond woman slurred. "I don't care how bad my foot is, I'm not taking any zeros, I'm going to make it to Canada."

"There's no shame in taking a break if you are hurting. The resource center has medical supplies and foot baths, it might help in the long run to get off your feet for a day." I piped up.

"I... I.. just can't though. I have to show them I can do this. My roommates."

"Oh, are they hikers?"

"No... they are just really athletic. They always make fun of me so I'm doing this to show them I can be athletic and strong too. So NO zeros, I'm not stopping!"

"Okay, well good luck. Hope your foot gets better soon." I said, confused. Hiking to spite your roommates, that's a new one.

The next morning we dumped any extra food and supplies we didn't want to carry into the hiker box and got ready to set off. I sifted through the box trying to see if there was anything good or useful to take. Sometimes just switching out a crappy small piece of gear for something nicer or smaller was helpful. I reached down and pulled out a slick white piece of paper.

"Temporary tattoos!" I laughed. Someone, somehow, put a large sheet of tribal armband temporary tattoos in the hiker free box. Of course while sipping my coffee I took them around camp to all the other hikers trying to get someone to put one on.

We were packed and ready to hit the trail, but first went to say goodbye to our hiker friends. The whole misfit crew was planning on getting off trail. They all had decided to skip ahead for various reasons, but first they were going to hitchhike to Las Vegas together. They said we could come with, but Tim and I were determined to continue our trek. We said goodbye, not sure if we would ever see them again. Now we were alone. It was just us and the herd.

A few miles into our day we arrived at a beautiful creek shaded by oak trees. I pulled off my shoes and soaked my sore feet in the ice cold water. It felt so good that Tim and I ate some food and then ended up dozing off in the shade. We woke up an hour later and the creek had completely dried up. It was gone, with no sign of it ever being there at all. We were planning on filtering some to drink too. It was bizarre. Thankfully we weren't relying completely on this stream, so we were able to keep going with the water we had until our next water source. Although we probably would have drank less during our break if we knew it had to be rationed.

Our next stop was trail angel Mike's house, which was only seventeen miles from Warner Springs. Our plan was to hike most of the way there, camp, then arrive at Mike's first thing the next morning. Mike's house was fairly off the grid, but it was off of a dirt road that would be accessible for my mom to meet us again. We weren't planning on meeting up with her again so soon, but my grandma had passed and we needed to get off trail to attend her funeral and be with family for a couple of days. Now we were going to be the ultimate zero-day-takers, but we had come to accept it. It is what it is, and we were doing the best we could under the circumstances.

The first thing you see when walking up to trail angel Mike's is a big water tank, and against it lay a sign reading "PCT HIKERS, WE ARE HOME, YOU POOR SOUL, COME DOWN AND REST FEET." His house was on a nice piece of land right off trail in the middle of nowhere in the high desert surrounded by manzanitas. It was 10:30 AM and two hikers we had met earlier on were helping to cook everyone eggs, pancakes, sausage, and tortillas, while another person was going around pouring Mexican Mimosas – tequila in orange juice. We partook in both, signed the registry, threw some cash into the donation bucket, and poked around in the hiker box which was an entire back patio room worth of stuff. After an hour of lounging we went to sit at the dirt road hoping my mom could find us.

A dusty old rusted tractor lay beside the road and Tim climbed it to extend his phone to the sky as if he was praying to the cell signal gods. I had no clue how my mom would find us on such a secluded road. The roads seemed unnamed and the houses were so discreet down their own private roads that trying to find a visible address would be laughable, if not dangerous. After an hour of waiting we were about to give up and see if there was a landline at Mike's we could use, when up rolled my mom's car down the dirt road.

We went back to San Diego to spend a few days with family in honor of my grandma, then Tim's parents took us back to the road Mike lived off of. Only a few days had gone by, but the trail felt like a different place. Instead of scorching and hot, it was cool and cloudy. We said goodbye then headed back into the desert mountains.

We started at 2 PM and hammered out ten miles before setting up camp for the night, then the next day completed twelve miles through constant inclines and declines through Anza's desert. We might have been easing in slow, but we had to keep in mind that some people were only just starting. We weren't behind in the season just yet, where increasing temperatures in the desert, and snowfall in the mountain ranges would make parts of trail dangerous or impassable. We also would be picking up our pace in time. In fact, we were finally to the point where five miles was starting to feel more like two, and our entire daily routine for desert hiking was becoming more fine-tuned in terms of when we would hike, cook, and nap in order to hike the most miles in the coolest time of day. Our spirits were lifted with our newfound confidence. We were still taking it fairly easy so we had no blisters or injuries, just sore muscles. We had been on the trail for half a month, yet we had lost count of how many half days, some still at ten miles a day, and zero days we had taken. Our zeros and half days weren't helping us from breaking through our snail's pace of attempting the trail, but it had been nice at relieving stress, resting sore muscles, and reminding us to focus on having fun while hiking instead of thinking of each day as a rigid, scheduled, chore.

After two nights back on trail we had only a few miles of walking before approaching the Paradise Valley Café. Our dinner the night before consisted of instant mashed potatoes with decadent instant brown gravy. I cooked the food and then portioned it out into our mugs as Tim blew up our sleeping pads and set up the tent. We each carried one plastic mug and titanium spork as our eating utensils, and had one small cooking pot and stove to share.

When we got back on trail a few days prior, we continued on with the food in our backpacks instead of buying more food in San Diego, even though we knew we were due to resupply in a few more days. We already had the exact amount of food we needed to make it to Paradise Valley Café and would rather not add any additional weight to our packs unless it was a necessity. The café was originally the next resupply point my mom was supposed to meet us at. It was also getting close to Mother's Day, so having lunch with her at the café was going to be our chance to celebrate the holiday with her as well.

We spent the morning walking up and down bare desert hills speckled in boulders and brush. It was mostly dusty and hot, but the cacti were blooming and the desert sage smelled amazing. Enjoying the desert's beauty and knowing we were about to get fresh food and coffee was enough to keep us excited. I was also looking forward to soon climbing into the forest of Idyllwild.

We arrived to the café and ran in excited for food and coffee. Tim and I ordered breakfast while I texted my mom to let her know we arrived. I didn't have phone service all morning, so per our original plans she intended to come later in the afternoon. It turned out that even though we were early, she wouldn't be able to come for a few hours anyway. This was perfectly fine with us. We and our hiker hunger were happy to wait at a diner that was practically on the trail, with coffee, beer, and all types of food. Not only did we eat breakfast while waiting for my mom, but lunch too. By the time she arrived we were stuffed, so we moved out onto the patio and ordered beer to sip on while we chatted. The sun was shining and we were more content than ever.

The thirty mile section between Paradise Valley Café and Idyllwild was completely closed due to a fire closure. When a wildfire comes through an area of a state or national park, they usually close it down for up to a few years so that the plants and wildlife have enough time to reestablish before humans come stomping back in. Disobeying the closure would mean a hefty fine, if you were caught. As we sat on the café's porch, hiker after hiker lined up at the stop sign across the street to hitchhike straight into Idyllwild. This went against the mindsight of hiking continuous miles on the trail, but there weren't a lot of other options, if any, in this case. Also it's imperative for hikers to remember HYOH: Hike Your Own Hike. Not all hikers want, or need, to hike every continuous mile of the trail. You need to hike the mileage and sections that feel good and safe to you, and complete your journey, not someone else's. Even though Tim and I were pretty shitty hikers, (okay he was pretty good - it was mostly just me who was shitty), we wanted to keep hiking continuous miles for as long as we could. One hundred and fifty two miles in, next destination: Idyllwild.

It was 3:30 PM which felt fairly late for hitting the trail, or... road. We sorted through our package and said goodbye to my mom, then started to walk along highway 74. As we were leaving we met a few hikers who had the same idea. They mentioned a campground half a mile past Lake Hemet they planned to stay in for the night, so we told them we would meet them there.

"There is a small store right off the road at Lake Hemet that sells beer. We should stop there to get snacks and beer for camp!" Tim suggested.

"That's an awesome idea! I had no idea there was a store, that's good to know." a hiker named Woolly, said. "We'll definitely be meeting you there for beer!"

"Sounds good, see you there!" Tim said as we walked off. It was nice to see that we weren't the only hikers doing the road walk, even if it was only these three dudes.

The walk felt so much different since it was a flat, paved path instead of a winding dirt horse trail, constantly changing in elevation. It felt like a nice change at first, but got incredibly boring fast. Tim and I discussed every little house we passed, deciding which ones we wished we could live in. Quickly our surroundings changed from desert to forest. We wanted all of the little forest houses. The mountains in the distance were beautiful, towering over green meadows where I hoped to see deer. The sky was bright blue with a few floating clouds. We passed a dead snake and poked it with a stick, then I stopped and squatted in a field to pee before the next cars came flying past. We walked up to the Lake Hemet store just as the sun started to set over the lake, completing nine miles from the café in three hours.

Tim and I ran up to the store anxious and out of breath. Then we saw the dreaded sign. The application to sell alcohol plastered in the window.

"What the fuck?" Tim said, as he barged into the store and I stayed with our packs outside. He came back out with his head hung low. "There was a change of ownership. No beer. Not for a few months, anyway."

"Noooo." I responded. Being sober for a night wasn't a big deal, it's just that we were close to Idyllwild and ready to celebrate and have whatever treats we could get. Kicking our feet up in a secluded campground with motherfucking toilets and a beer was like living the high life.

"We hyped up the other hikers," Tim said, "what are we going to tell them now?" Just then they rounded the corner to the front of the store. "No beer." we said, let down.

"What?!" said Woolly.

"They changed ownership and had to apply for a new liquor license. Sorry about that, I had no idea. We were really looking forward to it too." Tim and I walked with Woolly, Tarp, and Stealth back to the road and toward our campground.

The sun was going down as we walked in. The campground was technically open, but no one else was camping there and the ranger station was closed. We looked back and forth at each other. There was no way to pay.

"Maybe we could just pay in the morning." one of the hikers piped up. "I guess we'll have to." We wanted off our feet. We wandered the secluded, dark, paved driveway leading through the campground. It was eerie. Even owls hooted as we walked. We had the entire place to ourselves.

Tim and the rest of the guys sat up camp while I went through our food to see what we had to make. I pulled out two packs of ramen then started filling up the pot with water from a faucet in our campsite. I did a double-take as the water came out pure white. I dumped it and tried again, just to see if eventually the water would run clear. I held it up to the rest of our crew to show them.

"It looks like milk." said Tarp.

"Maybe I'll try another faucet." I responded. I wandered the campground trying all of the nearby faucets but they all ran milky white. This wasn't a big deal since I was boiling the water anyway, but it was a bit unappetizing. Eventually I settled on water from the bathroom sink which ran slightly more clear. We were excited for showers but they didn't have hot water so we decided to skip. Being dirty sounded much more comfortable than going to bed wet and cold with an incoming storm on the way. Stealth started filling his water bladder with water from the campsite faucet. We all laughed and joked that it was full of milk. After dinner, we all said goodnight and went to bed.

Idyllwild to Cabazon: The Day Drinking Hiker Trash of Idyllwild

The five of us woke up early, yet took our time packing while discussing our plans for completing the detour section around the burn area into Idyllwild. The guys said their goodbyes, then headed back to the highway to hitchhike the rest of the way into town. We were the last to leave, like usual, and packed up our stuff next to spying woodpeckers wondering what we were doing in their home.

Tim and I followed the other hikers up onto the road, but decided to walk as far as possible before resorting to hitchhiking. Immediately, our straight road through forest neighborhoods became a twisted highway with blind turns and no shoulder. Concerned for our wellbeing, we sat for a while between blind winding road deciding if we should hitchhike or what our other options were. We tried our hardest to safely pass the first turn, but it was both nerve wracking and seemingly impossible. Our only choice was to turn around and hitchhike as well. Our hiker friends had already been picked up, so we waited in the spot they had left from, a thumb out while simultaneously checking our maps for an alternate route. After studying the map, I found a short trail from the back of the campground straight to a dirt Jeep road leading into the town of Idyllwild. We couldn't believe our luck. Tim and I turned around and retraced our steps back into, and then through, the campground. Still, there was not one person to be seen.

By the time we found the trailhead an hour had passed since we left camp. It felt like the morning was passing us by and we hadn't even started hiking. The sky was grey as clouds hovered over tall pine tree-covered mountains in the distance. We climbed up for a few hours, until coming across a paved road leading into the residential outskirts of Idyllwild. We were at a point where the fog was rolling in thick and we had to decide whether to climb a steep hill, getting into town later in the evening, or take a two mile short cut into town. My calves were killing me from the last few days of climbing hills, and I was starting to shiver pretty bad every time we weren't in motion. I was rooting for the fast track to Idyllwild - dreaming of fried eggs, hash browns, fresh coffee, pancakes, and all the breakfast! We followed our map through serene house-lined forest roads, saying hello to woodpeckers and fenced dogs, and saying no to people trying to drive us the last mile. Of course people would only try to pick us up when we weren't looking for a ride. We made it to town in time to still catch breakfast.

Idyllwild was cold and cute. We got my favorite meal of the day at a breakfast heaven called Red Kettle. They had vegetarian eggs benedict and veggie sausage. People were giving us dirty looks for being glued to our phones, but it wasn't often we were able to post pictures and inform our friends and family we weren't dead, frostbitten, or lost.

After breakfast we ran into a fellow hiker we had met under the bridge at Scissors Crossing named Skips. We followed him back to a campground in town where he threw us each a Budweiser to drink with the other hikers who were camping there too.

The weather forecast for the night was snow. Many hikers were stopping into Idyllwild to avoid it, and tourists from nearby towns were arriving to enjoy it. We sipped our beer, discussing the weather and what our plans were to prepare for it. Tim and I could have stayed at the campground, but after chatting for a while we decided on checking into one of the last remaining available hotel rooms in town.

We checked into the Silver Pines Lodge, which was extremely accommodating to hikers and even had a resident dog to play with. Our room had a fireplace and a shower with a skylight looking up into the pine trees. We cuddled on the couch next to the fire until falling asleep, waking the next morning to the entire town blanketed in snow.

Tim and I bundled up and went out to explore, running into Skips again who told us about a hiker karaoke night happening at the burger joint after sundown. We took advantage of our day off, resupplying from the local grocery store and doing laundry, preparing to hit the trail again the next day. There were so many hikers partying in Idyllwild it was hard to want to go back to the trail, especially in snow.

The hiker karaoke was a huge party. About twenty hikers in puffy jackets waddling with sore muscles and slurring to every type of song imaginable, with locals looking on confused. People were swinging around, belting out songs in each other's arms, and swaying their beer glasses in the air. Just a simple night of hanging out in a random hamburger joint ended up being such a great memory of living the hiker trash life. Which is funny because we weren't even hiking. We walked "home" late, buzzed, and happy.

I woke up groggy and packed my things, checking out as late as we were allowed. We both were in dire need of coffee, so we sat on the back porch drinking cup after cup to wake ourselves up even though we had already checked out. Next thing you know, up walks Skips. He had stayed at Silver Pines the previous night because his girlfriend had come to visit with him before he got back on trail. We introduced ourselves to his girlfriend Anna and her pit bull Audrey.

I took a sip of coffee then looked up at Skips who was pulling out a cheap bottle of wine from a grocery bag. He popped the cork, took a sip, then extended the bottle out to me and Tim. We looked at each other and shrugged. We were kind of on vacation, and the pass was still covered in snow anyway. Why not spend another zero day as the day drinking hiker trash of Idyllwild? And that is exactly what we became... The four of us drank all over town next to melting snow, raiding hiker boxes, staring back at locals who were staring at us, and poking around in thrift stores with open beer in our pockets.

We visited a closed store that opened its back doors to hikers to get out of the weather, but we weren't into the "vibe." It reeked of cigarettes inside and many of the people didn't look like hikers at all. More like young runaway Juggalo types claiming to be. It was still cool the empty storefront had opened its doors for people to get out of the snow though, no matter who they were.

Even when we did meet other hikers we didn't know many of them or they ended up being slightly rude, so we avoided them. They were young and wouldn't stop talking about their gear or our tattoos and hair. Our adventuring through Idyllwild led us to meet a man who claimed to be wearing a five thousand dollar western suit, whose long brown wig was attached to his black cowboy hat. We knew this because when he went to wipe the sweat from his brow he would lift his hat and attached wig to give himself access to more forehead. We spent the evening drinking Bloody Marys at the diner with Skips until we set up our tent in the manzanita grove behind the Town Baker, where the snow was still melting but it was free. This was our last night in Idyllwild on trail, the night with the parking lot blanket and morning of biscuits and gravy before heading up Devil's Slide.

Once more, it seemed all of the hikers except for us hitched the two miles uphill to Devil's Slide. This trailhead was an alternate route which would hit the Pacific Crest Trail after climbing up 1,600 feet. It was the only real option to get back to the trail from Idyllwild's town center. Since we decided to walk the two and a half miles of road from the town of Idyllwild to the trailhead, we added another eleven hundred feet of extra elevation to our day before even reaching Devil's Slide.

Devil's Slide's climb wasn't nearly as bad as I thought it would be. Maybe I was just assuming the worst, but it wasn't too horrible of a climb and we flew up the mountain fairly fast. We had decided instead of following the Pacific Crest Trail once we met up with it again, we would take another alternate route which continued up the mountain to summit Mount San Jacinto sitting at 10,834 feet. This only added a mile to our day, yet added another 2,600 or so feet in elevation. We decided to camp for the night near the intersection of the Pacific Crest Trail and would summit San Jacinto in the morning.

Our tentsite sat on the edge of the mountain overlooking the tall peaks surrounding Idyllwild. The bright blue sky grew dark and fog rolled over the mountains as the sun set. It was too beautiful to describe in words. We were finally back on trail and it felt great. I kicked back on my sleeping bag as the sun set, listening to *The Hobbit* audiobook until falling asleep as soon as the moon and stars appeared.

In the morning, Tim and I packed up and followed the winding trail up the mountain, trotting on past patches of snow and singing birds with the sun shining brightly through the trees. We stopped to filter water, and I took the opportunity to make myself iced coffee with untouched snow. It's amazing what can make you feel fancy when surviving out in the wilderness. I put *The Hobbit* on again in my headphones to keep things interesting as I walked. The climb to San Jacinto's peak started as a winding trail through the snowy forest, until it turned to bare, rocky switchbacks as it climbed up to the top. It was nice and cool out, but I was starting to feel a bit of altitude sickness in headache form while approaching the peak. I hiked fast, so the Orcs wouldn't smell our footprints. Oops sorry, I think I'm starting to get my stories confused.

Reaching the top was definitely worth the climb and literal headache. There was a cool little cabin from the 1930's which was used as an emergency shelter. It was stocked with emergency bedding, food, whiskey, and mouse poops. The views from the tippy top of the mountain were beautiful, but it was crazy to look out into the distance to see just how far down and back up again we had to go. The desert floor was so far below us it was as if looking down at a city from the window of an airplane, and we would be reaching it within the next two days of hiking.

When we were done enjoying the views we descended down the mountain, which felt never ending. Down from the top peak to the flat bottom of the desert near Cabazon,

California. The forest turning into desert is one of my favorite landscapes. Seeing pine cones lying next to cacti, and chipmunks on rocks fade away then be replaced by lizards instead. The decline was brutal, although beautiful.

We camped on the side of the mountain hearing the rattling of freight trains ten miles below us on the desert floor near the 10 freeway. This decent was the most frustrated I had become on the whole trail. It was hard walking such an easy downward path, with my body disagreeing with it so much. At the end of the second day I was hobbling so bad from aching knees, ankles, and shins beaten to death from the rocky downhill that I told Tim to go ahead to find us a place to camp while I struggled to walk, expecting it would be just my luck for a mountain lion to pounce on me from a towering boulder thinking I was a sick deer.

We made it though. The next morning five miles of lingering downhill was quickly completed then we were able to fill up at a water source and make our way through an additional four miles of flat land. You think that would be easy, but there is always a catch. The sand was thick and hard to walk through, and the wind was beating us so hard that I wouldn't have been able to open my eyes if I didn't have my sunglasses. We arrived under the 10 overpass to a sign basically saying "We leave trail magic here usually, but locals keep stealing it so we've stopped. Sorry." We crawled out from under the bridge like trolls, and I called my mom to let her know what streets we magically appeared onto. Her and my grandma were coming to bring us a resupply package and take us to lunch. The neighborhood on the other side of the overpass was odd and didn't look like California to me at all. Scorched desert land with nice looking houses scattered in no particular order along the freeway. There was a lowrider parked in a dirt front yard with snow capped Mount San Jacinto as the backdrop.

There wasn't much in Cabazon, so we asked my mom to take us into Palm Springs since it was nearby and we figured it would have more options for food. Normally along the trail we had too much food, but we ditched a lot of it in Idyllwild figuring we would get rid of pointless weight. We ended up running out of most of our food early due to our miscalculation. When we pulled into Palm Springs our skin was red and wind-beaten and we had just hiked nine miles on zero calories. I ran into a Starbucks and ordered a large icy drink with lots of chocolate and extra espresso, then splashed my face with water in the bathroom, turning the sink brown from my hands. It had only been a few days since I had been in town yet my reflection looked like another person. A feral person. I felt that way too. The fluorescent light bulb in the bathroom felt foreign and the paper towels, soap, and running water felt luxurious.

I exited the bathroom to see my mom and grandma telling a few staring strangers that we were hiking the Pacific Crest Trail, although I'm pretty positive they had no idea what that was. Making small talk with strangers in this strange place was the last thing I wanted to do. Palm Springs is far from being a hiker town so people had no idea what they were going on about. These people were just trying to enjoy their coffee when there came my mom and grandma expecting them to treat two filthy sunburnt people who just crawled out from under a freeway overpass like celebrities.

The four of us left the Starbucks and found a restaurant to scarf down burgers and listened to my grandma's old stories of punching dudes in the face when she was a teen. They then said goodbye as they dropped us, and our resupply package, off at a Motel 6.

I had never been to Palm Springs before and man, was it odd. Rich women with fake tans would leave fancy restaurants on the same street, same block, as itching meth addicts rode their bikes against traffic and onto the tourist filled sidewalks. Boarded up buildings and "store closing" signs sat right next door to the fancy restaurants. All of this surrounded by flat desert with San Jacinto towering above. It was bizarre, but I neither loved it nor hated it.

The next morning I didn't know how to feel. My laundry was in the hotel washer so I only had my puffy synthetic down jacket and running pants to wear with nothing underneath as I walked down the street to get us coffee and explore the neighboring thrift store. Inside the thrift store my jacket was making me sweat and was sticking to my skin but I obviously couldn't take it off. I felt like I fit in to the homeless crowd as my eyes darted back and forth and I tried to flap the collar of my jacket to air myself out. My hair was poofy from washing it for the first time in a while, and I was carrying a cuben fiber hiker wallet around which looked more like a corn husk. I think I had temporarily become the weirdest person in Palm Springs.

I darted back to the safety of the motel and finished getting ready for the day. Tim and I left to walk seven miles across Palm Springs, checking out tourist shops, buying snacks at grocery stores, and I even got Tim to spend a couple bucks on casino games with me just for fun. We were kind of stuck for a few days because the next stop was Big Bear but again, a snow storm was coming. At night we found a street fair to walk through in the rain, drank a really crappy "World's Best Bloody Mary," then hung out in the motel jacuzzi.

In the morning we called a cab back to the 10 overpass so we could hit the trail again and start the incline toward Big Bear mountain. It was also Tim's 34th birthday so he shotgunned a beer on the street in celebration while we waited for our ride. We stopped into Ziggy and The Bear's trail angel house to buy fuel then headed back into the land of mile-counting and horny toads and dirt naps. Always feeling either hot or cold but never in between. Back to our job of working hard, traveling in a way no one seemed to understand, and was even harder to explain.

Friends, family, and Facebook always tried to offer advice or comment about how they would love to be where we were, but it was so much different than just enjoying nature or taking a hike, and it's definitely nothing like camping. This hike was a creature of its own. A routine of working your muscles and joints until they ache through the night, then doing your best to rise with the sun and do it all over again. Rationing every sip of water or sometimes drinking extra to relieve your back of the weight. Not thinking so much of Canada but instead seeing how far we could get in five months while stopping to poke snakes and whistle at chickadees and shower in motels instead of under thunder clouds.

Over the previous few weeks I had quite a few realizations about life on trail. At one point I was passing a campground and naturally started thinking about camping then came to the realization, *oh yeah, I guess I technically do that every night.* It doesn't feel like camping, it feels like hiking every day until you make dinner and pass out. I also never knew my feet could smell so bad. Some of my toenails had even changed colors. Although after about a week on trail my feet had become wonderfully blister free.

Hiking the Pacific Crest Trail was like doing "leg day" at the gym for months on end, as a full-time job plus overtime without pay. It was hard work, but I had become excited about the routine. At one point I was thinking I should just post elevation charts instead of pictures - right next to the day's weather forecast. It was also surprising that constant downhill could sometimes be worse than going up.

Everything felt heavy. Every ounce really does count. Every time I added something to my backpack, even snacks, I had to ask myself "would I risk being in pain to have this item?"

A hotel will never feel as good as it does after hiking for days while trading off between two pairs of socks and underwear, and not even remembering how many days it had been since you last washed your hands.

The trail has the tendency to make you curse the sun one minute and have you running up the trail towards the slightest hint of sunlight the next. No matter what I say, I don't think I could ever fully explain thru hiking - or surviving in the hot and cold in one outfit.

Cabazon to Big Bear Lake: A Mountain Lion Stole My Phone Charger

Ziggy and The Bear's held few familiar faces, so we bought our fuel and added to the hiker box then headed back into the mountains. The desert floor was flat and empty, but within the first few miles the trail took us up and down rolling hills surrounded by wind turbines. Soon we were scaling desert mountains in the middle of nowhere. It was very peaceful and quiet, with no one else around for most of the day. We had heard about a nature preserve called Whitewater Preserve which allowed hikers to camp there after hours. It was close to ten miles in, so we decided to stop there to camp and visit with other hikers. My knee had been bugging me ever since struggling my way down Mount San Jacinto, so I felt okay with completing only ten miles and then increasing the mileage as we went on.

We arrived fairly early, with the sun still up, and I was excited to take my backpack off and explore the grounds. It was a beautiful place scattered in man-made ponds filled with large trout. There was even a swimming hole, which would have felt amazing if the weather was warmer. The grass in the preserve was green and surrounded by tall, rock-covered hills that went back as far as the eye could see. Signs posted warned of both raccoons and mountain lions. We introduced ourselves to a few other hikers, who gave us the juicy updates about trail drama we had missed while we were in Palm Springs. Apparently the other hikers split up between Ziggy and the Bear's and a motel in Cabazon to get out of the rain, and supposedly the hiker motel party turned into an orgy. Tim and I laughed. It's funny how fast gossip can spread through the backwoods.

I slept great that night and was excited to start climbing mountains again in the morning. Instead of taking off right after waking up, we took our time making coffee and going through our backpacks. The hikers we had met the night before came over to join us as we packed our things.

"Did you guys hear the mountain lion last night?!" they said.

"What?? No! There was a mountain lion? Did you see it?" I replied, shocked.

"No we didn't see it, we only heard it walking through camp. Supposedly it stole another hiker's food!"

"It *stole* their food?!"

"Yeah, them over there. I think they even saw it."

"Crazy! I'm going to go ask them about it." Tim and I walked over to two other hikers packing up their tent. As we walked we searched the ground for mountain lion tracks.

"Hi! We heard you guys might have seen a mountain lion?!"

"Yes! Well... We didn't see it. We heard it! It actually reached into our tent last night and took a Ziploc bag of candy. The bag also had my phone charger in it. I spent the morning searching bushes around the preserve for the bag and it's gone." Tim and I met eyes.

"Huh, I've never heard of a mountain lion stealing candy out of tents. Are you sure it wasn't a raccoon?" Tim asked.

"It was so loud when it walked, it had to be something much bigger. It couldn't have been a raccoon." Tim and I assured them that mountain lions would be more interested in eating a small human or dog than a Snickers bar if they were actually desperate enough to venture into an occupied campground, but they didn't seem convinced. That and mountain lions are completely silent when they walk. We finished packing up and said goodbye, still giggling about the thought of a mountain lion out there with an iPhone charger.

We spent the next two days hiking up desert mountains, past our first sightings of poodle dog bush, and up into where the desert slowly fades into forest on our way toward Big Bear. Every morning we would hike as fast as we could, as a race to see how many miles we could do before the sun hit our face. Whoever led the way on early mornings was in charge of walking with one hiking pole pointed out to catch the dewy spiderwebs stretching across the trail before our bodies did. I was also getting surprisingly good at snot rockets. Our last day before reaching town we woke up ready to go and excited to press on for fifteen miles, which would leave us only six miles the next day before hitching into Big Bear and stuffing ourselves with restaurant food. Our tent was pitched at the top of a mountain overlooking a sea of pine trees layered in dense fog.

I bet you wonder by now if Tim and I had trail names. We had promised each other to let our names come naturally while hiking with other people, instead of naming each other. Other people only suggested things about our looks though, without actually getting to know us or base it off of a situation that happened on trail. I'm sorry but it would be pretty damn boring if half of the people on trail were called by their hairstyle. The short answer to the question is no, we never had trail names we introduced ourselves as. We never hiked with anyone else long enough for them to feel comfortable offering us names. But in reality we did have trail names, we just didn't realize it until a few years later. Within our first week hiking Tim and I joked that our trail names should be Burp and Thurp. Thurp being a comic book description of a fart, and Burp being self explanatory. Tim was Thurp and I was Burp, because that's what we did on trail. We never made it official because we thought it was lame to name ourselves. We had a blog called B&T PCT, which was for our real names but would have also worked perfect with our trail names. While we traveled Europe there were a few times we slapped up stickers which said in Sharpie "Burp 'n Thurp do Eur'p." I ended up telling a few people about Burp and Thurp years later, including some hikers I met while I cooked tacos on trail as trail magic, and they all said the same thing "Well there you have it, you are Burp and Thurp."

Tim and I descended the mountain we slept on, then zigzagged up and down for most of the morning. About half way through our day, we ran into some trail magic which was an amazing surprise. Imagine days of rationing water and food, and then your first unexpected sign of human life besides another hiker here and there was a cooler of ice cold drinks with a sign saying "BBQ" with an arrow. Tim and I each took a beer and popped it open as we walked the direction the arrow was pointing. In the trees were a few small log cabins, one with hikers sitting in the sun with their shoes off on the front porch and a beer in hand. Next to them was a man and his wife barbecuing chicken.

"I'm Lian and this is my husband Aloha." the woman said. "He is thru-hiking and I flew down from Oregon to meet with him for the weekend. We figured we would get a cabin right on trail so we could do trail magic!"

"Nice to meet you both! We're Tim and Bridget. Thanks so much for doing this." Tim and I introduced ourselves to the other hikers, one of them we had met a day prior. We joined them on the porch, spending an hour soaking in the sun. It was blissful and I wished I could stay, but Tim and I and another hiker named Transformer decided it was time we had better get going. We said goodbye to Ahola and Lian and took off down the trail to finish seven to eight more miles for the day.

As the three of us walked, we passed a property lined with cages and could see a few sad grizzlies inside. They were retired TV stunt animals who now lived in little chain link boxes in the forest. It was interesting getting to actually see bears right on trail, but I'd wished it was under better circumstances. There was actually a petition going around online to get the city to do something about their situation. The bears ignored us and we kept on walking.

Not long after we reached a water cache with a phone number for Papa Smurf and Mountain Mama, Big Bear trail angels who welcomed hikers into their home and offered rides to and from the nearby highway. Transformer had an injury and decided he wanted to take advantage of the highway being nearby to get a ride into town. Tim and I said goodbye and decided to press on with our intended plan of two more half days of hiking before hitchhiking in from further down the trail.

Within only a few yards my knee was getting bad quick and I was limping so bad it was starting to worry me. If I continued hiking I was scared it could be come damaged to the point I'd have to be off of it for weeks. Continuing on while limping also meant it could slow us down to the point we'd be spending extra days hiking which we didn't have the food for. After much debate and frustration we turned back toward the water cache and sat with our hiker friend by the side of the highway to wait for Papa Smurf.

Papa Smurf couldn't take us all the way into town, but he was nice enough to bring us to his house where we could visit with some of the other hikers and then get a ride from his wife Mountain Mama on her way to work. They also invited us to stay but the three of us were equally adamant about getting to town. An hour later Mountain Mama dropped us off at a more well known hostel in Big Bear Lake. We only saw a few other hikers at the hostel, which was musty and uninviting. We all sat on a bench outside searching the internet on our phones for what other lodging options and restaurants were nearby.

A woman who worked at the hostel walked up to us and asked, "So are you checking in, or what?"

"I don't think we will be." we answered back, getting up to leave. We decided on splitting a motel room down the street with two full beds. Between the three of us it was basically the same price as a hostel. We figured we could stay there for one night and find something better the next day if necessary.

I've been to some shady motels before, but this one was definitely one of the worst. There was an ice bucket but no ice machine. It might have been in the lobby, but after we checked in they locked up the doors and never opened it again. Garbage bags of trash were left piled under staircases and the remnants of a pool was filled with dirt and grass. Our bathroom sink had two different handles that didn't match, which also didn't work properly, and the glass in the bathroom window was shattered.

Nothing mattered more to us at this point than leaving our temporary home for a nearby local brewery, where we spent more on food and drinks than we did on our hotel room. I ate until I felt sick, which was worth it but made my time limping around town much more uncomfortable. Funny things happen when you're hiking and bumming around in towns. Lots of new experiences - like limping down a highway with a pack on while carrying a package from the post office in both arms, and someone pulling their car over to ask if you're okay.

We went back to the hotel full and sleepy, sharing a cold six pack from the brewery while we watched TV and then drifted off to sleep. After a good night's rest I woke up in the pitch black motel at 7 AM on a serious mission to ice my knee and drink some coffee. Of course the shady lobby was closed, as usual, so I hobbled to a coffee shop a few blocks away where the barista was nice enough to make me a hot mocha and a bag of ice. I lounged and iced my knee in the coffee shop for a few hours to let Tim and Transformer sleep in, then returned to the motel to check out. We stuck our key in the mail drop as we left since the lobby door was still locked.

I had heard about a different hostel for hikers and it seemed like a much better deal than the one we previously visited, so the three of us went to check it out. The Big Bear Adventure Lodge was a beautiful, red, historic lodge and hostel at the end of a steep, secluded driveway, not far from a few bars and restaurants. It was built in 1919 and is still the oldest active lodge on Big Bear mountain. As we walked up onto the big front porch filled with chairs and hammocks we were greeted by a large group of excited hikers. "Get in here! Have you checked in? Go check in! Want a beer?!" It was like a party was being thrown just for us. Transformer introduced us to another injured hiker named Gandalf the White, and the four of us instantly became inseparable.

The hostel was cozy and inviting, there was the large porch, friendly huskies, a pool table, fireplaces, free meals, card games, beer pong, I could go on and on. We ran errands with other hikers around town. First by car, where one of the hostel workers was nice enough to fit six of us in their one small car, blasting music through town with our heads sticking out the window while lap riding. Then we crossed town by bus, hitchhiking, and walking. We drank on the porch, walked down the street for one dollar tacos and jalapeño margaritas, and back to the hostel for more food, alcohol, and games by the fireplace until well past hiker midnight.

Most of the guests in the hostel were hikers, but there were a few other interesting characters as well. One guest who partied with the hikers and hostel workers was a Russian woman in heels and a fur coat, who drove a nice BMW. She woke our room up at 7:15 AM blasting techno in the shower, even though her private bedroom had its own bathroom attached. Instead she insisted on showering in the bathroom connected to the hiker dorm. Later that day she made racist comments about Mexicans at the diner table. After that we all stopped pretending to act nice to her. There was a rumor she gave one of the hikers a blow-job in her BMW while the rest of us went to the bar with the hostel workers, but who knows if that was true.

We spent a few days enjoying our time at the lodge, as did quite a few other hikers. It seemed a lot of people were injured or just needed a break. Since none of us knew what day we wanted to leave we would all get up and pay for another night each morning once we made our decision. It was the week before Memorial Day weekend and all of the hikers were informed that a family booked the entire lodge for a private event for multiple days on end. We would all have to leave. The three of us were still too injured to hike, and all of the other lodging in town was booked for the holiday. As we sat in the lodge with our heads hung down, not sure of what to do, one of the men working the hostel who we had been partying with had an idea.

"We normally don't do this..." he said, "but the three of us live in a cabin owned by the lodge owner right down the street. It's just a short drive away. In the attic is a bunkhouse. I think at one point he was meaning to rent it out but now we don't use it. We can charge you the same rate you are staying here to sleep there for a few days if you'd like?"

"Are you sure? That would be awesome, if it's not too much trouble." We all looked at each other and nodded in agreement.

"Okay, let us clean up here for another hour or so and they we can give you a ride." The four of us helped pick up around the hostel then were driven a few miles down the road into a residential neighborhood.

The cabin was dark and cluttered inside, but it felt homey. Upstairs were the bedrooms and bathroom, and a door with a steep stairwell inside leading up to our little attic bunkhouse with six single beds. We spent two nights there, watching movies in the living room by the fireplace and wandering back to the Mexican restaurant for tacos and margaritas.

Eventually we were all anxious to get out of Big Bear. We had been there for a week and it was time to move on. One of our hosts gave the four of us a ride into town where we thanked them profusely and said our goodbyes. Gandalf and Transformer were going to catch a ride about one hundred miles up the trail to Wrightwood so they could get back on trail with all of their friends. Tim and I hitchhiked back to the closest PCT trailhead in Big Bear, four-teen miles ahead of where we left off.

Tim and I were dropped off at the trail around 1 PM then stretched and started heading west up into the hills north of Big Bear Lake.

"I really don't want to ask this," Tim said, "but what would we do if we had to get off trail?"

I let out a long sigh. "Jeez, I don't know. Hopefully it won't come to that. We have pet sitters and time and money set aside for this though, we could always take off and go somewhere else?"

"If you could be anywhere else right now, where would you want to be?"

"Hmm, probably on a tropical beach."

"I've never been to the Florida Keys."

"Neither have I."

"We could drive there. Across the country."

"That would be cool. I don't want to leave the trail, but if we have to, maybe we can do that."

"I definitely don't want to either. But it's a plan, I guess. If you hurt your knees we'll go to the keys."

"The Florida Knees."

No other thru-hikers passed us by, but every now and then a day-hiking local would walk past and wave. Tim and I walked up a rocky hill as a father and his young son passed us by, saying hello. After them was a man jogging who went around us and up the hill. We trudged on for another half an hour before starting to hear a strange slap-ping noise combined with the sound of footsteps, look-ing up to see the same jogger running back down the hill completely naked. "It doesn't get any less steep!" He said as we stepped aside to let him pass. We thanked him for his advice and continued on while laughing to ourselves.

I was having a fairly easy day on trail yet was having a hard time getting into a happy hiking mood. I was worried about my knee. I was disappointed that we were all alone and the other hikers were so far ahead. I could already feel a tinge of pain in my knee, but kept on hiking through it, pretending it wasn't there. I was trying my best to push on through, but even Tim knew it was bugging me even though I said nothing about it.

After eight and a half miles of hiking we came to a creek and stopped to filter water. As we filled our water bladders, we were startled by a man on horseback coming around a bend in the trail. The elderly man greeted us, asking us where we were hiking and where we were from. When he found out we had last been living in Oakland he went on to tell us about how much of a shit hole he thought it was. Not only was this incredibly rude and awkward, but we were also both expecting him to just start spewing the N-word at any moment. Thankfully it didn't happen and he went on his way looking for illegal fire rings, but it only added to the lingering black cloud I felt enveloped me as I hiked. We walked on a few more miles before setting up camp under oak trees.

It grew dark and silent. We heard the sounds of some-one or something with us a few hours after we had gotten in bed, but it was too dark to see and we were too tired to care. It sounded like another person setting up a tent not far away, but in the morning no one was there.

The trail was easy and flat the next day, and we completed ten miles by noon, reaching our next water source. By the time we arrived I was crawling, practically dragging my bad leg. I had been limping all day long, and it was getting worse the more I walked. I felt throbbing and swelling to the point I could barely bend my knee. I wanted to cry in anger and frustration. The trail in front of me was flat and winding through the shade of trees, but it was a struggle to even move forward. We sat down to rest and I looked up to Tim with watery eyes. He knew what was coming.

"How much further do you think you could do?" he asked.

"For today - nothing. I'm swollen. I can't even bend it"

"And tomorrow?"

"I could try for five miles. I doubt I can do more than that in this condition. And I don't know what will happen if it gets any worse."

"We have to hike fifteen mile days from here to Cajon Pass or our food will run out."

"I know."

"Well," Tim sighed, "where do you want to get off. Should we look at the map?"

"Anywhere." I said, with my head hung low. "We could try from here since there is a parking lot. We can wait until one of these day-hikers comes back to their car and catch a ride."

"Okay. If that's what we need to do." Not much longer two off-road Jeeps pulled up to the end of the dirt parking lot on an unpaved road. One of them was having brake issues so they all got out to chat while the problem was being looked at. We walked up to the small group of people like sad puppies.

"Hey are you two PCT hikers?!" one of the drivers yelled out.

"Yes we are. But unfortunately she's injured, so we're trying to find a way back to Big Bear Lake." Tim answered.

"Oh, that's no good. I know how that is though, I hiked the trail in 1985! So you two are looking for a ride back to town?"

"Yes, we are. Wow '85?!"

"Yep! It was quite a bit different back then!" The man then looked over at his wife and shrugged.

"We are actually heading back to Big Bear Lake right now to get lunch," his wife piped up, "we should be able to fit you in."

We climbed into the back seats of their off-road Jeep and held our backpacks on our laps. We were both in a mental fog, trying to come to terms with the fact we were leaving the trail. At the same time we were incredibly surprised by our odd mix of bad and good luck, getting picked up by someone who completed a thru-hike the year before I was born. We zoomed through the backwoods bouncing up and down on the bumpy dirt roads with the wind in our faces. It felt so good and so bad to leave.

It was the Sunday of Memorial Day weekend around 1 PM when we got dropped off in Big Bear Lake Village. Tim and I sat on a bench in the middle of a crowd in silence, looking on our phones for a way out of Big Bear or somewhere to stay. We wanted to give my knee a break for another week or two then try again, but staying in town for all of that time would be too expensive. Plus it was time I saw a doctor. We needed somewhere to stay for the night so we could try to make our way to San Diego the next day. All of the cheap lodging was still booked and the only bus we could find that could take us to a train toward San Diego wasn't leaving for two days. We decided to go to the brewery for a couple beers and then find somewhere to sleep behind a building after the sun went down. The day after that we could move back to the hostel.

The brewery was crowded for the holiday weekend, but its small outdoor porch on the second story overlooking the lake had two seats open just for us. We sipped our beers looking out over the lake. It was bizarre that only a few hours prior we were in the trees on the other side. We were thru-hikers then. And now we weren't.

"ARE YOU GUYS HIKING THAT TRAIL?!" an excited voice yelled from behind us. "An old work buddy of mine left the job a few years back to hike it! The name's Rob, what's yours?" We turned to introduce ourselves to the middle age man holding a pint of beer who had approached us, and confirmed we had been hiking. Then the questions came pouring in. It was like we were celebrities. We answered each question as quickly and efficiently as we could, then explained our situation. "Where are you staying tonight?" Rob asked.

"Honestly, everything is booked so we're not sure. We have a tent and sleeping bags though, so we'll find a place eventually once the sun goes down." Tim answered.

"I see... Say, can I introduce you to my wife?" Rob asked.

"Sure." we shrugged. We had no clue what Rob had in store or how long he wanted to hang out. If anything we were thinking maybe our hiker fame would get us a free drink.

Rob poked his body back inside the door of the brewery and waved his wife over enthusiastically. "This is Helen. Helen, these are two Pacific Crest Trail hikers! Tim and Bridget."

"Oh, uh.. Nice to meet you!" Helen said confused, not sure why her husband was so excited.

"They were hiking from the border of Mexico to Canada, but Bridget here hurt her knee. Everything in town is booked so they are just going to sleep outside tonight. What do you think about them coming back to our place and staying in the guest bedroom?"

"Oh, well, we should make sure it's okay with the girls. But I don't see why not? We have laundry, showers, food, wine..." And then she said the magic word. "We also have a jacuzzi." Tim and I nearly spit our beer. We were sold.

Their house in Big Bear was a shared vacation home they owned with another family and took turns using. Rob and Helen had one twelve year old daughter and she had brought a friend with her to stay for the weekend. The couple explained to the girls two strange broken hobos would be making dirt tea in the jacuzzi that night, then drove them home before coming back to pick us up with more room in the car. This worked out perfectly since we had food and drinks to finish anyway.

The minute we stepped into Rob and Helen's home we were introduced to the two girls then given a tour. We were shown to the red wine, guest bedroom, laundry room, guest bath, and the jacuzzi. Helen handed us clean towels and was very adamant about us taking showers and doing laundry first thing. In our eyes two nights on trail was still fresh and clean, but we had to remember we were back in normal people land now. Plus not only was it convenient for us, but the least we could do to make them happy. The family got in their nice dinner outfits as we greeted them again, this time fresh and clean. Wearing our clean base layers as the rest of our clothes went through the wash.

"The only thing about you staying here is that we have dinner reservations tonight. I hope you don't mind." Rob said.

"Oh, no problem. We don't mind just relaxing and maybe using the jacuzzi. Thank you so much for everything." I said, surprised at how trusting the family was to leave us in their house alone.

"We will be back in a few hours." The minute the family left the house we threw on borrowed bathing suits, poured ourselves some wine, and jumped in the jacuzzi.

We spent the entire time they were at dinner in that jacuzzi. Not only was it relaxing for our muscles, but it helped to ease some of the stress and frustration we were feeling. Or maybe that was the wine. We stayed in that hot tub under the Big Bear stars for what seemed like days, but was only about two to three hours. Even when our hosts arrived back home from dinner we stayed in for just a "little bit longer."

Not long after the family returned we all had another glass of wine together and Helen made me an ice pack for my knee. As luck would have it, Helen just so happened to be a physical therapist, so she gave me general tips on how to help with the swelling as we discussed the physical aspects of long distance hiking.

They had so many questions and we were more than willing to answer them all. We discussed all the logistics of our hike and regaled them with stories of the trail leading up to Big Bear. We even took out our cooking setup to show them what and how we eat on trail.

"Thanks so much for being our trail angels!" Tim said to Rob.

"What is a trail angel?" Rob asked.

"Oh, a trail angel is someone who helps a thru-hiker for nothing in return. By offering lodging, food, rides, or anything really."

"Did you hear that honey?! We're trail angels!" We said good night and crawled into the luxuriously soft and warm queen bed of "our" room.

After a great night's sleep we woke to Helen cooking a big breakfast, complete with fried eggs, toast, coffee, and orange juice. We scarfed down our food and thanked our trail angels once more, then Rob drove us back to the front porch of the Adventure Lodge.

The men at the hostel were surprised to see us back. We explained our situation and paid for one night, but they upgraded us to a private bedroom at no extra cost. All of our hiker friends were gone. We were at the hostel alone with just the workers and a few strangers, but it felt so good to have our own little hotel room in the lodge. It felt like we had a few days of being spoiled before going back to uncertainty. Even though at this point we hoped we could still get back on trail, even if we had to skip ahead, it didn't happen. At least, not for me. And neither of us finished the trail. A month later Tim ended up skipping ahead and hiked from Kennedy Meadows to the summit of Mount Whitney before deciding he'd rather not hike alone.

I continued to remind myself that this was just the start of our two-year adventure. My hike on the Pacific Crest Trail took me almost three hundred miles on foot instead of 2,650, but my feelings of excitement and accomplishment overshadowed any feelings of failure. I tried, I got dirty, I climbed mountains, I held lizards, I slept under the stars, I left everything I knew to work toward a goal and got all that I needed out of the experience. To quote Bill Bryson's *A Walk in the Woods*, "I got a great deal else from the experience. I learned to pitch a tent and sleep beneath the stars. For a brief, proud period I was slender and fit. I gained a profound respect for the wilderness and nature and the benign dark power of woods. I understand now, in a way I never did before, the colossal scale of the world. I found patience and fortitude that I didn't know I had. I discovered an America that millions of people scarcely know exists. I made a friend. I came home." Except there was no home. Home, for now, was my teal Osprey backpack.

Big Bear Lake to the Florida Keys: A Case of the Florida Knees

I tossed and turned while sleeping in the van, it was well past midnight and the raindrops were loud on the roof. I was trying to ignore the dripping water hitting my forehead, not wanting to fully wake up again. I assumed it was condensation dripping from the little plastic fan dangling above me, cranked on high, but then it started to burn. I patted my forehead and smelled my hand. *Battery acid, great!* It was August in Miami and I was almost more upset about my fan being broken than the fact I had been an inch away from possibly becoming blind. Tim and I had been driving across the country for weeks and were only a few hours from our destination, Key West. We had a spare month with no plans and randomly decided driving from California to the Florida Keys and back in late summer would be a good idea. Not only were we battling heat and mosquitos, but there was also a hurricane approaching with a fifty percent chance of hitting the Keys. Thankfully for us, this hurricane never hit land.

The weather in the Florida Keys was hot with random showers here and there, and most of the tourists had fled due to concern over the hurricane warnings. We spent a week finding the best hidden beaches and cheap local food spots. We drenched ourselves in bug spray to sleep next to random dead chickens near a hidden cemetery in a residential area. We drank our morning coffee across from clear beach water, the temperatures already approaching 108 degrees.

I thought back about our trek to the island paradise we were in and all of the random events that took place. We had swam in a river near Auburn, California almost immediately after a body had been removed, wandered smoky casinos in Reno, walked into a midnight dance party at a squat in downtown Salt Lake City, won discounted tickets to a Broadway play in Denver, taught myself how to embroider in Kansas, slept in a child's bedroom in Tulsa, watched homeless men chase down a shoplifter in Austin, slept on floors with dogs in Houston, drank abandoned green goo grenade drinks while almost getting hit by lightning in New Orleans, bought Hot Pockets in Mobile just to say we did, and trekked through alligator swamps in Gainesville. Though we had made it across the country, we were only halfway through our drive.

We zoomed back across the country quick this time, with storms following behind. Each time zone passed gave us an extra hour, cooler weather, and less bugs. We broke our own records of how many times we could be the first to visit friends that had moved, as well as how many people with face tattoos we could stay with in a row. We listened to podcasts while falling asleep in gas station parking lots, stayed in motels with mystery blood stains, and Googled unknown bugs. Often while passing through new cities, I was envious of the wealthy tourists who had actually planned their stays. They had their air-conditioned rooms with a view, jacuzzis, and gourmet meals, while I found luxury in finding a Starbucks to brush my teeth in. I can only imagine their relaxing vacation to be not much more than that though. While ours may had been the rougher way to travel, our adventure was more than just an island vacation, but a month's worth of sweat and scars and sunburns to remind us of each place we had been.

Crossing The USA: Hitchhiking Our Way to Europe

"Nothing is more damaging to the adventurous spirit within a man than a secure future. The very basic core of a man's living spirit is his passion for adventure. The joy of life comes from our encounters with new experiences, and hence there is no greater joy than to have an endlessly changing horizon, for each day to have a new and different sun." - Jon Krakauer, Into The Wild fter spending the summer hiking the Pacific Crest Trail and then road tripping California and the southern portion of the country, Tim and I spent the winter doing odd jobs for cash before heading to Europe. A year prior we had booked round trip tickets to London from Philadelphia because it was the cheapest option we could find. How would we get to Philly? We'd figure it out. We had to leave our van in San Diego since we had nowhere to park it on the East Coast for most of the spring and summer. We planned on taking a few buses up California to stay with friends before making our way across the country in whatever ways we could. We had one month to find our way to Philadelphia Airport.

It took me six months to get a diagnosis for my knee because I had state-provided health insurance for people with low incomes. It took three months for them to tell me it wasn't broken (*shocking!*), and another three before I was allowed to get an MRI. For the time between I was sent to a physical therapist and told I most likely had a torn meniscus. This terrified me, so I spent as much time possible elevating and icing my knee without using it. What I didn't know is that this routine was making it worse. I developed atrophy, made my tendons angry and constricted from all the ice, and ended up on crutches. When I finally received my MRI it came back negative for a torn meniscus, and the doctors decided I had a bad case of tendonitis. This was good because I didn't need surgery, but also not so good because it's something I will probably have to struggle with forever. I was so frustrated I gave up the ice, threw the crutches outta my sight, and started using it as normal. It quickly got better as I eased it back into regular use and practiced stretching. As long as I was biking or walking and not scaling mountains with weight on my back it usually didn't swell or feel pinched with pain.

San Diego to Auburn: Ask Him What Year It Is

Our second trek across the country in six months started Tuesday March 1st, 2016. We woke up early in San Diego, ran around like chickens with our heads cut off, grabbing every last item we would need or want to carry on our backs until August. My brother Patrick drove us downtown to the Greyhound station where some of our friends were waiting to say goodbye and give us homemade gifts. Our first stop would be Los Angeles, where we would board another bus straight to Oakland, arriving a little before 11 PM.

Since we were going straight to our friend Alina's house, I had packed a full handle of vodka I was given for my birthday a few weeks earlier. I wasn't going to drink it all myself, in fact I probably wouldn't have drank it at all. And Alina wanted to make Bloody Marys, so it just made sense for me to bring it for that. Tim may or may not have been working in Humboldt during the fall, so was carrying a small supply of product (which neither of us partook in), I guess to pass the last bit off on friends who might be interested in said product as a gift for letting us smell up their house. We also each had a small pocket knife. Basically, we had *EVERYTHING ON THE PROHIBITED ITEMS SIGN* except for a gun. And they were searching bags! Somehow I had been on many a mode of transportation, and didn't realize Greyhound is the only one of them that has TSA-like security to make you feel safe on their squeaking, smelly, mystery-stained, walk-in freezer of a bus.

While walking nervously up to the bag-searcher-man we were stopped and told by Greyhound staff we needed to get on the bus *immediately* to make it in time. The man working security looked from side to side then just waved us on. We threw our bags under the bus so fast we didn't even think to grab jackets for the two-hour ice bucket ride. Everything was, somehow, working out in our favor though. We finally had time just to sit and relax, so nothing else seemed to matter.

After arriving in Los Angeles, we walked the two miles or so with heavy prohibited item filled backpacks to Union Station, where we got on our comfy Megabus with no problems. We spent the night in Oakland playing dice with Alina, drinking Bloody Marys with fifty pound dogs in our laps. We woke up the next morning to rain - a whole week's forecast of it. We drank coffee topped with scoops of vegan vanilla ice cream, and a crackhead told me all about his old dog "Donut." We watched an all-female punk band practice, learned how to make exploding glitter bombs, then decided at 2 AM to head down to the train tracks in Emeryville. The weather had cleared up a bit so it was as good of a time as we were going to get to leave town for free. I relaxed on our crinkled strip of hiker Tyvek ground-sheet, surrounded by long grass and chirping chickadees, until falling asleep with my face tucked into a homemade scarf. About thirty minutes later I jumped up to the sound of a train horn only a few yards away. *It's Amtrak*, I thought, then laid back down. It wasn't, I was just too delirious to notice the obvious. It wasn't stopping anyway though, so it didn't matter.

A freight train didn't stop near us until 7 AM, four hours later, but it was surrounded on both sides by security and train yard workers so we were out of luck at catching a free ride. It was also starting to rain on us. We walked back toward the nearby shopping center to get coffee and split a bagel. We weren't getting any luck from ride shares and both buses and trains were too expensive. Finally I tried Megabus again, desperate for anything soon and sleep-on-able, and found tickets to Sacramento for ten dollars a person. But it left from San Francisco. To San Francisco we went, free bus to BART, to two miles of walking in the rain, to a two-hour bus nap.

In Sacramento we got food then found a bus to our next destination Auburn, to visit friends. Except the bus driver confused Auburn, California with Auburn Boulevard in Sacramento, so we were going to have to transfer from bus to bus to bus. We were disoriented, trying to figure out what neighborhood exactly we were in, so Tim asked a man walking through the bus station for information.

"Excuse me, where is Sacramento?"

"Uh, you're in Sacramento," he responded.

"Yeah but which direction is downtown?" The man kept walking away from us, confused.

"You should have asked him what year it is." I said to Tim.

I found our location on the map, and we were a twenty-five minute drive from the northern edge of Sacramento, and it was going to be a three-and-a-half hour bus ride *just* to Roseville, which was only halfway to Auburn. It was already dark and most of our stuff was damp. We called our friend Chris and he ended up driving over to pick us up, making the trip only thirty minutes by car.

We were on our way to Auburn, and stopped to grab a few six packs of fancy beer on our way to Chris' house to watch bluegrass videos and drink whiskey sours. After probably my tenth second-wind of the day, I fell asleep on the couch around midnight while Tim and Chris continued to talk. I woke up again around 2 AM to more friends around me drinking whiskey sours and discussing everything from skateboarding to politics. We went to bed again around 4 AM, woke up at noon, and had a few hours to eat breakfast and watch a very addictive TV show before our ride share would be there to pick us up. We considered trains again but decided against it. Not only was it pouring rain nonstop, but it was also snowing up the hill on Donner pass. Tim found a rideshare online going east, so at 4 PM a scruffy, thin twenty-eight-year-old man with a ponytail loaded us into his small Toyota truck. Destination: Wyoming.

Auburn to Green River: Getting Cold Feet

We drove straight to Wells, Nevada where we ended up splitting a cheap motel at 1 AM. I was set on falling asleep the minute I got into that room, but our driver offered us each a cold beer from his six pack, and we ended up talking and relaxing for an hour or so before falling asleep. He was set on reaching nearby hot springs in the morning before getting to an orientation he had to make in Wyoming around dinner time. That meant going to bed at 2 AM, realistically 3 AM if you want to include the time zone change we'd soon be passing, and waking up around 7 AM.

In the morning, snow was scattered on the ground and the wind felt icy. We took some random Wells, Nevada backroads through the tiny town which was completely closed up on an early Sunday morning. The sky was grey, and rain and snow were on the forecast for mid-day. We found the dirt road to our hot springs but it was looking pretty muddy. We decided to go down the two-mile road for as long as we felt safe in the mud, which ended up being about a mile in. The well-packed mud quickly became large puddles of sticky mess. The guys jumped out to shovel off the thick layer of mud sticking to each tire, and to their shoes. It was everywhere. At this point we definitely weren't continuing forward, but there was no place to turn around for us to go back. And it didn't help that this little old truck was two-wheel drive.   Our driver was worrying about becoming stuck, while Tim was informing him that the real danger was the possibility of us sliding off the road. It's not like we were on a cliff or anything, but sliding would definitely mean flipping the truck horizontally down a hill and then really being screwed. We started to slowly roll backwards, but the slipping and spraying of the mud kept scaring our driver into slamming the brakes. Tim started to coach him out, and he was determined to get it right. After a few tries of forward, backward, and forward again, we zoomed backward through the mud, sliding past pond-sized puddles and cheering as we backed up right into a turnaround spot. We all glanced around at each other relieved, but our driver then mentioned he was still determined to see the hot springs, although he didn't want to do anything we were uncomfortable with.

The weather app on my phone said two hours until snow storm, and we would have to walk two miles through thick mud, wet, in 39-degree weather with no towels or warm jackets. All while trying to beat a storm, and leaving the truck to the whims of whatever the locals were like in this part of town. Thankfully our driver was okay with just getting back on the freeway. On our way to whatever Wyoming would have in store.

We said goodbye to our temporary adventure buddy while pulling our backpacks out of the back of his Toyota at a gas station in Green River, Wyoming, which was the furthest he could take us. We walked the small-town strip, only the length of a few blocks, checking out what the town had to offer. A dive bar, two or three gas stations, and lots of small motels. We sat down in a nice park that had a gazebo with power outlets. Behind us were impressive towering rock formations, and in front was the train yard in a lone field, surrounded by trees speckled in glistening snow melting in the sunshine.

The snow made me nervous. I'm one of those people who are always cold. I'm like a shivery 117 pound Chihuahua. Hypothermia is something I sincerely hope to never experience. When planning to hike the Pacific Crest Trail, besides injury, snow was my big issue that I felt was worth leaving the trail over. Besides hypothermia, the risks of hiking in snowy conditions are also losing the trail and getting lost, sliding off of a mountain, or walking off of a mountain in low visibility. A lot of hikers still do it successfully, but they know what they are doing and I don't. I'm from San Diego! Land of three hundred and sixty five days of desert heat.

We went into a gas station for supplies. I bought food and drinks, a beanie, and some cheap cotton gloves. My warmest outfit now consisted of cheap black jeans over Merino wool leggings, two pairs of hiking socks, a thin sweatshirt over a button up flannel, over a T-shirt, over a tank top, a cheap beanie, thin cotton gloves for hands twice my size, a homemade scarf, and a paper-thin ultralight rain jacket. It sounds warm but it felt only slightly warmer than a T-shirt and jeans. During the day I was fine, but night time wasn't so fun.

To pass the time, we had a few drinks and snacks in a local dive bar. We were getting stared at by locals, yet everyone who talked to us was nice enough. After getting a little buzzed, we wandered to the train tracks and threw our stuff under a bridge next to a half-frozen river.

I shivered waiting for a train to come. Tim had heard of a better spot to wait at under the bridge on the other side of the river, but the only way it seemed we could cross was over the top of the train bridge. I don't think I need to explain why that was not a fun idea, although we were desperate enough to try. It seemed like no trains were coming, so I jogged in place to warm up my feet, then walked as fast as we could single file next to the tracks over the river. About half way there we saw lights peering out from behind the bend. "Walk fast, don't run" Tim warned as we quickly turned back. My heart was beating and I walked as fast as I possibly could, pretending walking on train track rocks with numb feet wasn't comparable to walking on Legos in heels. We made it to our spot under the tracks and of course the train didn't even stop.

After a while, we knew we would only get comfortable if we pulled out our sleeping bags and cuddled for warmth. A few more trains passed without stopping, and it was impossible to sleep due to the cold. My face hurt if it wasn't buried inside my sleeping bag sealed in a sack of hot breath, and my feet burned from the cold even with my shoes on inside of my sleeping bag. An eastbound train never stopped, and through most of the night trains didn't even pass through. Once the morning came I was done. I wanted real sleep. I wanted to scald the cold off of me with burning liquid. I wanted a shitty motel.

We hobbled with frozen feet back to the main strip. My toes had lost feeling to the point I wasn't sure if they were curled or straight inside of my shoes. I swore one foot's toes were curled, which made it awkward to walk but

I didn't want to look to fix it until I was in a warm room. We checked into a cheap motel and jumped onto the bed feeling ecstatic. Tim turned on the TV and I defrosted in a steaming hot shower. Of course you could see the train yard from our room's door, and a train headed eastbound stopped right over the bridge a few acres away.

We checked out the next morning and headed back to our spot. No trains came the night we waited under the bridge, but plenty came throughout the day. Our new plan was to head over to the better spot we had heard about on the other side of the bridge. We would get there early then bask in the sunlight while we waited. A highway was the only way we knew of to cross the river besides the aforementioned train bridge. Walking the highway for miles across town didn't seem like a great idea either, so we walked to the gas station and asked the first nice local for a ride to our "hiking" spot. The man who offered us a ride was nice. He told us about his hiking adventures and we talked about ours. He mentioned his wife was also from San Diego and came from a strict Mormon family. He dropped us off in a neighborhood and we walked down the hill to our spot under the bridge.

We basked in the sunlight, still bundled since the air was cold, sipping cold drinks and listening to a murder mystery podcast. I read the graffiti under the bridge for close to an hour, trying to find familiar monikers, and successfully finding those of a few friends. Including one from Chris, who we stayed with in Auburn. The sun started setting as I wandered the neighboring field, tracking raccoon prints and poking at the frozen river edges with a stick. No train came our way the entire day.

The sun went down and again it got uncomfortably cold. My spirits were low. I felt stuck in this stupid town. I took to jogging in circles for nearly an hour trying to keep my limbs from going numb again. Then, I tried jumping jacks and pacing up and down a trail, hidden from the nearby dirt road by tall bushes. During my pacing two large German Shepherds bolted out of nowhere heading straight for me.

"*Dogs!*" I yelled to Tim.

He looked over from a few yards away and started yelling, "*Go, Shoo!*" The male went straight for Tim, growling and baring his teeth, a female ran up to me looking more inquisitive.

"Hi doggy," I said, trying to use an upbeat greeting to hide my fear.

"Get back here!" a voice yelled out from the road on the other side of the bushes. "I'm so sorry about that!" he then said to us.

"No problem," we yelled back, surprised he wasn't interested in why a couple would be hanging out at night under the train bridge. Or maybe he was used to it, I don't know.

We sat down and calmed our nerves, still shaking from the cold. Eventually a train horn blew from out in the mountains and we ran up onto the bridge and into the neighboring field to try our luck.

Finally, an eastbound train stopped right in front of us. We jumped up and walked as fast as we could, me bumbling again with numb feet, walking car to car trying to find one we could ride on. I don't know what was with our bad luck in Green River, but the train quickly aired up and pulled away again without us finding one rideable train car in the ten or so we jogged passed. They were all grainers with no holes and no floors. It was just the two of us again, alone in a field under the stars.

I thought we could stay up in the bushes, since it seemed warmer than the cold wind tunnel the bridge created. After another hour of waiting I was done. I didn't want to go through another night under the bridge. I was freezing and numb and our sleeping gear wasn't nearly warm enough for this kind of weather. Normally while traveling like this we'd have no money, and no options, but today we did. We saved for years for these trips, and we didn't have to be out in the cold. It just meant blowing the minimal Europe funds we had, but at this point I didn't care.

Now how would we get back to the main road to reach the motel? Crossing the train bridge was the only way. It shouldn't have been that bad since there were no trains ever, right? Plus, one had just passed us not that long ago. Walk fast, don't run. I wobbled my frozen meat stumps as hard as I could. Trying my best not to roll the ankles I couldn't feel, but knew I had down there somewhere. We approached the bridge from the field then heard another horn. "You have got to be kidding me!" A train was slowly making its way through the train yard westbound toward us in the field, going the opposite way we needed. We ran into the bushes to hide and watched the front of the train slowly pass us and roll to a stop. We walked along the side of the train and back down under the bridge to wait for it to leave. Time went by, and it wasn't going anywhere. We wanted to go, the train wasn't moving. We walked up on the bridge again and considered walking across along the train's side. Even if it started to leave we would have enough time to make it across before it picked up any speed.

"Go, go, go!" Tim took off ahead of me and I walked fast and steady, meticulously placing one foot in front of the other. I was calm and confident, but peered over the edge and started to convince myself my foot was going to slip and I would slide off the rocks on the bridge and into the river below. It was a horrifying thought. My anxiety was getting the best of me but I kept walking quick. The minute we reached the other side of the bridge the train aired up to leave. I practically dove into the dirt, rocks, and plants, just to feel real ground under me and not sketchy train rocks over an icy river of death. I dusted myself off, wiping my oversized gloves on my pants to knock off some of the bird poop from the wire bridge railing.

There went more of our Europe funds to another motel. We walked the dark town strip to the store for food and drinks, relieved yet somberly disappointed at the same time.

"A creepy little park, in a creepy little town.
I tried to cross the bridge, but the train ran me down.
The dogs tried to bite us, I wish I'd had a treat.
But now I'm where it's warm, so I can finally feel me feet!"

I sang. "Delirious diddies by Bridget, I'll be here all night".

I threw open the motel room curtains the next morning to see multiple feet of snow piled against the window. We bundled up and stepped outside to everything covered in white. I was so thankful we wussed out. I wussed out. We were over Green River and not willing to wait another day with not one train headed in our direction, so we grabbed some gas station coffee and went to a freeway on-ramp to try our luck in Cheyenne.

Tim held up a cardboard sign reading "CHEYENNE OR EAST" and I sipped my drink cupped by both hands swimming in faded black gloves too big for my hands. Across town we could see a train round the bend, heading east. *"There she goooooes, there she goues ugain,"* I sang, Tim glared back at me with an evil look in his eye.

Green River to Denver: The Big City

A woman in a rickety little car pulled over to let us in. She asked us how we had ended up in Wyoming and told us about the different hitchhikers she had picked up over the years. She mentioned how her friends thought she was crazy for picking up strangers but all of her experiences had been positive, leading to meeting new people and hearing their unique stories. The woman could only take us to the next small town a few exits away, just slightly bigger than Green River, but she dropped us off at a spot she swore more people would be driving past because of the bigger truck stops located around the on-ramp. It was nice to have better food options, but getting back out on the road again was rough. I gave a friendly smile and wave to the constant stream of cars driving by, none of which were stopping. After a full day on two Wyoming on-ramps we decided on another motel. In the morning we put a rideshare ad out online just in case, then headed over to a Denny's.

It's funny how when you have backpacks servers come to see if you're "okay" every other minute. "You still here?" "Still planning on payin' for stuff?" Tim went to the bathroom once we had finished our meal and the lady asked me if I was "okay" four times while he was gone. Maybe I should have asked for a ride to Chicago.

I put on my best fake smile at the on-ramp and soon enough we were doing a double take as a big red truck towing a trailer actually pulled over on the awkward, curved on-ramp to give us a ride. It was a young couple who owned a business transporting trailers across the country, and they were headed to Cheyenne.

The truck was nice and new, so we had a comfortable two-hour drive before we said our goodbyes at a truck stop a mile or two from downtown Cheyenne. I was excited to be somewhere new. We walked past fields and cute houses, dogs in yards, and a cute little park with an old train caboose.

We came to a stoplight blocked by a train headed into the yard, and waited aside the car traffic for it to move down the line. The train pulled in and out, back and forth, and we took a seat on our backpacks to wait and watch. Once it moved we crossed the main street and headed into downtown. "*Woohoo, the big city!*" I yelled out with a sarcastic Southern accent.

We passed a lot of cheap motels, a few gas stations, then ended up in front of a bar a friend of ours had told us about. We heard this local's bar was right outside the train tracks. You could enjoy a beer while watching the trains, then run and jump on one with locals cheering behind you. We walked in, excited for nothing more than to just have a beer and sit down.

"*Outside!*" the woman behind the bar yelled, "take your houses *outside!*" The locals turned to look at us and we stepped outside to leave our backpacks by the parking lot lined picnic tables. Some locals at the tables asked us if the woman was giving us trouble.

"She doesn't like backpacks at the bar," they warned a little too late. We walked back inside and up to the bar to buy our drinks, but the woman still wasn't having us.

"No backpacks on the property, you have to leave, you can't be here." On the opposite side of the bar was a drive-up liquor store where they sold beer to go.

"Can we buy beer to go then?" Tim asked.

"Yes, but then you have to *leave* the property." The woman grabbed the attention of the man selling beer to go and informed him, "They can buy beer but then they have to *go*." We were too caught off guard to be offended, mainly just confused. We weren't dirty, smelly, drunk, we had even spent the last three nights in motels. I assume they had too many bad experiences with drunk train riders and it was obvious we didn't walk to Cheyenne to go hiking.

We stepped outside, bought some beer, and instantly two cop cars started circling the block. I was not feeling good about Cheyenne. We heard there was a good spot under a bridge near the not-so-welcoming bar, so Tim went to check it out while I stayed with our stuff along a road behind a closed business. He was gone for a while which was making me more nervous. I figured the cops would pull around and question me any minute, so I tried to duck into a shadow with the backpacks and beer, trying to think of what I would say if questioned.

"Yeah, I'm just waiting for my fiancé."

"Oh yeah? Where is he?"

"Oh, I don't know, walking around..." *Imagines Tim then crawling out from under the bridge.*

He came back out before the cops came back around, and told me there was another man down under the bridge he was talking to. Not really the type we would want to hang out with. Plus, there was a lot of water under the bridge. It was pretty flooded out from what I could see. The bar knew we were there, the cops knew we were there, we could see the train workers from the main street so obviously they knew we were there. It wasn't a good situation. And we had no spot to wait in. We were both sick of waiting. We need to get all the way to the East Coast and we were running out of time. We walked back down the street then paid for an extremely creepy cheap motel. The hallway looked eerily similar to the one from *The Shining* and the room was awkwardly gigantic with big open spaces. The couch and bed were dusty, and the bed was filthy. We pulled out our sleeping bags and slept in them on top of the comforter. Out of curiosity we looked up cheap flights to the East Coast just as a possibility to fast track our way there. Denver to Boston for $100 each. Tomorrow we would hitchhike to Denver.

The next day we spent some time exploring downtown Cheyenne, then walked the four miles back to the original truck stop we were dropped off at. It was already late evening so we were hoping to get a ride before the sun went down, or else we would have to sleep in a neighboring field and try again in the morning. We received a reply to our online rideshare ad, but it seemed questionable. It was from a "good-looking, fit trucker" who thought we sounded like a "fun couple."

Soon a man pulled over and we ran up to his souped up two-door 90's hatchback with a bad flat black paint job, and jumped in. The man was skinny and pale, with a shaved head and splotchy facial hair which grew in light patches scattering his face. He was much younger than us, probably early twenties, and was covered in poorly scribbled prison tattoos. Immediately after introducing himself, he told us he was crossing the border from Denver to Wyoming and back to sell weed, then went on to talk about how he lived with his girlfriend and newborn daughter in a hotel in Denver and worked for the mafia. I'm sure the first thing people who work for the mafia do is tell strangers that they sell drugs and work for the mafia. I didn't care to judge this man's life though, if anything I felt sorry for him since he was struggling to care for his family.

We sped down the freeway, and by sped, I mean this guy started driving so damn fast I was starting to question what the hell we had done by getting in his car. He got into the fast lane of the four-lane freeway and from the backseat I watched the speedometer dial slowly pass 90, 95, and keep going. I tried not to look. Very low profile for a so-called mobster with weed and who knows what else in the car.

Within ten minutes we hit traffic that brought the whole freeway to a stop. I had never been so happy to be in traffic in my life. *Whew,* I thought, wiping sweat from my forehead. *Glad that's over.* Boy, was I wrong. Every time the car in front of us moved forward our driver would hit the gas, gun it, shift into second gear, then have to quickly brake and shift back into first a second later before coming a foot from slamming into the car in front of us. I was sweating. Tim was sweating. I assume people in the cars around us were sweating. The jerking was making me nauseous so I was trying to figure out if I should concentrate on not puking, or use my nausea as an excuse for him to let us out. It had been forty-five minutes and there was no possible way I was going to ride with this guy for another hour to Denver.

Our driver was getting jittery, checking his phone more and more, which was something he had been doing the whole time he was driving like a maniac. He was getting irritated with the traffic and slamming the wheel with his hands in frustration. It was obvious there was somewhere he had to be. I looked up the traffic on my phone and informed him of an accident quite a ways ahead. It looked like there was no way we'd be avoiding it. I also informed the driver of an alternative freeway to the city outside of Denver he was trying to reach, a pit stop he was planning on taking with us in the car. He looked at the map himself and agreed as if having a revelation. Thankfully this new route was much too far out of our way, which was a perfect excuse for thanking him for the ride but opting to be dropped at the nearest freeway exit. He continued to repeatedly lurch forward then hit the brakes behind a flatbed semi-truck, just the perfect height to decapitate us with if he failed to slam the brakes fast enough while simultaneously checking his phone. We jumped out of the car at the next freeway exit, grabbed our bags and waved goodbye, then ran into a gas station to buy a beer to chug in the parking lot together not caring who was watching. That was by far the worst hitchhiking experience either of us had ever encountered.

We found a fancy hotel next to the freeway on-ramp to try hitchhiking from one last time before the sun went down. We were left in a little farm town right on the edge of Denver with nothing but hotels far out of our price range. We entered one and took advantage of their bathrooms, WIFI, and live music in the bar until we were ready to sleep behind the neighboring gas station. It didn't take too long the next morning before a nice man in a big truck took us closer to the city, dropping us off at a transit station with a bus to downtown Denver.

Denver to Philadelphia: Pure Hell

We arrived in the city with nowhere to go. We had three days until our flight. A bus took us to a neighborhood punk bar to sit in as we figured out where to stay. Last minute, I found a man renting his dining room futon out for twenty bucks a night. And it was only a few blocks from the punk bar. It seemed perfect enough, so we went to meet with him, excited to put our backpacks down for the rest of the night.

Tim and I sat outside of an old brick building as a tall thin man named Ryan opened the front entrance door to greet us. Ryan showed us to his studio apartment on the second floor, popping his key off the keychain and handing it to Tim as we walked. Instantly as we entered the apartment Ryan took his shirt off, changing in front of us into his work clothes.

"Sorry, but I'm already late for work." he said. "I do security at a cocktail bar downtown, so I'll be getting home after midnight."

"Okay, well, thanks for letting us stay." Tim said.

Soon Ryan left and we were alone in his apartment. The place was a mess, and smelled how food does when it's rotting in a drainpipe. It smelled worse in the kitchen, so I figured that was the culprit. The apartment was scattered in clothes and food wrappers, as was his bed which was in its own corner of the living room. Between the living room and kitchen was a small dining room containing only a futon mattress. There was a wall between the futon and living room, but no door. Tim and I went out once more to walk around Denver, before coming back to the apartment for an early night in.

I buried my face into my sleeping bag as the front door swung open and lights went on at 1 AM. Not just Ryan returned, but he had friends with him as well. A few men lounged around the living room drinking beer, talking loud, and Ryan even came over to ask us for the key back since he needed to let his girlfriend use it. The men talked as they occasionally walked into the kitchen to use the fridge or sink, saying hi to us loudly even though it was apparent we were trying to sleep. Eventually we woke up and browsed the internet for a bit, then I put ear plugs in and tried to fall back to sleep.

An hour later Ryan's friends left and his girlfriend popped by to spend the night. I don't know what this guy did wrong, but she was not happy with him. His girlfriend screamed and cried and fought with him, calling him every name in the book at the top of her lungs for the next few hours. I had lost track of how long it went on. Basically all night. They fought for hours on end while chain smoking inside. It was pure hell. A few times I seriously thought about leaving, but what would we have possibly done wandering Denver's streets at four in the morning? It sucked, but I didn't feel like our lives were in danger so we were better off hoping the two would wear themselves out eventually and pass out. It was five or six by the time they dozed off, and we did too.

Three hours later Ryan and his girlfriend were somehow up and starting their day, so Tim and I threw our sleeping bags in our backpacks and took off. We spent half of the day in a coffee shop trying to keep ourselves awake. I was desperate for sleep and somewhere to go. I wanted to wash off the cigarette smell and change my clothes. Tim and I looked online and found a private hostel room available about ten blocks away. We walked to it and checked in, thinking it was the best we could do last minute without spending too much money.

Two days later we stepped off a plane into Boston. With all of the adventure we had been through, I somehow didn't face any danger 'til almost losing my thumb in the door at the airport coffee shop. See, all this travel truly *is* dangerous. I had never been to Boston before. We had arrived just in time for Saint Patrick's day, which neither of us really wanted to go out of our way to celebrate. Mostly because hanging out in a packed pub full of drunk people screaming while slamming Irish Car Bombs wasn't really our thing.

The plan was to stay with an old friend of Tim's named Jamel for a few days before catching a bus to Brooklyn to stay with my high school best friend, Lewis. From there we would find another bus to Philly where we would board our flight to London. We were finally only two weeks from leaving the country.

We took a subway train to Jamel's house in the Jamaica Plain district of Boston, where he showed us his apartment and then took us out for drinks. We spent a couple of days with Jamel and his girlfriend, visiting museums, sifting through record shops, and cuddling with their dog and cat in our sleeping bags. We were almost ready to leave for New York when Jamel ended up in a predicament. He and his girlfriend were packing to catch a flight out of state when their pet sitter canceled. They had no backup and it was extremely last minute for finding someone to stay at their place for a whole week. Tim and I met eyes and shrugged. It was all too convenient that they already had two people in their house with nowhere to be. Of course we stayed, lounging around the apartment and taking the dog to see all the tourist sights of downtown Boston. While tourists posed for selfies next to statues of historical figures, Tim and I took pictures of the shiba inu, Cooper, posed next to each statue. Later Tim compiled them into a slideshow video to the song *America, Fuck Yeah!* And sent it to Jamel.

We only had a few days in Brooklyn, but it was just enough time to visit with Lewis and his wife Kim. They took us out for Ethiopian food; then, the next morning, we made them vegan breakfast burritos. They also got us discounted tickets into the Brooklyn Museum. It was a quick stop in New York, but we were ready for Europe! Tim and I said goodbye to Lewis, Kim, and their cats, then jumped on a bus to the Philadelphia airport.

Europe: Four Months, Nineteen Countries

'Ever bike? Now that's something that makes life worth living!... Oh, to just grip your handlebars and lay down to it, and go ripping and tearing through streets and road, over railroad tracks and bridges, threading crowds, avoiding collisions, at twenty miles or more an hour, and wondering all the time when you're going to smash up. Well now, that's something! And then go home again after three hours of it... and then to think that tomorrow I can do it all over again!" - Jack London, *The Letters of Jack London*

The United Kingdom: Alan's Granny's Big Ding Dongs

Tim and I arrived in London around 8 PM and took the Tube from Heathrow Airport to Victoria station, emerging to dark, empty streets. My entire life I had wanted to explore big cities on other continents, and here I was. It felt unreal. Here and there a person would walk past us with somewhere to go as we stood on the sidewalk like deer in headlights not knowing where we were or where we were going. We didn't even realize we were nearly three blocks from Buckingham Palace.

In order to save hundreds of dollars each month on phone bills and roaming fees, Tim and I had turned our phone service off once our plane hit the ground in London. We still had cell phones, but they would be used strictly as cameras and clocks unless we were connected to WIFI. For the entire four months we would be navigating the old school way – maps or pen and paper notes.

"We're supposed to walk South on Buckingham Palace Road, then take a left onto Sutherland Street." I read off my notes. That's all I had. Those directions and an address.

"Which way is South?" Tim asked.

"Where even are the street signs?" I asked back. Tim and I walked to the nearest intersection and searched all four corners for a street sign. There were none. Even if we found one we had no idea which direction to walk.

"There it is!" Tim said, "The street signs are up on the buildings."

"How do they expect anyone to see that?"

"Okay, we're on the right road, but which way do we go?" Tim and I leaned against a closed coffee shop trying to see if we could steal any WIFI to pull up our maps, with no luck. A man walked by and I stopped him to ask which way Sutherland street was. He pointed us in the direction and told us we would have to cross a bridge a few blocks down at an intersection.

We walked with heavy backpacks down the dark streets, except we ended up walking too far. We walked and walked with no sign of the bridge or Sutherland. Eventually we turned back. We stood on the corner of each intersection we had passed, looking up and down confused. There was no Sutherland street. Eventually we spotted a bridge a few blocks away and just decided to cross it. On the other side was Sutherland. I didn't realize while jotting down directions that we would have to take a street named Ebury Bridge to get to Sutherland street. It took us nearly forty-five minutes to walk the four and a half blocks to our hostel.

Our hostel was a beautiful old flatiron style building painted white, with tall windows stretching down each of its three stories. The bottom story was a low-lit pub with a vintage wood bar and decorative shelves of liquor going up the wall behind it. The wood shelves were backed with mirrors, and curved around the rounded corner of the triangle-shaped building. Supposedly underneath were passageways once used for smuggling liquor and gunpowder.

To one side of the bar was a door with a keypad which opened to a stairwell leading toward the hostel above. We were shown to our beds, where we ditched our backpacks, then went back down to the pub for a drink before bed. It was finally dawning on us we had made it. We were drinking beer at a pub in London.

After tucking into our bunks and dozing off to sleep, I woke in the night delirious, reaching for my phone to check the time. Twelve?! How the hell was it noon?! I sat up so fast I nearly launched myself off the bunk, ripping the window curtain open to look outside. It was dark. How was it twelve? It couldn't be midnight, I went to sleep around twelve thirty or one and that had to be hours earlier. I focused my eyes into the dark, and there were sleeping bodies all around me. I realized I had forgotten my phone hadn't yet adjusted to the different time zone. I shuffled through my backpack at my feet and pulled out my tablet, which had connected to the WIFI earlier on in the pub, correcting its clock. Five in the morning. Back to sleep I went.

I slept hard our first night in Europe. I adjusted to the time change easily and was ready for bed at a decent time, since we had poorly slept for two hours in the Philadelphia airport the night before after drinking free shots with some locals. After staying between Boston, Brooklyn, and then Philadelphia for two weeks, London really didn't seem much different. The currency changed and all of a sudden everyone had funny accents, but the hordes of tourists, chilly weather, and old historic buildings on every block remained similar. We spent four days in London eating nothing but grocery store snack foods, which were surprisingly cheap and tasty, in order to save our money for accommodation, future tourist attractions, transportation, and beer in local dive bars.

Although I really didn't care what people on the street thought of me, I still felt like an odd sight strolling around Piccadilly Circus. I was used to walking into stores fresh off of the Pacific Crest Trail, sunburned and sweaty, chugging water in workout clothes covered in dirt. I grew up with people pulling their children away from my friends and me with our spiky hair and studded jackets. Now I was thirty years old and still getting side-eyed for wearing tight black jeans, big grey trail-runners (a very 90's Jerry Seinfeld-looking combination), a T-shirt sporting a graphic image of Donald Trump shooting himself in the head, and sunglasses... *inside*. I had forgotten my eyeglasses in the hostel and was wearing my prescription wayfarer-style sunglasses indoors to successfully see what I was browsing for and most likely not going to buy. It didn't help that during my indoor sunglasses wearing shopping I was giggling at packaging labels such as *American pizza* and becoming audibly giddy about vegetarian chorizo ravioli. After roaming the store just to see what UK markets had to offer, Tim and I ended up purchasing a blood orange cider to split while exploring London's tourist attractions.

During our second night sleeping in the hostel, I was startled awake in the night again. This time by what could have been nothing other than a major earthquake. My body sloshed back and forth in the bed, violently rocking me out of my sleep. I was on the top bunk of a three story bunk bed that really should have been bolted to the wall. I mean at least when my lower bunk mates moved in their sleep my mattress surrounded by metal poles didn't bang into the ancient wall, but being seasick in my sleep wasn't much better of a situation.

Most of our time exploring London was spent around Tube-riding businessmen and hipsters all wearing the same ripped-knee pants. Finally on our last day we found a metal bar which seemed like a glimpse at London's version of our hang out spots back home. The bar's exterior was painted bright red and beer signs hung in every window. Inside, a woman with rainbow colored hair ordered Iron Maiden's Trooper beer in her black fringe leather jacket with a hand-painted portrait of either 80's Madonna or the singer from Hanoi Rocks on the back. I couldn't tell which they were going for. A bartender who looked like he had stepped out of the movie *Airheads* trained a new hire with long green hair falling down the back of her black dress. We enjoyed our drinks while listening to the music on the jukebox. A few songs by Judas Priest and then *Breadfan* by Budgie, which as far as I knew I had never heard in a bar before. We then made our way back across town to the hostel. I cozied up into my three-story earthquake bed, pulled a bandana over my eyes, and hoped for sleep. Next stop, Belfast.

The Tube took us back to Gatwick airport where we planned to board a quick Ryanair flight straight to Belfast for only twenty-five American dollars each. Ryanair is an Irish airline known for its no-frills flights at a cheap cost. They often get a bad rap for being generally unreliable.

For us it was worth taking the risk in order to save money. We had planned to take a few Ryanair flights across Europe seeing as you could jump across the continent in a few hours, without spending hundreds of dollars like you might on Eurail. And if our flights were delayed, who cares. We had nowhere to be anyway.

After checking in and passing through security, we followed a herd of people up to the big monitor of flight information, staring and waiting for our flight number to appear. Once it appeared, we followed the signs to the other side of the airport to our gate number. The problem was, the gate was empty. No employee at the podium, no one in the seats, and nothing on the screens. It was getting close to boarding time, so this was not only confusing but also worrying.

Tim and I walked up and down the terminal searching for another monitor of flight statuses, but there were none. We split up, running up and down the entire wing of the airport searching for any information. With no luck, we had no choice but to walk back across the airport to the original information screen we checked after passing security. Out of breath, we arrived at the screen, and this time our flight wasn't even listed anymore. It was just gone.

We paced back and forth for over ten minutes, sweating, hoping for something to pop up again. I started looking for a Ryanair desk in an attempt to find help from an actual human, but one of those didn't seem to exist either. Our flight appeared on the screen once more, this time displaying a new terminal. Again, it was far from where we were standing, and it was listed as *boarding*. We ran across the airport as fast as we could, finally arriving at a gate with a long line of people waiting to board two different Ryanair flights. Another hopeful passenger of our flight confirmed we were at the correct place, so we took our spot in line, trying to catch our breath.

The line led out the door of a room beyond a wall of windows. Inside was a private seating area for the gate, and two podiums of employees checking tickets and passports. After this check in, we were led into another secluded room of seating where we would wait for our flight, which was actually delayed by an hour.

Once they were ready for us to board, we walked on and took our seats. Ryanair planes are very similar to a Southwest plane, except the no-frills flight experience means no drinks for free, or to purchase. Not even water. Supposedly checking bags costs as much as the ticket. Which seemed fine for us, seeing as most flights across Europe are not very long, and you can buy almost anything you need in the airport and carry it on. Even open beer. Which might actually be against the rules but I ended up doing it later on a flight out of Greece anyway. The backpacks we traveled with were also carry-on size, so that made things very convenient.

We were on our plane, ready to go when an announcement came over the loudspeaker informing us of a new bump in the road to Belfast. Our plane didn't end up in the queue for gas so it would be another hour of sitting, waiting to squeeze in line for a turn to get fueled up. Passengers tapped angrily on their phones, sighing, or buried their heads into folded arms trying to nap against the trays. It was a bit annoying, since the wait alone was nearly the same as the flight itself, but soon enough our turn came and we were gassed up, in the air, and on our way to Belfast.

It was just our luck that things couldn't have continued smoothly from here. Halfway through the flight, another announcement from the captain came over the speaker, "I apologize for the inconvenience, but due to an unexpected minor mechanical problem, we are going to have to land in Dublin to switch planes." Everyone looked at each other wide-eyed. *Mechanical problem?* Sighs made their rounds across the plane once more. After a while I looked back and forth across the plane, wondering if I should ask any of the strangers if in Ireland they celebrate April Fool's Day, which was what day it was. Once I convinced myself we weren't going to die, I couldn't stop giggling about the irony of it being April Fool's, which I ended up just keeping to myself.

Since we didn't even have lodging booked in Belfast, I almost thought we could just jump off in Dublin instead. We had already paid for a flight all the way to Belfast though, so we had might as well continue on with our original plan instead of complicating things further. I know it seemed like Ryanair had truly shown itself as a shitty way to travel, but I was still on my way to Belfast. At this point I just wanted to follow directions and go to the place I paid and planned to go. And after many rough patches, we were still on our way there.

After safely landing in Dublin and switching planes, we successfully made it to Belfast without another issue. People like to complain and make jokes about Ryanair, which are apparently well deserved, but I'd say I would still stay loyal to their brand. A twenty-five dollar flight is a twenty-five dollar flight.

We stepped out of the airport onto the ground of our second European city. Belfast is part of the United Kingdom, so it didn't differ much from London when it came to stores, currency, food, and so on, but the countryside, pubs, beer, and people were obviously very Ireland. Belfast was another town mixed with old and new. It was much smaller than London, but that made it easy to explore on foot. We walked into an overcrowded hostel with no reservation, taking our only option of a private room for three nights. The other hostel guests were young – high school age at most. Loud and giggly, bolting across common areas screaming and chasing each other, while others whispered secrets in a corner. After seeing the other guests, paying more for a private room didn't seem like much of a bad thing.

Belfast was constantly cold and rainy, much gloomier than London had been. Although despite the bleak weather, the locals were warm and friendly rather than the busy and standoffish people we often came across in London. As we walked the town, we passed a large Guinness mural and rows of shops. Wet brick buildings covered in graffiti murals sprouted green plants poking through crumbling brick. I felt chilly and tired, but the constant new sights around every corner were enough to keep me going.

I crossed my arms, trying to keep warm in only a sweatshirt under a flimsy ultralight rain jacket. Tim and I had an immature inside joke that the ninety-nine cent stores of the UK should be called "Pound Town." We turned a corner and there it was. "Pound Land." Close enough. Close enough to make us die laughing as we entered. We bought scissors, which became a ritual across Europe, ditching them before flying then re-buying in the next country. Scissors were just a nice thing to travel with for various reasons, including hair trimming. From there we went to do the only thing I had on the itinerary for Belfast – to drink a Guinness in a historic pub once ravaged by car bombs.

The "Crown Bar" is both Belfast's most famous bar and most bombed, due to its proximity to the IRA's primary target and most bombed hotel in the world, the Europa Hotel, located directly across the street. The Crown Liquor Saloon was full of swirling decorative wood and tile mosaics. All of the windows were stained glass, including those that separated one booth from another. Each booth, called a snug, had its own door which could be closed for more private beer consumption. The wood and stained glass made the booths look almost like church confessionals. Tiled pillars with lion and griffin statues lined each snug's doorway as well. Even the ceiling had an intricate floral design in carved wood, cleaned and restored after decades of buildup from cigarette smoke. The pub's style was that of a Victorian gin palace, which it once was in the late 1800's.

Visiting old dive bars has always been a priority of mine while traveling, the more historical the better, so I loved the Crown Liquor Saloon. It was much more fancy and sophisticated than a real dive, but the age and history behind it was intriguing to me, even if it was a bit morbid. It was the perfect place to drink our first Guinness in Ireland.

On our way back to the hostel from the pub, we decided to walk one block over than we previously did, avoiding the main street for a quiet neighborhood road. The neighborhood was lined with British flags, and walls of graffiti, murals, and monuments inscribed with "Sandy Row." I did a quick Internet search when we got back to our room to find not only were we in one of Belfast's oldest neighborhoods, but also in the heart of Unionist territory. The Unionists believed in a strong union between Northern Ireland and Great Britain, and had bloody battles spanning mostly between the late 1960's to the late 1990's with opposing groups such as the IRA, who wanted a united Ireland. Northern Ireland's "Troubles" took place in the Belfast area, and sometimes continue to this day. Less than six months prior to our visit, there were weeks-long riots over British flags flying on downtown government buildings. I read stories of bombings and Catholics being brutally murdered by Unionists in Belfast's past. It was interesting to read since my Catholic great-great-grandparents grew up only about two hours away, although I doubt they ever came to Belfast.

We were still trying our best to save money by eating grocery store or gas station food. This was less disappointing than it sounds. For less than £3 you could get amazing caramelized onion hummus, as well as chicken or beef cup-o-noodles, called Pot Noodles, which were unintentionally vegetarian. On our second day in Belfast, we decided to eat out to try one of the extensive local breakfast fry-ups we had heard about. We had our pick from such breakfast items as "Cheesy Doodle Soda Bap" and "Alan's Granny's Big Ding Dongs." I used the little WIFI I could get in my room to stream Stiff Little Fingers while packing my bag, which took on a whole different connotation being in Belfast. Songs that once brought me back to teenager-hood in Southern California suburbs now reminding me of Belfast's not so distant past.

> *Take a look where you're livin'*
> *You got the Army on your street*
> *And the RUC dog of repression*
> *Is barking at your feet*
> *Is this the kind of place you wanna live?*
> *Is this where you wanna be?*
> *Is this the only life we're gonna have?*
> *What we need is...*
>
> *An Alternative Ulster*
> *Grab it and change it—it's yours!*
> *Get an Alternative Ulster*
> *Ignore the bores and their laws*
> *Get an Alternative Ulster*
> *Be an anti-security force*
> *Alter your native Ulster*
> *Alter your native land*
>
> *They say they're a part of you*
> *But that's not true you know*
> *They say they've got control of you*
> *And that's a lie you know*
> *They say you will never be*
> *Free*

On our last night in Belfast, we met up with a friend of a friend for dinner and drinks. She was an artist and mom, and old freight train-riding friend of some of Tim's old friends. She grew up half in Northern Ireland and half in California due to her parents each being from separate countries who bounced her back and forth here and there. As a young adult, she fled some unhealthy ways in California and ended up later marrying and starting a family in Belfast and continuing on to have a fairly successful and happy life.

Out of anywhere she could have taken us, she chose a "Mexican" food joint. Tim and I were incredibly skeptical. Being from San Diego makes us irrationally harsh burrito critics. Ask anyone from San Diego about burritos, and you're in for an earful. Most San Diegans have a hard enough time even finding decent burritos as far away as Los Angeles, let alone Northern Ireland. We walked into a clean, hip little restaurant with burrito fillings laid out in little bins behind the glass wall customers line up to order from. It was similar to a Chipotle, which is blasphemous as Mexican food for us at home, but better than I was expecting. After our new friend nicely treated us to burritos, we went back to one of the old pubs on the main strip not too far from our hostel for a drink. We shared an old booth with stained glass to sit at and chatted about old memories with mutual friends, or stories from when we were younger.

Belfast excited me for Dublin, imagining the bigger city would mean more history and interesting people. Tim loved the small town feel Belfast had. It wasn't really a tourist destination, so he felt he could stay there for days longer, exploring and living like a local. During our last day in Belfast, I started to agree, there was just something about being in a smaller city that was so real, and not covered in tourism signs, bustling crowds, or duck tour busses. But Dublin was calling.

Dublin: Póg Mo Thóin

We took a bus through the countryside from Belfast to Dublin, on our way to a hostel in the Temple Bar area. This was another hostel we didn't book in advance which meant spending each night in a different room, whichever had two empty beds available for each night. Our first night was spent in a twenty-four-person dorm full of club-going young Australians, and the next two nights we spent in smaller shared rooms. One of the rooms had a window facing the church next door where Saint Valentine's bones remain.

We walked the cobblestone roads daily, gawking at Viking ruins and medieval churches. We stopped to picnic on a bench at Christ Church Cathedral, founded around 1030, which was once the center of medieval Dublin. Although we did not enter the cathedral, I had read that its crypt contained the oldest known secular carvings in Ireland, the town's stocks from 1670, Roman candlesticks from around 1690, and a case containing a mummified cat and rat that died together in an organ pipe in the 1850's. Taking up most of the bench next to me was a lifelike bronze statue of a homeless man, sleeping with a blanket pulled over his face. As I was packing my things to move on, I noticed the homeless man's bare feet peeking out of the blanket had holes through them. The homeless man was supposed to be Jesus. Years later I read the artists who made the statue scattered some around the United States as well, where locals continually called the cops on each sleeping bronze Jesus. Calling the cops on Jesus sounds like the epitome of white America.

After going up to Tesco for some nibbles and crisps for our picnic near Viking ruins and the old cathedral, we went to go get craic on the black stuff, which ended up being a €20 entry fee, so we told 'em to "póg mo thóin" and went over to Fibber Magees for a Bavaria. To clarify, the Guinness brewery had an expensive entry fee, so we ended up at a so-called punk bar for cheap beer instead. The next day we ended up at the Jameson distillery for Irish coffee after accidentally stumbling upon it while searching for church catacombs filled with mummified friars. We spent the evening at another punk bar, listening to Billy Idol and reading the old flyers hung on the walls, until our booth was engulfed by locals there to take part in a folk music jam.

When I wasn't slurping down Pot Noodles from gas stations or corner markets, we were blowing money at late night "Pizza and Kebab" shops. You find them everywhere across Europe, and I don't exactly recommend them. Stopping by during the day for some falafel is one thing, but buying a large overflowing Styrofoam to-go box of cheese fries after a night out at the bar is definitely a regrettable decision. I was always down for curry or "beef and tomato" Pot Noodles, but Tim questioned my sanity, seeing as the "tomato" part of "beef and tomato" was a packet of ketchup you squeeze into the broth. And obviously, it didn't actually contain beef either. Months later, after we had returned back to the states from traveling Europe, many friends and family approached me saying the same thing. "Wow, you must have learned so much seeing so many European countries. Your life must really be changed." But what would really go through my head was how I had now started pouring curry powder into my Top Ramen.

Our little hostel room had two more backpacks propped up against the opposite bunk. The familiar first sign of new roommates. Tim was dying for a haircut, so we decided to go for a quick trim in the room's private bathroom. I'm sure it was an odd sight for our roommate's first impression of us to be with the bathroom door open, Tim seated on the toilet, and me cutting his hair.

The backpacks though... the belongings of people backpacking Europe were an anomaly to us after our experience as "hiker trash". When you hike a long-distance trail, you often need multiple liters of water, compact cooking gear and utensils, shelter and warmth, a sleeping pad, emergency supplies, up to a week's worth of food, sometimes a bear canister, and some even bring solar panels for outdoor charging. You know a thru-hiker when you see one because they have all of this stuff, yet their backpacks are tinier than even the day hikers. It's all about taking the bare essentials. European backpackers have almost twenty-four-hour access to *real* mattresses, food, water, a full kitchen, outlets, pillows, lockers, toilets, and shelter, yet their backpacks are enormous. When most people go into

REI and see the monstrous, small-human-sized backpacks that tower three feet overhead and knock over anything in a four-foot radius, they think, "Wow, that person is going on a *long* hike." In reality, hauling that canvas trailer up and down five months' worth of mountains would kill you. I'm convinced those backpacks are strictly for young Eurail riders. I can't help but wonder what all is in there.

Sometimes I'll catch myself and think I'm being too judgmental. Not everyone knows about ultralight gear or has spent years saving to afford it piece by piece, constantly scouring the Internet for good deals like I have. But then I think about how their giant backpacks, towering over their heads, with removable daypacks and fancy clipped on water bottles probably cost at least twice the price of mine, and are being used for most likely no more than a few weeks abroad, so I'm starting to think they have no excuse.

What could be in there? I can assume club wear, beach wear, shoes for wearing in the shower, a towel, many changes of clothes, a book or two, selfie sticks, I don't know? We did share a hostel with some young French club-goers who would walk around the large shared dorm blasting the hottest radio dance tunes and farting while wearing nothing but little underwear. Every night they would comb and straighten each other's hair before going out to the clubs. So I know for a fact some people *do* carry flat irons. Not just women trying to look hot, but straight men as well.

In no way would I actually be able to entirely pull off ultralight gear while backpacking Europe. In the woods no one cares about how you smell, and shampoo is easy to come by in free hiker boxes. You just use the amount you need then put it back. No need to carry anything in excess, besides water. And there are no knickknack stores along the way. So in some ways, I can see where the extra stuff comes in. Even then, we were planning on doing some camping while we were in Europe and only brought tiny camp pillows, sleeping bags, and a tarp. Our bags were still half the size of the backpackers hosteling for two weeks.

You have to strive to find that comfortable spot between necessary and luxury items. My balance for both hiking and Europe consisted of around seventeen pounds of stuff, including a small dSLR camera stored in a beanie, a pee rag, condiments, and only two to three pairs of underwear. Having backpacks sized as carry-ons also saved a lot of time, money, and headache no matter where we were headed. For those wondering what a pee rag is, it is a cloth or piece of a bandana used as toilet paper for pee. Very environmentally friendly and dries quickly when dangled off of your backpack while walking in the sun. The sun also disinfects the pee rag, although it still needs to be washed often. Yes, I did bring my PCT pee rag to Europe. It's so small when folded up and stuck through a loop on the outside of my backpack that it looked like a dark green bow. A teal backpack with a cute little green bow on top that no one knows is meant specifically for wiping pee.

We were two weeks into exploring Europe, and a month and a half had passed since we left California. We hadn't really hung out with other people since we were in Boston, besides the one night in Belfast. It was nice for Tim and I to spend time exploring together, especially since our goals and desires for traveling were exactly the same, but I was hoping to interact with more locals or go to punk shows. To have a bit more of a social life from time to time. Next on our list was Amsterdam and Antwerp, where we would be staying with American expat friends in both cities. I was excited for them to take us to do more than what a tourist map might suggest. We had planned for a week in Amsterdam and a week exploring Belgium, so we had plenty of time to both relax with friends and see the sights. It had been a brief stop in the homeland of my ancestors, but I was ready to see what was next.

Amsterdam: No Pimps Allowed

We took another cheap Ryanair flight from Dublin to Amsterdam. Fortunately, we had a better experience than our nearly disastrous flight to Belfast. The airport's information window helped us find a bus going straight into the city where our friend Buster would be waiting for us. I'm sure the info desk attendant thought we must have been mega tourist stoners since, unknowingly to us, the reference meeting point we needed directions to was one of the biggest and most famous "coffee shops" in Amsterdam. A weed café which we didn't even enter.

Buster was an old friend of Tim's from the US who he met back in his days riding trains across the country. He stayed with us for a few weeks when we lived in Oakland, then sold off whatever personal items he had to buy a one-way ticket to Amsterdam. By the time we arrived Buster had been living in Amsterdam for three years – squatting for free rent and dumpster diving since he couldn't legally work. The last few squats he had lived in were busted. Abandoned buildings to open as squats were becoming scarce because of a new system called Antikraak. Instead of leaving empty schools, offices, libraries, and other buildings to potentially become squatted illegally, agencies started renting them out to students or anyone else looking for bare bones, temporary housing where the owner could walk in to show the building to potential buyers without notice. Basically, the city wanted people to pay to stay in empty buildings without having any rights or permanence in them just to keep out the low income people who were harder to remove due to squatter's rights laws.

We followed Buster through town with cold twenty-five cent beers in our pockets, which we drank canal-side, catching up for a while, before visiting his girlfriend at work. Buster's girlfriend was a Scottish woman named Mhairi, who worked at an Irish pub in the tourist center of Amsterdam.

After a second beer at the pub, we rode back to Mhairi's apartment on an extra bike Buster brought for us. At first I tried to hold onto the back of the bike Tim was riding, sitting on less than half of the seat as he sat forward, but we kept having to stop because it was hard to hold on without swaying the bike around too much. Buster was riding his favorite of the two bikes, called a bakfiets – a Dutch cargo bike with a long open compartment in the front. We tried again with me in the compartment of Buster's bike with the backpacks which made for a smoother ride.

The bike roads were pristine and flying through a dark park at night in the cool breeze felt amazing. It felt exciting to be around familiar faces and new friends after spending the last two weeks in new countries, rarely talking to anyone else outside of the two of us.

We dismounted our bikes and climbed the old steep staircase to the top of Mhairi's canal-side apartment. Dutch canal houses are tall, skinny, and deep. They have basements, tall stoops meant to protect the entrance from flooding, and an attic with a large window originally meant for hoisting in goods from the outside via a pulley. Sometimes behind a canal house would be a second house, a courtyard, or a warehouse. The canal house Mhairi and her roommates lived in had each story turned into a different apartment.

Inside the apartment, Buster offered us dumpstered Heineken, candy, pastries, and other goodies while we streamed TV episodes onto a wall with a projector that, yes, came from the trash. Even the joints he was smoking came from hostel trash cans or just picking them up off the street. He had also found multiple brand-new hiking backpacks and a guitar.

The apartment had the tiniest bathroom, with a toilet Tim deemed the "shit-shelf." Others might call it a Dutch toilet, or another smart-ass name is the "inspection shelf." Instead of a deep bowl of water for your poo to plop into, you have a dry, waterless shelf with a small hole of water below it. During this process the poo lands onto the shelf, where you can smell it in all its glory, or dissect if you accidentally ate something of value, then afterward is flushed across the rest of the shelf and down into the hole. As you could imagine, but might not want to, this is very messy. A toilet brush becomes almost as necessary as toilet paper.

Another interesting Netherlands toilet quirk were the public urinals. Those with the appropriate parts could admire a famous statue or building, then turn and publicly whizz freely behind a small slotted metal barrier. We experienced almost every odd European toilet trend while in Amsterdam. When thinking of European toilets, a bidet would probably be the first thing to come to mind for most Americans, yet in all of the nineteen countries we visited, we never came across one.

I sat on the apartment's shit-shelf-style toilet and looked up in the small bathroom, into the shower which was only a foot or two in front of me. On a shelf was a bottle of conditioner staring back at me. *Palmolive Anti Klit*. Hmm, well that sounds sexual in an unfortunate way. I went back to the couch and consumed dumpstered candy, pastries, and beer next to Mhairi's elderly cat.

Her roommates were out of town but okayed Mhairi to let us stay in one of their bedrooms, which was in the attic of the five-story brick building. We went up the stairs, past a broom closet, and there was one small room with a little window looking out.

"No one is supposed to stay in here but the landlord doesn't know, and our neighbors don't care." she told us. The bed was comfortable, and I took out my sleeping bag and burrowed in. Tim went back downstairs to hang out a bit longer before going to sleep.

The room was eerie in the dark, and I tried hard not to think about how the room Anne Frank lived in was only about a ten-minute bike ride away. It was an eerie, anxiety-inducing thought, but I couldn't really stop it from popping into my head.

When I woke up the next morning, I went downstairs and took a seat on the couch. Mhairi instantly brought me tea and asked if I wanted sausage for breakfast.

"Oh, that's alright. I don't eat meat." I said, feeling embarrassed about rejecting her offer.

"It's veg meat," she said in a thick Scottish accent, "I'm vegetarian myself."

"Oh, in that case, I'll definitely have some!"

A few minutes later she returned with a plate of toast and what looked like an enormous hot dog, cut in half straight down the middle. *What the fuck kind of sausage is this?* I thought. I cut a small piece with my fork and took a bite. *It's like a giant Smart Dog.* Smart Dogs are a brand of veggie dog that, to me, taste similar to your everyday bottom of the line grocery store packaged hot dog. If the ninety-nine-cent store sold a hot dog, it would probably taste like a Smart Dog. Except, rest assured, there are no assholes and earlobes, just plant matter. Some people don't like them, but I can't get enough. I was one of those kids who ate hot dogs cold out of the package on a hot summer day though; so my standards might be low. I also ate those little Vienna sausages right out of the can. Never even had them cooked or prepared. I don't even know how one would cook or prepare them?

This is why it's just best that I don't eat meat. I was a leave half of the chicken meat on the bone, and would eat Vienna sausages out of the can, but didn't like steak kind of person. I was the pickiest of eaters until I stopped. Even as a kid I would have to dissect my fish sticks to make sure there weren't one of those little poop string looking things in it before I ate it. I would only eat the boot-shaped Mc-Nuggets, not the round ones, because they seemed to have less veins. I tried to go vegetarian as a kid, after making friends with a big turkey who disappeared after Thanksgiving, but my parents laughed at me then took me back to McDonald's and Taco Bell. I couldn't actually figure out how to do it until I was nineteen, then went vegan thirteen years later, but that was after Europe.

I stared down at my sausage. It was like if you took the whole package of Smart Dogs and smooshed them into one dog. I felt as if I could give or take the sausage. I was apathetic to whether I would ever want to see one again. But then things changed. For the next few months I craved them, scouring every grocery market meat shelf across Europe for the sausages. They came two in a pack, saran wrapped on a green Styrofoam tray. The delicious faux meat filled my thoughts, and I became obsessed with scanning the shelves trying to find such a quick, cheap meal. When I did find them, I would cut them in half long ways down the middle and fry them, like Mhairi did, or slice them into circles and fry each side. Unfortunately for me, Belgium would be the last place I would see them.

It was Buster's birthday, but we were in an extremely lazy mood. With only a few days each in London, Belfast, and Dublin, we were going nonstop trying to see as much as we could in a short period of time. Even though Amsterdam seemed amazing and beautiful, sitting on the couch was our biggest priority for the day.

We went to get a crate of beer from the Albert Heijn grocery store down the street as a present. To our surprise, they offered free gift wrap for anything bought from the grocery store. We poorly wrapped a long piece of the decorative paper around the plastic crate of glass bottles, covering only the widest side. You could still read "Grolsch" on two sides. We went back to the apartment and handed Buster his birthday present, and Mhairi started making him a weed cake.

"Ah, shit!" Buster yelled. "The cat peed in the bag of candy. I'm going to have to throw it all out." It wasn't funny the candy was wasted, but we still laughed. At least it was free.

In the evening a few of their friends came over for a small birthday get-together. His friends were nice. Many of them were from Poland and had lived in some of the same squats as Buster at one time or another. We listened to music, chatted, and drank beer well into the night. An hour or two before going to bed I decided to try a few crumbs of weed cake. I never got into smoking weed, so I didn't want to overdo it. I didn't feel much, yet I did send a goofy nonsensical message to Dionna that kept me laughing until I fell asleep.

Since Mhairi's other roommates would be coming back from being out of town the next morning, we were swapped to another room for the night and would be sleeping in the living room the night after that. We still had another half of a week left in Amsterdam after staying with Buster and Mhairi, but would spend those nights with a friend of theirs named Alex who lived on the other side of town.

Staying up too late then sleeping half the day became our norm for Amsterdam, but no one seemed to mind. When we were finally ready to explore the next day, Buster and Mhairi mentioned a large flea market next to a canal, and Tim and I couldn't say no. We packed into Mhairi's car and made it just in time to browse the aisles of tents before they started to close down. I bought a pair of cheap hoop earrings to stick through my stretched ears. Once the market began to pack up, we walked over to the canal to relax in the sun. The canal was lined with small sailboats. Buster and Mhairi dreamt out loud about wanting to buy one to live on and travel in. Tim and I told stories about the little sailing we had done.

We went back to the apartment to grab our backpacks, sticking them in Buster's bike and then riding together to a windmill turned into a brewery. The bar was pretty crowded, but the beer was good. We met more of Buster and Mhairi's friends, who we joined on the outside patio. It was kind of awkward having our backpacks with us, but we didn't really have a choice. We were already halfway from Buster's to his friend Alex's house, so it only made sense to keep them with us until we ended our day there. The backpacks made things more awkward when one of the men we were introduced to asked us why we felt the need to be homeless in their city. "We already have a home," Tim responded. Which was only partially true. We were definitely not in Amsterdam to *be* homeless though. It was a weird and obnoxious question. Especially coming from someone who seemingly left Poland to squat in Amsterdam. The man softened up after a while and eventually became a bit friendlier to us. Buster mentioned a time where someone thought his name was Mustard. I thought it was hilarious so I started referring to him as such. He seemed not to notice.

After a few beers, the group started talking about a party at a nearby squat. "Do you guys want to go to the party?" Buster asked.

"Sure." we both responded. I got into the front compartment of Buster's bike, and we headed to the party with a few of the others, the sun setting as we rode.

Everyone locked their bikes up outside of the building. The neighborhood looked nice and was lined with old brick houses. The inside looked like any other punk house. There was a big kitchen, dining room, and living room on the main floor. One whole wall shared by the dining room and living room was painted red, with a quote in blue letters going across most of the brick wall. *The dune of my house glass cocoons the sleepy sands my tomb labyrinth of wrinkles conceived on an alchemist's loom to weave the ancient tune of the infinite moon full to the womb of...* I couldn't read the rest. Another read something about the theory of Anarchist Capitalism being killing, stealing from, and then eating someone. A few stuffed Teddy bears hung from the ceiling next to a brassy colored chandelier.

Instead of a party, the house was throwing a small dinner for one of their friends becoming a legal citizen.

I *now* felt like an awkward American squat tourist. Holding my backpack and everything, inside this quiet dinner party. The dining room table was filled with housemates and friends sipping cocktails, so I followed Tim, Alex, and Buster to the neighboring living room couches. A black and white cat rubbed against Tim's leg as he sat.

We talked for a few minutes, and then two women came over bringing snacks and mixed drinks made with fresh fruit. "Oh, wow! Thank you so much!" I said, taking the drink. When I was halfway through savoring my drink they were back with another, this time with different fruit. Food was passed around the table, and a few of us got up to make a small plate. I was trying not to intrude any more than I already was, but I was hungry, and the food looked great. The room got quiet, someone talked, and we all applauded for the person who was getting citizenship. We didn't stay too long after that. The dinner was wrapping up, so we said goodbye and thanked our hosts again.

All four of us crammed onto the two bikes and started riding towards Alex's house. I jumped back into the front of Buster's bakfiets with the backpacks, and Alex awkwardly hung off the back of Tim's bike. We rode the bikes onto a ferry platform and went across the IJ, a large canal cutting through the Netherlands that connects to the sea on both sides. We followed the main street, with Tim and Alex in front, and Buster and I drifting further behind. We came up to a roundabout and had no idea which street they turned down. Buster took a right, and we rode up and down streets of houses searching for them. He had forgotten where Alex's house was, so we couldn't just meet them there.

We rode back to the roundabout and Buster dropped me off on a corner so I could wait to see if they would come back for us, and so he could ride down the streets faster to look for them on his own. I waited under a street lamp with the backpacks at my feet. The entire neighborhood was asleep.

Buster swung back around, "Any sight of them?"

"No, only a person walking their dog."

"Fuck. They took off so fast. They've gotta wonder where we are? I'll try another street, be back in a few minutes." After Buster left, there came Tim, walking without the red bike.

"Where were you guys?" he asked.

"We lost you! You guys were too far ahead, and we couldn't see which street you turned down. We picked one, and I guess it was the wrong street."

"Where is Buster?"

"He dropped me here to wait while he sped off searching down each street. He just left so it might take a few minutes for him to come back."

"Oh, well the house is just another two blocks that way." Tim pointed across the street in the one direction we hadn't yet tried. "The red bike broke."

"What? What happened to it?"

"Alex wanted to steer, with me on back. I didn't think it was a good idea, but I let him switch. He then rode off a curb and it bent the front wheel. It's back at his house now."

"Uh oh."

"Which way did Buster go? Maybe I can find him and call him back." I pointed, and he jogged off to do a quick search for Buster, leaving me on the corner with the backpacks again. I was expecting it to be like some British comedy skit. Next thing you know, Buster would come back without a bike, leave again, and then Tim would come back riding in the cargo bin of Buster's bike with an old-timey stranger with a top hat peddling. Then they would both show up simultaneously from opposite directions with no bike, and we would all have to split up again to figure out where the bike went. They both came back to get me and we walked the next two blocks.

It was getting late, but Buster sat with us for one last beer at Alex's dimly lit kitchen table before riding all the way home. Alex introduced us to his girlfriend, Lena. She was in her mid-twenties with pale skin, a lip piercing, and a blue mohawk left down to one side. She was also from Poland. They lived in a two-story townhouse with a roommate. Alex had kids, but since they were with their mom, we were able to sleep on a blow-up mattress on the floor of their bedroom.

We sat and talked about where they grew up in Poland, and about funny Dutch words. I guess the worst cuss word or insult you could say in Dutch translates to "child cancer." Implying you would be wishing it upon the person or their family.

In the morning Lena made us coffee, which I drank in their porch garden in the sunshine, watching the neighbor's chickens pop over to eat worms out of the grass. I walked down the brick pathway to see the canal in the daylight, and the chickens followed. The neighborhood was awake, but it was still quiet. Everyone inside the house was either already at work, or preparing to leave. Alex and Lena told Tim and I we could use whatever we needed and gave us a spare key in case we wanted to leave.

We went out in search for a grocery store, which was harder than we thought it would be. After finding nothing but a few corner stores with no breakfast foods, we went back to the house to use the WIFI to search for a real grocery store. "Baby Dump." I said. "There is a store nearby, called Baby Dump."

To our luck, we found an Albert Heijn within ten blocks, which had everything we needed for a veggie version of English breakfast. Including giant Smart Dogs. Buster had also given us some of his roll of 25% off stickers the Albert Heijn store clerks use to discount products. Another useful thing he found in the trash.

I had been missing cheap UK food. I noticed that Pot Noodles were now not a thing - unless you found them at a British import store for twice the price. Which, yes, I still paid. DIY English Breakfast definitely hit the spot. We spent the rest of the day showering and going through our things, having a lazy day until our hosts came home from work and wanted to watch a movie.

The next morning we took off bright and early to finally explore the tourist sights of Amsterdam. Our fifth and last full day in town. Before leaving the house, we heard Lena scream upstairs and ran up to see if she needed help. Their cat had killed a big bright green parrot and brought it in to display its kill. An explosion of green feathers covered the bedroom. I didn't even know there were parrots in Amsterdam. I Hoped it wasn't a neighbor's pet. Later I found out there were nearly four thousand wild parrots living in the city.

We stopped into a coffee shop next to a park on the way to the ferry, so we could share a muffin and get some caffeine inside us. The ferry was quick and free and led right up to Amsterdam's main transit center. From there we walked to the canal-lined houses, whose rails were covered for blocks in locked bikes. We passed and admired the outside of the Anne Frank house, and drank a beer at a bar's outside café tables in the Red-Light District.

Some of the sex workers danced in the windows to music passersby couldn't hear, some motioned with their finger for men to come to them, and some tapped away on their phones looking bored. I thought it was interesting that their businesses were all run on their own, and they even had a union to protect them. No pimps allowed. We skipped museums and restaurants to save our funds and eventually went back to our room to get a good night's rest. Amsterdam was beautiful, and the city was amazing to explore. After six days, it was time to visit more friends.

Belgium and Beyond: Penis Death

It was Wednesday, April 13th, 2016, and this American couple was flying through the Netherlands' fields on a high-speed train. Or maybe a regular speed train – I really don't know. After six days in Amsterdam we were now headed to Antwerp, Belgium, where we would spend another week with friends as well as travel back and forth between nearby cities such as Ghent, Brussels, and Paris. This was just sixteen days into our four-month journey through Europe, plus the month we spent traveling across the United States prior to flying into London.

Our train pulled into Antwerpen-Centraal which was one of the most beautiful train stations I had ever seen. It was originally constructed between 1895 and 1905 out of iron and glass, and was made tall enough to fit steam locomotives. Although it didn't damage the structure of the building (and was not something I noticed), the hall's roof contains wave distortion from V-2 bombs during World War II.

"Amanda said she'd be under the big clock," I said, scanning the building after departing the train. We went up a tall escalator and above us we could see a giant decorative clock surrounded by light pouring in from the stained-glass windows, and Amanda on the platform underneath it with her hands in the air for us to see. She flailed her arms and jumped up and down next to two Belgian military dudes with machine guns who didn't look impressed.

It was only a month or so after three suicide bombings had killed thirty-two people and injured more than three hundred at the Brussels airport and central metro station. It was the deadliest terrorist attack in Belgium's history. Things like this were something some of my family members and friends were concerned about when it came to us traveling, but honestly I didn't think I was at risk any more than being in any big city in California. Terrorist attacks could unfortunately happen anywhere. I've been robbed at gunpoint, I've hidden from drive-bys, I knew multiple people who had witnessed a school shooting. The terrorism in Europe was heartbreaking, but not anything I wasn't already used to fearing in my own country. It was similar to the reactions when we left to hike the Pacific Crest Trail. "You better bring a gun!" I'm sorry but two of the deadliest things on the PCT are rattlesnakes and snow, and I don't feel the need to shoot either of those.

We knew Amanda from San Diego, where just a year prior she took off to Europe for a solo trip for her 30th birthday. During this trip, she fell for a guy from Antwerp who was a friend of friends whose bands had toured across Europe together. She had moved to Antwerp four months before we arrived to visit, and was in the process of becoming a legal resident.

Amanda and Hans' place was only a block off of the main strip in Antwerp, not more than four blocks from the main station. Their apartment had views of old statues on elaborate buildings and a medieval cathedral. It was sunset, and the warm colors reflecting off of the ancient buildings looked beautiful. We dropped our stuff off in their apartment and were instantly handed glasses of the best selection of Belgian beers we'd ever had at our immediate disposal. The four of us stayed up late talking while trying different Belgian beers, as their orange striped cat playfully bolted across the room chasing toys.

"Would you like a digestif?" Hans asked.

"Um, I think I'm okay." Tim responded, confused.

"Liquor? Like, a shot." Hans clarified. He scooted his chair from the dining table to the closest wall, where a literal treasure chest of booze lay against it. Their full liquor cabinet sat inside an old chest, decorated with skulls and other trinkets.

"Oh, in that case, yes." said Tim, his eyes focused on the treasure.

We talked about politics and about how children are raised in Belgium versus the US. Hans told us in high school, Belgians pick a trade and graduate with the certificate needed to find a job in that trade at the end of their final year. He talked about his union, and the three of us Americans had to explain to him how and why American jobs don't typically have unions. *And* that some people are strictly against them. Hans nearly spit his digestif across the table in disbelief.

"No unions?! How do you not have unions?!" He yelled and slammed his hand on the table. "Amai!"

"Amai." Amanda solemnly repeated in agreeance.

We stayed up late, then Amanda and Hans retreated to their loft while Tim and I laid out our sleeping bags across a blow-up mattress on the living room floor. The apartment was lit only by candles and a dim ceiling light over the dining room table behind us. The walls were decorated with skulls and crucifixes from different countries. The cat nestled into my hair, and I fell asleep.

I forgot Belgian beer had such a high alcohol content, so I woke up groggy and dehydrated. Thankfully not completely hung over. Hans had left before the sun had even risen. He had an important work meeting to attend with a client, which he showed up to still drunk. Fortunately, it went smoothly, and he was then able to come home and nap. Belgium quickly became the current trip favorite. Castles, beer, savory stuffed waffles, and good weather. More than what we had expected from a place rarely mentioned by so-called world travelers.

On our third day in Belgium Tim, Amanda, and I took a train to Brussels for an overnight trip to wander the city and see a punk/metal show. Our friend Justin was in town with his band Usnea from Portland. People speak French in Brussels which was new to me since The Netherlands and a large portion of Belgium, Antwerp included, speak different dialects of Dutch. We got turned around a few times trying to find the small apartment we would be renting, but finally found it in a cute little French neighborhood. Down the street from our place was an outdoor market lined with fresh pickled veggies, and all of the meat, cheese, beer, wine, and olives one could want. People walked with baguettes and drank champagne next to a park while their children ran on a playground. Bright blooming flowers and statues were everywhere we went.

Our apartment was unbelievably cheap and beautiful. Two bedrooms with large windows and high ceilings. Little red slippers and clean towels were left at the edge of each bed. The family who owned it greeted us at the front door to let us in. Only the father spoke English but his French-speaking pregnant wife and their daughter, no older than four years old, were there to greet us as well. Right when we entered the building's front door, the little girl took my hand and led me through the building and to the apartment. She then stopped and ran back to one by one bring Amanda and Tim to the apartment by hand as well. We were all laughing and thanking her, even her parents. We bought fancy cheese from a fromagerie on the corner, and it was the best I had ever tasted. We lounged in our apartment snacking and getting ready; then, in the evening, we took a bus to the venue for the show. Typical of our luck, as we headed out the door the blue skies turned grey, then rain started to pour for the entire walk from the bus station to the venue, and then stopped once we arrived and went inside.

The venue looked like a muraled warehouse on the outside, with the interior of a normal bar with a large stage. The bands played backlit with red and blue lights inside of the dark building. We sipped on cheap beer, enjoying the music. Before leaving, we spent time chatting with Justin and followed him on a tour of the venue. What looked like a regular little club with a stage and a bar, had a separate room for bands that included a living room area and bunkhouse. If only our country would take note. Amanda and I spent the last part of the night laughing until we cried about some French graffiti in the bathroom I wrongly translated to mean "Penis Death." As the lights came on in the venue and the people cleared out, we said our good-byes and headed back to our apartment.

The next day we did our tourist duty of seeing the famous Manneken Pis - a statue of a small boy peeing. While window shopping near the statue, a random man approached Tim to compliment his *Bumbklaatt* T-shirt, a band from San Diego and Tijuana Tim had been friends with since he was young. The man said he had purchased an album of theirs at a record shop in Europe years prior, and was excited to find someone else who knew of them. They were both excited about having a random small-world connection, so Tim took a picture with him to send to the band.

We continued strolling the tourist area, and Amanda found a specific rare beer glass as a birthday present for Hans. The three of us then jumped on a train to Ypres to meet up with Hans for his birthday show and a night of camping.

We arrived at the venue early while the bands were setting up, since Amanda was supposed to bartend. Ypres was another beautiful little town filled with medieval architecture surrounded by rolling green fields. While the bands set up and the bar was being stocked, Tim and I wandered the streets in search of food. The small town was nearly empty, leaving us to settle on coffee and pastries from a coffee shop. Back at the venue, the lights were dimmed, and the music had started.

The lineup was a mix of crust punk, black metal, and even straight edge hardcore. A child in a flip hat and denim vest, no older than ten, bobbed his head to the music and ran to pick up a broken drumstick off the floor. He was smitten. His dad stood a few yards behind him sipping beer with a smile on his face. Tim and I drank cheap beer after cheap beer, but my stomach was rumbling. "At some point there should be food for the bands in the back, you guys can have some. It should be meat-free." Amanda said.

I went back and sat at a brightly lit table to relax, but the food wasn't out yet. I picked at some chips which were almost gone, feeling bad about taking the last of anything, since it wasn't technically for me.

"Are you two the people from Oakland?" a man across the table said.

"Yeah kinda." Tim answered. "We're from San Diego but spent the last four years in Oakland, plus we each lived in the Bay Area for some time years before that."

"Oh, we are from Oakland! On tour across Europe."

"Nice! How funny."

"Where in Oakland did you live? Did you even go to shows? Why haven't I seen you before?"

"We lived at 30th and Linden. We went to shows but worked a lot over the last few years too. I'm sure we know a lot of the same people."

"Yeah, maybe. I guess it's just weird I've never seen you guys before." the man said to Tim, doubting the fact I spent the majority of my twenties in the Bay Area. He went on to boast about himself and his band; and eventually, Tim and I went back out to watch the show.

By the time I came back to check on the food, most of it had been eaten and was heavily meat-based anyway. I made myself a plate picking around meat, trying to get what food I could into my stomach, which wasn't much. The last band finished their set as Tim and I stood by the sound booth having another beer. Hans came over to furiously vent about the Oakland band. They had taken off after playing without payment, and had supposedly been complaining about not being promised a large guarantee. A guarantee they had decided to ask for only a day before the show, months after it was booked. While leaving unannounced, they also either purposefully or accidentally took some of another band's equipment. Hans had booked a cabin at a nearby campground for the Oakland band and us to stay in for the night, but since they weren't even answering their phones, it looked like it would be only the four of us. Which by this point we all preferred anyway.

The last band's set came to an end, and a dance party was announced. The bar kept selling beer and a DJ started playing *Total Eclipse of the Heart*.

As I'm sure most people wouldn't know, sometimes at the end of the night American punk shows turn into an 80's or 90's dance party. A night of people with mohawks and black studded vest calmly bobbing their heads to live music or thrashing around a mosh pit suddenly evolves into punks doing the worm or even breakdancing. I had been told tales of friends' bands who tour Europe being confused by punks and metalheads playing techno after shows and the crowd being into it (American punks do *not* like techno). So after this show in a small town in Belgium, we were excited that an 80's dance party was happening! Which quickly turned into techno.

A lady danced over to me and said, "I remember when this song came out in '98!"

Then I got it. "*Oooohh*, this is *their* 80's dance party!" I said to Tim.

A man overheard me and said "Yes! This is our Bon Jovi!" then danced away. So there, I figured it out for those who are confused!

The end of the night was a blur. We made it to the small log cabin surrounded by tall trees and thick grass. It was only a few miles from the venue. A perfect place to crash. The cabin had two small rooms of wooden bunks topped with plastic encased mattress pads probably purchased fifteen years prior. If you had been to sixth-grade camp or partook in some form of scouts, I'm sure you know the ones. They were like crib mattresses for adults. We pulled out our sleeping bags and were out the minute our heads hit the sweatshirts we were using as pillows.

We woke up earlier than I would have liked in order to check out and help clean up the venue. I felt delirious and haggard in the most beautiful setting possible. The sky was so blue, and the grass was so green. The sun was shining, and the temperature was perfect. We went back to the venue to help break down and clean up, then on our way back to Antwerp tried stopping by a Trappist brewery attached to a monastery located on a long winding road through green fields.

This was a place where monks made beer that was said to be one of the best in the world, but they refused to mass produce it and distribute it to chain stores. The only way to taste it was to either pay an outrageous amount of money for one bottle, if you could find it, or visit the brewery attached to the monastery if they decided to open. It was just what lil' old hungover me needed.

We entered the brewery, Westvleteren Abdij Sint-Sixtus, which was fancy and crowded with mostly elderly people. Amanda and Hans ordered a meat and cheese plate, and Tim and I ordered whatever beer they were having, since they knew their stuff. It was heavenly and helped to settle my stomach. The cheese plate, not so much. I nibbled on a slice of cheese with nausea waving over me. I wobbled past grannies sipping on some of the world's best beer midday, making my way to the bathroom hoping I only had to pee and not disgrace the Trappist monastery by puking their amazing beer up after only drinking half a glass. I made it through a second drink, then slept my hangover off in Hans' van during the drive home. A ride I could have only made it through by remaining horizontal.

I woke up a few hours later in Antwerp with Hans yelling at traffic. There just so happened to be a large ten-mile marathon blocking off the entire city, and all entrances from the highway into downtown. It was a Sunday, Hans' birthday, and all we wanted was to get "home," especially Hans since he wanted to relax before having to work the next morning.

We were in traffic forever. At one point an ice cream truck pulled up next to us, and we saw the driver go to the back to grab an ice cream to eat while he was stuck in gridlock. Ten minutes or so later Amanda asked us each "chocolate or vanilla," then jumped out of the van with a fistfull of change to grab us all ice cream cones.

Since sitting in traffic felt pointless, we turned around and drove all the way around Antwerp to try to take side roads in from another direction. Half an hour or so later we got in *just* as they were opening the tunnels we were trying to enter from in the first place. We pulled up a block or two from the apartment, but all streets which led up to it were blocked off. Hans asked a cop if there was any way we could get through to their parking garage and she told us no. She said to go park, eat dinner, and try again later. She also told us it would be cleared by 6, which was confusing because it was already 6:30. Hans rolled his eyes and tried a different way, through the main street which people were usually not supposed to drive on, even on a normal day, yet for some reason it wasn't blocked off like it usually was. It took us almost to the apartment, yet right back up to the same cop lady who was not happy. Thankfully there was a guy with her this time who was laughing at Hans' creativity and moved the cones to let us through. We took turns showering and went to bed early. In the morning Tim and I would be leaving for Ghent.

Here's what Europe is basically like in one long sentence: you travel across the globe, take trains to a little medieval town, go to the oldest existing bar, climb tiny treacherous stairs to a little nook to drink your local beer, not found anywhere else in, sit down, look out over the castles, canals, and cobblestone streets, just as the theme song from *Friends* begins to play over the stereo.

It's like you're always stuck in second gear,
Well, it hasn't been your day, your week, your month,
or even your year.
But, I'll be there for you, when the rain starts to pour.
I'll be there for you, like I've been there before.
I'll be there for you, cause you're there for me too.

We decided on spending one day and one night in Ghent, which was probably the most breathtaking place in Europe we had seen so far. A friend of ours who had toured Europe a few times with his band told us we had to go to Ghent just to visit this ancient little pub. Because of this, we chose Ghent over going to Bruges.

Ghent was lined with canals and beautiful buildings towering over the water's edge. Some of the tall waterfront buildings dated back to medieval times, such as the Graslei row, whose bottom floors were sidewalk cafes, seated not far from the old pub we were searching for. Some of this area originally dated back to the fifth century A.D.

We found our little pub between Graslei row and the Gravensteen castle. It was a small white two-story building with a basement. When I say small, I mean there was only enough room for twenty people inside the bar, and seven on the second story, which was a little loft overlooking the bar. And that would be if the bar was packed to the brim. To get up to the second story, you had to take a tiny spiral staircase that was so steep you could reach out in front of your face and touch the next rows of steps. The pub was called 't Galgenhuisj, which translates to the Gallows House. It's the smallest and oldest café in Ghent, being continuously licensed since 1776. It was named the Gallows

House because it was the last place convicts could have a beer while waiting to be hung - directly behind the building. The brackets used to hold these convicts at the end of their lives were still bolted into the wall.

We walked in and up to the bar, which was relatively empty. The bartender asked what we'd like to drink and Tim and I stared at each other, caught off guard. We had no clue what even one beer was on tap, or how much they cost. "What do you recommend?" Tim asked. He mentioned the house beer, which was what we went with.

We walked up the stairs and sat at a little round table overlooking the bar. I got up to peek out the windows. I could see the castle and people walking the streets, and sipped my beer while listening to the theme song from *Friends*, shaking my head and laughing.

We booked a hostel for the night, maybe fifteen blocks away, in a more modern part of town. It was a clean, seemingly hip hostel with space-pod looking bunks and free breakfast. It was a nice enough hostel that I wished I could have spent more time relaxing in, yet with only one day in Ghent we spent the entirety of our time exploring the town by foot. We spent the rest of the day wandering random streets and peeking into Saint Bavo's Cathedral to take in the medieval paintings and jaw-dropping Gothic architecture. We walked back for an early night in, and to prepare for Paris in the morning.

Paris: Stories of a Distant Toilet

From Ghent, we went straight to Paris, which was a rough one for me. We showed up in the piss-covered train station surrounded by trash, crowds shoving into subway cars for rush hour, and homeless people sleeping against buildings. My mood went sour quick. How the hell did I go from quaint European oases to a dirty Los Angeles sister city? My first impression of Paris was that it was a complete shit hole. I hoped I was just having a bad first impression during rush hour, and that I'd be wooed by Paris eventually during the twenty-four hours we squeezed in to stay there.

Things weren't looking up. After being swarmed by scammers trying to rob us at the train station, we walked dog-shit-smeared sidewalks to our €20 a night studio apartment. Got lost, found it, and then walked past the broken elevator and up seven flights of stairs to our temporary home.

The studio apartment was small but somewhat quaint, except for the odd setup where the shower was positioned right next to the mattress on the floor. There was a small kitchenette by the apartment door just big enough for a sink and microwave. On the other side of the room, by the bed, was a mini-fridge against one wall and the shower near the other. While showering it was nearly impossible to keep the shower head from slightly sprinkling the pillows on the bed. We opened the large windows to exchange the faint rotten drain smell with the Paris breeze while taking turns using the one communal toilet which was down the seventh floor hallway.

It was already evening by the time we had reached our room, and we only had the rest of the night to see the Notre Dame and drink French wine while eating French cheese under the Eiffel Tower. This was our itinerary for day one, day two was set aside for the Louvre and traveling back to Antwerp.

Back on the subway to the downtown area we went. We had a whole two miles or so to walk to Notre Dame and then the Eiffel Tower. Of course there would be some sort of store in a vast downtown tourist area right? No. No stores. Anywhere. For two miles. No wine. No cheese. Nothing. Just aching legs, sore feet, and the sun disappearing fast.

We could see the sparkling glory of the Eiffel Tower at night glowing in the distance as we approached it, dragging our slumped, sore, wine and cheese deprived carcasses toward it. Then two blocks away *aaaaaahhhhh* a glowing grocery store in the dark, like a green oasis in the desert. We ran grabbing snacks, cheese, wine, and a lemonade to quench my thirst. The store clerk even uncorked our bottle of wine as we paid for our things.

We went to the bottom of the tower expecting to finally get off our feet and relax while enjoying the view. And we did - It was just interrupted every three minutes by men trying to sell us stuff. Knickknacks, glow sticks, roses, and of course wine. Oh, the irony. "No thanks," "We already have some," "Nope," "No," "NOOOO," it was never-ending.

We enjoyed what we could, but I was exhausted. I wanted nothing more at this point than to lay my head on a stranger's wet pillow up seven flights of stairs ten minutes away on the subway.

The next morning we were supposed to be up early to get to the Louvre at a decent hour in hopes of not being stuck in line for half of the day when we didn't even have a full day in the first place, but my body was refusing. I woke up puffy and tired at 10 AM. I woke up ready for a nap. I wasn't going to miss the Louvre though. I'm an art history nerd, so this was my big museum ticket purchase for Europe. To save money, our few priority museums were picked out in advance. On top of that, we had gotten a hook up through friends on museums in Brooklyn and Boston before flying to London, where we visited the impressive and free British Museum. So becoming museum burnt was a real possibility no matter how much we loved exploring them. We felt we had to pace ourselves.

We flew on the rickety metal Paris metro toward the Louvre. I appreciated the trains for being faster than your average subway, and found joy in watching the doors slide open just before the train had made a complete stop. The locals seemed professional at still jumping off anyway. Even with my subway entertainment, I was still a little irritated with Paris. After having to battle men attempting to scam us in the metro station I was in no mood for bullshit when approaching the Louvre.

We charged through crowds, speed-walking toward the museum entrance when two women each cornered us separately, shoving clipboards in our faces and mumbling in

French. "No!" I said, but the woman shoved the clipboard into me further. I consider myself a fair and reserved person, but my first instinct with this pushy woman was to slap the damn clipboard out of her hand and into outer space. Which, as if on autopilot, was what I ended up trying to do. "NO!" I repeated, slapping the clipboard upward as hard as I could, aiming for the herd of parked taxis beside us. The clipboard flew upward, but the woman held on tight. She looked at me silently with wide open eyes and instantly backed off to let me through. I walked up to Tim who was on the other side of the sidewalk pressed against the wall with a clipboard by the second woman. "NO!" I interrupted. I shoved her hand and pen out of Tim's face, leaving a black streak of ink across the paper. With both women silently stunned and standing out of our way, we were on our way to the Louvre.

We found an alternate entrance to the Louvre which the Internet told me had shorter lines and closer access to baggage lockers. We had our backpacks on, which drew scammers and pickpockets to us like magnets, and after much research I still had no idea if the Louvre would let us in with them. No food or drinks were allowed, and we arrived at the security line with backpacks full of beer and snacks, with coffee in hand. And of course, the lockers ended up being past security. We only had a few hours to see this massive museum, yet we had no idea if we would be allowed in or how long it would take us to even get tickets. The few employees wandering outside of security didn't speak enough English to help us. *Screw it*, I thought. We jumped in line for security and tried our luck.

Not only did security not care about coffee, beer, or snacks, but the free lockers were before the museum entrance so we could ditch it all without having to try and explain ourselves a second time. The ticket line looked unusually short, and while standing in it we saw do-it-yourself ticket machines which had no line at all. We jumped out of line to try them, hoping it wasn't some too good to be true members only situation. We successfully paid for our tickets, which made the total combined wait from security, to ticket purchase, to museum entry a quick five minutes. Long lines be damned.

The Louvre's building was absolutely amazing, yet many of the exhibits were unexpectedly familiar to the British Museum. Of course the Venus de Milo and the Mona Lisa were there in all their glory, screened by a veil of selfie sticks and duck faces. After walking the entire museum, we grabbed our backpacks and headed to the train station to make our way back to our temporary home away from home, Antwerp.

We said goodbye to Hans and Amanda after another day or two sipping Belgian beer under impressive towering cathedrals and prepared ourselves for an overnight bus ride towards Freiburg, Germany at the edge of the Black Forest. After two weeks of having a blast exploring and partying with friends, it was time again for Tim and me to hit the road on our own.

Freiburg: A Tube of Mustard a Day Keeps the Doctor Away

I boarded the bus and snagged two empty seats, awkwardly stretching out in hope of sleep. I get motion sickness easily, so I curled up and closed my eyes to get some relief as the bus sloshed my body back and forth like a boat at sea. It's fun when you finally start to drift into slumber; yet, the bus slowing then accelerating again jerks you into a wide-eyed panic as you try to stop your body from catching air and hitting the back of the bus seat in front of you. Yes, so much fun.

When we arrived it was almost four in the morning. We grabbed our stuff from the bus we had just spent the last eleven hours on and sat against a curb in a freezing cold, dark parking lot in what definitely seemed like the middle of nowhere. We were in a suburb of Stuttgart, Germany, where I had ignorantly planned for us to nap in the train station until a decent hour when we could get on another train going to Freiburg. The only problem was, there was no train station. Just an above-ground transit platform in a quiet suburb outside of the city center, where I accidentally scared the shit out of a man trying to do graffiti in the stairwell.

A path led from the parking lot through some bushes to the station, and we made our best guess at booking tickets to Freiburg at the ticket machine. The machine let me print an itinerary showing the five trains we would need to take to reach our destination. Thankfully it was only €28 total which was a reasonable price for that long of a trip on European trains. According to our itinerary, we had over two hours to wait for our first train, so we decided to wander a few blocks into the night, or early morning, to explore what was around us. It was Sunday, so nothing was open and probably wouldn't have been even if it was a reasonable hour. I deliriously welcomed ourselves to our sixth new country by calling out "Hello, Germany!" down the dark cobblestone streets.

We wandered into an open lobby of a hotel hoping someone at the front desk could confirm the correctness of our train itinerary. A little old man was poking around the back and almost had a heart attack when he turned around and saw the two of us, bundled up in black jackets, black beanies and hoods, peering into the hotel bar to ask weird questions in English. He caught his breath, took a look at our train schedule, and confirmed, "To Freiburg, yes, Freiburg." We walked the streets a bit more, making bets on how long it would take for the locals to call the cops on us, then we walked back to the station and curled up on a dark bench half shielded from the wind. Tim pulled out his phone to play podcasts to pass the time, and I pulled out my sleeping bag to stop my shivering. After only fifteen minutes of waiting, our train came early.

Groggy and sleep deprived, we boarded a subway train where half of the passengers looked like professionals starting their morning, and the other half were headed home drunk from a night of partying. A small group of men in their early 20's were yelling German cuss words, screaming laughing, and falling out of their seats. They were obviously wasted.

The main station was extremely confusing and filled with more rowdy young dudes with beers in hand at 7 AM. I guess Germans know how to party. We tried to not act lost, the last thing we needed was the attention of slurring local bro-dudes. Eventually, we found the part of the station we were looking for and enjoyed some coffee before boarding our train.

When I researched a summer in Europe, everything I read said to prepare for heat, besides a bit of rain in the northern countries. It didn't help that I was reading this from San Diego in a 90 degree February. After attempting a Pacific Crest Trail thru-hike, I have become somewhat obsessed with trying to pull off poor man's ultralight packing, so let's just say I was not prepared whatsoever for Spring weather across the United States and Europe. It was mid-April, and I woke from my dozing off on the train to the most beautiful sight of towering pine trees being blanketed in pure white snow. My eyes said "Wow!" While my inner thoughts said, "What the fuck." We hit snow in Wyoming, Boston, and now Germany. I spent the last two months in rain and snow and wind thinking "Eh, just a few weeks more, I'll tough it out, I don't want to buy warmer clothes I'll just have to carry for months." And now it was 37 degrees midday. Sunshine warming my skin was becoming a distant memory of my past. Something I was now assuming I'd have to tell tales of to my children's children, "Back in my day..."

We half-slept on each train, dozing off for a few minutes then waking to meet friendly dogs and watch tiny
towns pass as we traveled through Germany's Black Forest.
By 11 AM we were in Freiburg, walking cobblestone alleys
to our hostel where we immediately took naps and then hit
the town to explore and stock up on drinks and snacks at
a grocery store.

The entire town was closed for Sunday, which we were
starting to realize was a Europe thing we would have to
start anticipating and preparing for. We walked for hours
not finding anything, and it began to rain. We stopped
into a coffee shop that was also a cocktail bar to hang out
in until we were ready to go back and sleep. We were excited for our first taste of real German beer, and a small
café such as this was the only place we'd be finding it on
a Sunday evening. A little old lady a few seats over sat for
hours reading a book by herself with three full glasses of
the biggest beers I've seen. I joked about how they were all
for her, which later we realized they indeed were. By the
time we decided to leave, she was finishing the third glass.

The little I knew of Freiburg was that it was a tiny town
of castles and cobblestone roads on the edge of the Black
Forest, home to Hansel and Gretel and the cuckoo clock.
While this was true, the medieval cathedrals and Bavar-
ian architecture were combined with odd sights of ye olde
McDonalds and Burger King on what seemed like every
corner. Ancient clock towers were scrawled with modern
graffiti, and homeless men and women sat outside of the
H&M stores hoping for change from tourists.

You can't really be too disappointed by this when visiting a new city or country though. It seems like a very privileged American belief that beautiful tiny towns should hide real life issues so they, as tourists, can pretend it doesn't exist. I feel thankful enough that these medieval towns haven't been bulldozed and turned into condos, and I actually get to experience seeing the buildings and cities I had for thirty years only heard about or seen in pictures. In some ways, political street art and murals next to ancient towers were an amazing sight. Old next to new. If anything, it makes it feel more real.

After struggling to get out of bed, we got to see the town awake with open stores, and even found a large grocery store! I got a tube of strong mustard we tried in Belgium, vegetarian cordon bleu, German beer, fancy cheese and bread, fruit, and cheap packets of ramen, which is a pretty accurate list of everything we survived on for our entire four months in Europe. We spent most of the day hiking to a 99-foot-tall lookout tower overlooking Freiburg, in the ruins of what once was a French military fortress. It ended up being closed off once we got to the top. The views were beautiful either way though, so I wasn't too disappointed.

"They should have had a sign saying it was closed off," Tim said.

"The signs were all in German, so they probably did," I responded. It was overcast and chilly as we walked through the thick green woods. We could see the Schneeburg castle ruins in between pine trees across town and Freiburg's ancient cathedral towering over the city center as we climbed down the hill.

Freiburg Minster is the name of Freiburg's big cathedral. It was constructed in a Romanesque style around 1200, then continued being built in a Gothic style in 1230. Freiburg Minster was Built on the foundations of Freiburg's original church which was built in 1120. The 380-foot tower was described by the Swiss historian Jacob Burckhardt that it would "forever remain the most beautiful spire on Earth." Freiburg Minster's tower was the only Gothic church tower completed in the Middle Ages in Germany, surviving from then until now, even through bombing raids in 1944. It was truly picturesque seeing Freiburg from above with its mix of forest and spiraling ancient architecture. After descending down the trail to the bottom of the hill we went back to the hostel to relax, snack, and meet some of our fellow travelers.

The unfortunate thing about finally leaving to travel extensively in your 30's is that a lot of hostel goers were so much younger than we were. This was the second hostel we stayed in which had a big group of young kids screaming and running like chickens with their heads cut off at almost 10 PM, pillow fighting and flailing as if they had never left the house without their parents before. It was very sixth-grade camp feeling, except I was closer in age to the camp counselors. Thankfully we weren't sharing a room with them.

Our dorm mates were already soundly sleeping so we went to a common room to drink a beer and blog without waking them. Not all who stay in hostels are young, one man in our dorm had to be well over sixty. The differences between travelers can make it hard to make travel buddies too. I missed days on the Pacific Crest Trail where no matter what our ages were or what we were into, we were all in it together. All just as tired, just as desperate for beer and burgers.

Life is funny, you could be hiking the Pacific Crest Trail daydreaming about walking European cobblestone roads, where you could stop for beer and burgers at any time, then exactly one year later you are walking down rainy cobblestone roads between medieval buildings wishing you were napping on the trail in the sun. I don't know how I even did those 300 miles. I was walking quite a few miles a day in Europe, usually with no backpack, but I was *tired*. So tired. But then again, alcohol was often involved, and even if we weren't staying out partying just a beer or two before bed was a higher percentage than we were used to in the United States. That Belgian beer made it worth it though. We spent a few rainy days exploring Freiburg and drinking German beer, then hopped on another long distance bus to the big city.

At this point we were very close to being one month into our Europe trip and I had learned a lot. I learned that French people really do run around with baguettes, and sometimes don't wear deodorant (go French people though, I'm not here to judge). Good cheap beer flows freely in every country we had been to, where people often drink in unconventional places compared to our country, such as while window shopping or eating a meal in a train station. Flying is cheaper than trains. Sex workers have their own unions, in fact everyone does. I'm sure there are a lot more things I could list off, but for real: I know we would not be experiencing this the same if we hadn't been taking multiple months, at least weeks to explore Europe as we wished. I was glad we chose to not do it any other way. I knew I was going to desperately miss parts of European life when we left.

There were things I wished we could have that Europeans have, like free or cheap college degrees (I had met squatters with master's degrees), healthcare, and so on. Plus Europeans just live so simply. And why not? The status symbol of how wasteful you can be in America, especially Southern California, is disgusting. Europeans don't feel the need to prove how masculine they are by hanging truck nuts off of their giant *Earth Fucker* 5000. And I'm not even a hippy or anything. I swear.

Munich: A Lot to Drink

We were only in Munich for less than two days, so my exposure to the city was fairly limited. When we arrived, our hostel's front desk told us there was a traditional German Oktoberfest-style beer festival going on right down the street. This sounded exciting. "Traditional German Oktoberfest," and we didn't even have to wait until October. Tim and I were starving so we hurried over in search of local beer, food, and fun before it closed.

We walked up to the festival, but it wasn't what we had expected at all. It ended up being just a regular fair. The small fairs they throw in a park or empty lot once or twice a year with carnies and tilt-a-whirl rides. Not even like a big county fair with all the crazy fair foods. We did find a beer hall, but everything was so expensive we continued our walk towards downtown hungry instead.

After exploring for a while and finding a decent Vietnamese restaurant for food, we went back to our hostel for happy hour. This hostel was nice and clean. A few floors of small, modern shared bedrooms with a real sports bar connected to the lobby. The party was kept in the bar, so the rooms remained relatively quiet. Both nights we stayed, the bar was packed from happy hour until late into the night. The first night was filled with crowds clinking glasses and yelling over a soccer game broadcasted on the large flat screen TVs. Our second night we had to book last minute due to a schedule mix up on our part, so Tim and I had to split up and take separate rooms due to limited availability. He stayed in our original room while I moved four floors up to a room with a small balcony and fewer bunks. I was the first person in the room for the night, so I picked what I thought was the best bed and stashed my backpack in a locker. We explored for the day, thrift shopping across Munich, and came back again to enjoy happy hour, free WIFI, and maybe meet some of the other travelers.

It was a good night of chatting and enjoying a new beer we discovered, when we decided to get up from our bar stools to head back to our rooms. We had to be up early for check out and to catch a ride share to Vienna. Tim stepped away from his bar stool first and felt his foot slide. We turned to see the entire floor and wall behind us, only about three feet away, completely covered in fresh puke.

We quickly checked the back of our clothes and hair to make sure we were free from any splatter ricochet from this stealth puker, and thankfully we were clean. By this time the people nearby had noticed our disgust, and a drunk young man was awkwardly giggling. He had been acting weird the whole time, so we had a hunch it was him. There was also a crying drunk girl earlier in the night, but I never saw her walk behind our stools.

As we made our way out of the bar, I got the attention of a bartender and told her what we had found. She was not happy but thanked me profusely for telling her, after questioning me a few times about whether I had seen the culprit.

Tim and I parted ways at the elevator, and I went, slightly buzzed, up to my new room full of sleeping strangers. As quietly as I could, I unlocked my locker, pulled out everything I needed for a quick shower down the hall, then locked it back up again. I took a warm shower, playing music on my phone since no bedrooms were nearby, then headed back for bed. I reached the door to my room with my toiletry bag and clothes spilling out of my arms, dressed in my pajamas with bare feet.

I fumbled around for my key card and couldn't find it anywhere. I didn't want to knock and wake up my roommates, so I left my stuff outside the bedroom door and went back to check the bathroom. No key. *I must have locked it inside the room*, I thought. It was really late, I was tired, I had to be up soon, and I paid a deposit for that key card. I was not having the best night.

I did an embarrassing, half-naked with wet hair, locked-out-of-room walk of shame back to the lobby situated right next to the bar entrance, to plead for them to let me in my room. They gave me a loaner key attached to a giant stick to take back up with me. It was impossible trying to be quiet while I entered the room and searched through everything I owned with my phone as a flashlight. No key. I lost it. I would have to go back down and tell them I lost it.

I checked the bathroom one more time, scanning the floors around a girl using the mirror. "Did you lose your key?" she piped up. "There is one on the floor near the toilet." I thanked her, picked my plain white key card off of the plain white tile, brought back the giant wooden stick to the front desk, went back up the elevator, then slid into bed.

In the morning I packed my bag dehydrated and groggy. The women in my room asked me where I was from and I apologized for making so much noise during the night, explaining how I had temporarily lost my key.

"Oh we didn't even hear you," they responded, "we had a lot to drink."

Vienna: Good Brad

It was our first time trying a ride share in a stranger's car in Europe with a man who may or may not speak English. He pulled up in his nice car and threw our backpacks in the trunk, excited to hit the road. "We have to drive a few minutes out of the way to pick up one more passenger. I hope you don't mind."

Fifteen minutes into the drive we pulled into a quaint neighborhood with little white houses and big green gardens. A well-dressed middle-aged woman with short poofy blond hair arrived outside of the car with enough bags to make it look like we might be helping her move. Our driver cheerfully Tetris-ed her belongings into the trunk, and Tim moved into the back seat with me to let the woman up front. She swung open my door and smiled, then shoved in as many bags as she could into every open space around my legs. Into the front seat she climbed, scooting the seat hard into Tim's shins to fit more bags at her feet. Our driver followed her around doing damage control, rearranging her bags and scooting the seat back into an appropriate position. Once we were all in and the bags were in order, we hit the road.

I slept my nausea away while opening my eyes from time to time to see rolling green trees, hilltop castles, and the woman's jewelry reflecting rainbows onto the ceiling of the car. So far Austria seemed beautiful. Halfway through the drive we stopped for gas and I ran into the convenience store to grab anything I could to appease my growling stomach. There wasn't much. I needed more than potato chips. *Chips and salsa, I guess that'll do.* I sat on a curb outside in the sun and opened my snacks. I took out a triangle shaped corn chip and inspected it. It was covered in a colorful flavor dust, like a Dorito. This wasn't mentioned on the bag. There were no better options for the salsa anyway. These were the chips that were supposed to go *with* the salsa. I opened the salsa and shoveled a scoop into my mouth. It was sweet. Sugary sweet. It was like ketchup with too much sugar. My nausea instantly returned, but my hunger got the best of me and I ate it anyway.

We arrived in Vienna in time for the last two days of a three-day punk festival and benefit for Anarchist Black Cross. We got to town fairly early to be heading to the show, so we went to the nearby central train station to use WIFI and eat lunch in the large mall-like food court. Hans and his band were playing the festival, and even though we knew they hadn't arrived at the venue yet, we thought we would go check it out and see if things had started. We were off to a rough start since the address on the show flyer was confusing. It took us to a maternity store on a deserted street which hilariously said "baby lump" in the window. Definitely not a well-known squat surviving since the 1990's. We went back to a free public WIFI spot in a park to double check our address and realized our mistake. This time the address was only two blocks from the park bench we were sitting on.

As we approached, the building was impossible to miss. It spanned almost a whole square block and was covered seven stories high in political statements, anti-Nazi, and pro-refugee graffiti, and wheat-pasted flyers as far as the eye could see for punk shows and protests.

We walked up to the large steel front door which was wide open. Inside, staircases were leading up and down, with open doors on the right and left sides. Straight in the middle was a sign indicating what was on each floor, where the information booth was, where the bars were, what floors had free lodging for guests, and a schedule for the fest. We were still early, and Hans and his band had still not yet arrived. We poked our heads in the information room, where we were greeted by a woman in her late twenties with dark baggy jeans and blond dreadlocks with parts of her head shaved. She instantly offered us a place to stay for the next few nights in the attic of the squat, which was also a gym next to a free box area (like a free clothing or gear swap) the size and quality of a small thrift store. It was also next door to one of the many bunk rooms for traveling bands.

We hid our backpacks in some gym lockers in our temporary bedroom then went down to the outside patio bar for €1 beers and pay-what-you-can vegan food. For the second time in Europe we were surrounded by punks, but this time we knew no one. We gawked at the large murals, sipped our drinks, and watched as dogs sniffed around, and a woman with black dreadlocks and tattoos greeted friends with an infant in her arms. When we started hearing the stereo blasting from inside the venue part of the building we moved inside.

The inside was amazing! The entire building was amazing. It blew my mind, and I was so jealous California didn't have anything similar. Seven stories of stores, classrooms, gym, free store, guest lodging, bathrooms, kitchens, private apartments, a basement practice space, a garden roof terrace with kiddie pool, outside bar area, and venue complete with inside bar, commercial kitchen, multiple lofts to sit in, and two underground stage rooms, one with another small bar. Not long after we had moved inside Hans and his band arrived, and the first band started playing downstairs. We browsed the anarchist and feminist literature tables, one which offered free vegan brownies and fliers on consent. Every band we heard was great, and since there were two stages, each band flawlessly went from one to the next with no waiting time for set up in between.

Hans and friends came up to us after their set with rounds of shots. A neon green substance in a little plastic shot glass called "Pfeffy." We had not yet heard tales of Pfeffy, but we soon learned many bands touring Europe near Germany were notorious for having experiences partying with it, usually resulting in quite the hangover. We toasted our Pfeffy and downed our shots, which kept coming. Soon the basement liquor bar had scratched Pfeffy shots off of the menu. We cleaned them out. Pfeffy is actually just short for Pfefferminz, which is a German peppermint liquor. Like Peppermint Schnapps, but neon green. After the music ended, we went up to our attic nook and went to sleep.

In the morning we slept in then went to explore. I felt groggy from staying up until wee hours of the morning, but besides that Pfeffy's wrath had not come for me as promised. For Tim that was not the case. We walked the large muraled stairwells through anti-cop doors that resembled steel castle moat bridges. We had been so cold for so long, when I saw people and dogs sunning on the rooftop terrace I couldn't stop myself from joining in.

We spent most of the day drinking a few leftover beers we had while laying out in the sun, toasting our skin to make up for multiple months of cold winter weather we weren't prepared for. Our friends had continued on their tour, so we would be attending the last day of the festival by ourselves. When the venue doors opened, I jumped in line for the vegan food. It was burritos the previous night, but I didn't have the cash on me to afford one. This time there was schnitzel cordon bleu with a side salad topped with marinated veggies. It was absolutely amazing restaurant quality food. And it was pay what you could afford!

The bands started up again, and I was already tired but determined to stay awake for the after-show activities starting at 1 AM. This night's activity was karaoke. I did my best to groggily remain awake and made it to 1 AM. Because of technical difficulties karaoke didn't actually start until closer to 3. During about an hour of waiting for them to get the projector working, 80's dance party broke out. A drunk man was singing into the microphone and flailing on the floor, and a girl with short pink hair and most of her head shaved was trying to get me to dance with her. After an hour or so of watching some pretty hilarious dancing and singing, I was ready for sleep. Tim came up with me to set up our bed then went back down to enjoy the party for a little longer.

In the morning we stepped outside to grab a coffee from the gas station across the street, and came back to the pink-haired girl and a few other residents of the squat already drinking beer on the front stoop. We drank our coffee, and I offered my potato chips to the people letting us stay in their home. We had been there for two nights, but were hoping we could stay for one more, if possible. Tim talked to a small bearded guy with dreadlocks who offered us a place to stay in Leipzig, Germany, while I introduced us to the others. A homeless man who seemed like a regular character to the area drank beer while standing on the sidewalk, trying to keep his balance while dancing (or violently flailing) to the American pop music one of the guys with us was blasting from his car parked on the street. Next thing you know a bottle of Pfeffy appears and begins making its rounds across the stoop.

One of the men we had met, the one who owned the car, started dancing to the pop song *Call Me Maybe*. Jumping up onto his car and sliding around, humping the roof while we laughed and the city bus drove past full of confused onlookers. The bus driver purposefully ignored us, since the squat had a tradition of clapping for the bus every time it passed the front steps on a Sunday morning after a show. As the alcohol continued to flow, polite clapping quickly turned into standing ovations with cheering and whistling. Complete with continuous chanting of the bus number, as if it was a sports team who just won a point. We fit right in, talking politics, music, travel, then pausing to clap, whistle, and scream for bus number 14A, or vierzehn-A, without missing a beat.

We lounged on the front stoop sipping beer and the girl with the pink hair, Sarah, kept checking her phone. Her boyfriend was across town playing a game of American football. She wanted to move the party there so she wouldn't miss her boyfriend's game, but no one was in good enough shape to drive. Instead, we were invited upstairs to one of the private apartments and into the bedroom of the *Call Me Maybe* dancer to finish a crate of German beer and listen to records.

After a few punk records, our host put on *The Village People*. The song *In the Navy* blasted in the dark room with sunlight peeking through the only two windows, which were half covered by black curtains. A poster hung on the wall saying "When You Cuddle Alone, You Cuddle with Hitler." It was odd seeing a joke poster involving Hitler in Austria, but I had seen the image before somewhere and knew it was just that. A cow skull hung on a wall by a sink, and two gas masks on the wall served as lamps, holding lit light bulbs which were displaying colorful patterns on the wall.

Tim left to use the apartment's shared bathroom then chat with another resident in the kitchen. The kitchen resided behind a massive steel locked door covered in murals in the main staircase of the building. Attached to the kitchen were private bedroom doors scattered around the kitchen's perimeter walls, one door being the bathroom for the apartment. There were multiple of these apartments, about two to three on each floor above the ground floor.

Tim came back into the bedroom as our host turned off the music, and the sun started setting outside of the windows. "This is time for our show," a man informed us.

"What kind of show?" Tim asked.

"A murder show," another person responded, popping their head up from the bed in the corner of the room. The murder show seemed very similar to an Austrian version of *Law & Order*. We watched and slowly each person started to fall asleep, including Tim. I left the room and wandered back up to the seventh story gym, where I had a pack of ramen buried in my backpack I was hungry for. I was already inside two giant steel doors after leaving the apartment door without a guest key, hoping I'd be let back into the third. Thankfully when I returned someone was going through the door, and I followed. I made myself at home in the kitchen, finding a bowl and fork and doing the kitchen's dishes while I waited for the water to boil. People walked through here and there usually greeting me with a "hallo." I ate my soup alone at the table, washed my dishes, then went back to the room of sleeping people watching the Austrian murder mystery. By this time it was night, so I woke Tim to move upstairs to go to sleep.

In the morning we packed our things and I went to the free pile and grabbed a big black peacoat to better prepare me for the non-summer weather we were continually having and were perpetually unprepared for. We started down the seven floors and ran into our host from the night before leaving his apartment. We had just spent three nights in the gym of the squat and felt we were overstaying our welcome now that the show was over, even though none of the residents specifically seemed to mind. Still, it was their house not ours, and there wasn't a spare guest key so if we came and went we would most likely get locked out with our belongings inside. We had no direct contact here and no working phones without WIFI either way. The people we had met said there could be a possibility of us staying longer and getting a guest key if a few of them could discuss it, but at this point we were ready to move onto a different sleeping situation and not make things harder on anyone else. We grabbed our things and said goodbye, not knowing if we would come back or not. We still had a few days left in Vienna to find cheap bikes to ride to Budapest.

Tim and I walked back to the central station for WIFI and started looking up hostels in the city center of Vienna. We found a decent one, booked a reservation, then took the subway train into town. We had already been in Vienna for what would normally be a full length stay for us visiting a new place in Europe, yet while stepping out of the station we were just now seeing what Vienna had to offer outside of its large and impressive punk community. A Gothic cathedral towered over us, spacious bike lanes flashed their own stop lights, and billboards filled the tops of tall buildings. We walked to a lead we were given on a bike kitchen, from the woman working the info center of the squat. Yet when we arrived, the man working the shop seemed caught off guard and said he had no bikes for sale. He did tell us about a bike flea market coming up within a few days, so we thought we would stay in town and try our luck there.

We turned around back toward the metro station and headed to the hostel. It was a nice place with funny images poking fun of pop culture and political references, like Donald Trump's face surrounded by pictures of poop plastered on a non-working door. We cozied into our new room which was occupied by one woman in her 50's, and rested until the bar opened in the hostel's basement. We were tired, and I felt as if I was coming down with a sore throat, but the hostel offered us each a free welcome drink so we thought we'd partake and see what other guests were around.

The bar had good WIFI, so I did a quick video chat with a few family members back home while enjoying my drink. Tim met two Australian men who were playing a euro-coin throwing game to win free shots of liquor from the bar. When I came back from video chatting in another common area, they had more shots than I could count lined up down the entire length of the bar. They also had a young man from Pakistan accompanying them who instantly started pestering me as I walked toward them. I guess he had shown some interest in me from afar and one of the snarky Australians had jokingly told him I was interested in him as well. I still had my mom on video chat so she could say hi to Tim and be introduced to the group, yet this young man stepped right in front of the screen to not only greet my mom, but to go over his entire resume of skills with her, apparently trying to prove himself as a viable suitor for her daughter. I laughed and rolled my eyes. What did he see in me? Some grimy punk chick eight or so years his senior in a dark hostel bar. I guess I was really the only target around besides the bartender, who later told me she had her fair share of harassment from this kid as well.

Tim and the Australians pushed a handful of shots my way, and I chatted while blatantly ignoring the young man trying to win my attention. Tim was ignoring him as well. He started to get pushier, not leaving me alone and begging me for attention. I was drinking more liquor and becoming increasingly annoyed. I began to demand he leave me alone. I called him names. I told him he was creepy. I told him he was gross with women. I told him I owe him nothing and for him to continue to pry is sexual harassment. Tim sat back and let me handle the situation myself instead of barging in to claim me as his property, but when he wouldn't stop Tim then started to aggressively hit on him in return. He blew kisses and winked from a few bar stools away until the man became uncomfortable.

Eventually Tim and I ended up having a drunken heart to heart with the man, giving him advice on how to speak to women and how not to. He seemed to be all ears, taking everything in and apologizing. He even went to shake hands with who he embarrassingly learned was my fiancé, then offered him a game of pool.

While they played, I remained at the bar chatting with the bartender about the situation. She told me he had said some nasty things to her, much worse and more vulgar than how he had acted towards me. This made it obvious his apologizing was just a show. He hadn't changed. He didn't care. I walked up to the game of pool, grabbed Tim by the arm, and dragged him away yelling out "screw this guy!" then told Tim what the bartender had said to me. We made it perfectly clear he was not to speak to us, and we went back to our room to go to sleep.

I laid in bed, my throat hurting even more, and my nose starting to sniffle. A new roommate came in late to crawl into what he thought was his bed, yet was occupied by the woman in her 50's loudly breathing away in a deep sleep. He jumped back, using his phone as a flashlight which was shining brightly onto the woman's dead-asleep face, then crawled into the unoccupied bunk above her.

The next morning we approached the breakfast buffet to load up on free cereal and bread when this familiar sound echoed in from a distant corner of the room. Ah, the American accent. Something we hadn't heard in at least a few weeks. Not only was it an American accent, but the screeching squeal of the valley-girl American accent. Multiple of them, each one trying to talk over the other.

"Whut is thiz *BRAD*? The brad that comes in a loaf, that you cut yourself. It's *GOOD BRAD!*" a blond-haired young woman in flip-flops announced to the kitchen staff about their baguettes.

We left the hostel breakfast buffet and made it to the bike flea market, successfully buying bikes for about €100 each. Mine was a purple and black rusty clunker I named Purple Badass, and Tim found a vintage teal and white Puch he appropriately deemed Pfeffy. Purple Badass was a five-speed Dutch-style bike with a rusted black bell, a rack over the back wheel, and shrill squeaking brakes. The handlebars were also positioned slightly off center. I had found a small belt pouch from the free pile at the squat and attached it to the handlebars for quick access to my phone and tissues. Pfeffy was similar in style, with straighter handlebars, road bike tires, a basket in the front, a working bell, and permanent head and tail lights which were powered by a small crank resting on the front tire. Someone had also knitted about four inches of Pfeffy's frame with light teal colored yarn. I thought Pfeffy was nice. Tim liked Pfeffy's sock. If bike touring was based on quirkiness alone, we were set. But for now, the real test was seeing if they could get us back to the hostel.

We happily and awkwardly rode our bikes back to the hostel, excited for our upcoming trip. Because I had come down with a cold, we spent an extra day at the hostel to rest. Thanks to the Australians and the game they introduced us to, Tim needed the rest as well. We thought this would also give us time to buy groceries and other items required for our trip, yet we didn't realize that we would be shopping on a Friday which was the first day of a three-day holiday weekend. We planned an extra day besides our sick day to buy and research what we needed to at least get to Bratislava, but *everything* was closed. Not only that, but the hostel was booked so we couldn't extend our room to get groceries once the stores opened again. We found a hostel to move to about two miles away.

The next morning we mounted Pfeffy and Purple Badass while wearing our backpacks and rode the two miles uphill, along a river running through Vienna, into the green hills just outside of downtown. The hostel was in a beautiful area overlooking tall trees and some of the city. We would have liked to leave Sunday, but of course, the entire town was still closed. By that time we had run out of snacks and food.

We walked the neighborhood for an hour hoping something would be open. A gas station and McDonalds who shared a parking lot would have to be our only source of meals for the day. We swung open the McDonalds' doors, both of us starving. There were no veggie burgers, which other European McDonalds sometimes had and was a decent meal if I was desperate for something cheap and quick. I ate salad and fries with "American dressing", which seemed to be Thousand Island, and Tim got a burger. We went to the gas station and grabbed a bottle of wine, chips, and a cold sandwich each to save for dinner.

I stayed up late stressing out over our lack of maps to Budapest along the Danube bike trail, a section of the Eurovelo 6 bike trail spanning from Nantes, France on the Atlantic Sea to Constanta, Romania on the Black Sea. The Eurovelo is a network of fifteen bike trails spanning the entire continent of Europe in almost every direction. The bike paths span over 28,000 miles, and are currently being expanded. When we learned about this network of trails that zigzagged across nearly every country in Europe, it immediately became our goal to ride a portion. Vienna to Budapest on Eurovelo 6 became the plan.

I woke up still stressed. *I need to get out of bed so I can get ready to bike to Budapest.* That's something I never thought I could say. We were still completely unprepared, yet on our way to bike approximately 275 miles to Budapest, a trip that we could hopefully complete in ten days. That is - if nothing went wrong. Quite a few of the days would be reserved for not cycling, but exploring new towns along the way. We allowed ourselves a few days to explore Bratislava which would give us more time to iron out any issues with our bikes, maps, or food supply. We also planned an extra break day we could use somewhere between Bratislava and Budapest. Low daily mileage would give us more time to explore the countryside at a snail's pace, which was probably our bikes' top speed anyway.

We saw more of Vienna on our last day than we had in the six days we had spent there. The day started off wonderfully, with us walking the first four miles downhill into downtown Vienna instead of riding due to Pfeffy already having a flat tire. We still had to run all of our last errands while trying to get on the road, er... bike trail, as well as bike all of Vienna (about ten miles including what we had walked) just to get to the trail. After that we would ride another thirty-one miles to Hainburg, our first destination.

The flat tire was a great start to trying to bike fifty-five miles to Bratislava through backwoods on flea market bikes without a way to secure our backpacks, extra tubes for our tires, or even a pump. Finally, we found a Wiener Pumpe (yes this is what the public bike pump is called), and spent the rest of the amazingly sunny, warm day biking downtown Vienna while running errands at the same time. Sometimes we stopped to check out a street market or take in the beautiful architecture we would pass.

We stopped and loaded Pfeffy's basket with food and water then rode off once more, teeter-tottering off balance with the wind blowing against our heavy packs. We stopped to check our maps to make sure we were on the correct road through the city toward the Eurovelo trail, when we noticed we were right up against what in the US we would call a 99-cent store. A euro store! We lit up as if someone had just handed us a hundred bucks. Tim was determined to make us baskets for the backs of our bikes to hold our backpacks.

We ransacked the store scanning every inch of the shelves for helpful items. I found a crappy plastic bike pump and bungee cords. Tim found plastic baskets and spent about ten minutes trying to describe zip ties to the people working the register. Eventually we found them on our own, since it was a hard one to get past the language barrier. "Cord ties," the packaging said, in English. Tim fashioned us rickety plastic basket and zip tie backpack holders. Our backpacks were placed inside upright and held in place by bungee cords. The bikes still wobbled a bit, but it was much more comfortable and as good as we were going to get with what we had. There was enough room to squeeze our grocery bag of snacks inside the basket too, and our water bottles could fit pressed against our backpacks under the bungee cords.

We reached the trail around 5 PM, which started on an island on the Danube river. I was instantly reminded of the Pacific Crest Trail, except with hot dog carts, ice cream carts, and beer gardens spanning miles of paved bike trail. Ah yes, and lots of fully nude sunning elderly folk. A head to toe naked granny walked across the bike path where we had stopped for water, passing a family with children. She continued into the parking lot to grab something from her trunk, then back to the water's edge to accompany the other sunning elderly people. Not the parents, children, or anyone else even did a double take. I thought it was awesome people were nonchalant about the human body, but if this had happened in America not only would the children's parents be screaming and shielding the eyes of their young, but I'm sure the SWAT team would be loading granny into a paddy wagon at gunpoint.

Soon the trail became even more Pacific Crest Trail-like when we left the water's edge and started to pass "No food or water for thirty miles" signs. Except it said kilometers and was in German. We cycled a straight trail through farmland and then the Donau-Auen riparian forest for almost the entire distance to Hainburg, which is on the border of Austria and Slovakia.

We rode in dense, dark forest with sunlight only reaching the raised trail. Past furry cows, big jackrabbits, and deer. It was mostly quiet until I started to hear crunching in the trees. I stared into the darkness between the trees as I rode, trying to get a glimpse of whoever was moving about. A huge brown animal showed itself and I almost flew off my seat. *A bear?! Is that a small bear? There are bear in Austria??* I thought. I was used to black bear in California, which can sometimes be more on the brown side, so small bear was my first instinct. Only a second had gone by yet Big Brown, who had to be over twice the size of my 60 lb dog, was still crunching through the trees allowing me to suddenly get a glimpse of his face. I was eye to eye from my bike on the raised bike path with a wild boar. Tusks, back mohawk, and all.

Hainburg: My Butt Was Dead

I woke up the morning of our second day on the bike trail and was glad I was still alive, although I could swear my butt was dead. My muscles ached, and my bottom half felt bruised. Touching my butt to the hard bike seat shocked me with pain, even just to scoot around from our camp spot to a park trash can.

We rode into Hainburg around 9 PM the previous night, and I was beat. Our trusty clunkers had taken us forty miles on the Eurovelo trail and through Vienna. We were towing heavy bikes weighted down even more with our heavy backpacks poorly strapped to the back. We approached the little town on a bridge going over the water and could see two castles lit up on the hill. The bike trail was dark, and I was tired and physically uncomfortable. All I wanted was to reach town and get my butt off of that seat. We stopped to look at a sign to make sure we were headed the right way and I waddled with pain, inching by foot and walking my bike on the path until it was time to ride off again.

The trail continued winding toward town, lit only by the moon and distant street lights. The path took us through the trees around a large dark open field. *BANG... BANG...* gunshots rang out across the field from a direction I was unsure of. This was not the first time Tim and I had been alone in the dark at night in some rural area with people shooting out into the darkness in our direction. I was panicking internally, yet the only thing we could do was keep going to get out of the field. I was sore, I was tired, and now I had to try not to get shot. I thought this was a problem we only had to deal with in America? We yelled out into the dark, making any noise we could to make our presence known, while pedaling quickly in an attempt to pass the field. I'm not sure who the shooters were targeting, but we were on a known continent-wide bike trail so shooting around it in general didn't seem very smart. I did see camouflaged hunting platforms a few fields back, presumably for the boar or maybe deer. The edge of the field led us onto a potholed paved road with houses on one side and forest on the other. We used the last of our strength to press on and make it to the quiet little cobblestone roads of the medieval town.

Sleepy Hainburg was quiet and eerie. Before we could stop for the night, we had to throw our bikes over our shoulders to climb ancient steps into the center of town. A few young men were drinking and partying on a park bench, and we felt no choice but to take the only other available bench next to them to rest and figure out where to go.

We didn't have anywhere to stay in Hainburg so after snacking on cold baked tofu, which brought me back to the distant memory of bologna lunch meat, we wandered with sore muscles for over an hour until realizing the only place we could find to throw down our sleeping bags was up against a medieval castle along the Danube. We never passed any grocery stores or markets, only little restaurants and stores that were closed for the night. Even though we were technically urban camping in town it seemed pretty primitive. We leaned our bikes against the castle wall and locked them together, also slipping our backpack straps through the cable lock. Our sleeping bags laid out on a thin blue tarp were fairly invisible to the nearby road, but would be glaringly apparent come sunrise.

I got into my sleeping bag and tried to relax, something I had spent hours longing for, but I couldn't stop thinking paranoid thoughts about the possibility of someone finding us. A car blasting music passed, then circled around and passed once more. I could see the man who was driving the car's face from my sleeping bag in the castle's dark shadow. He circled again, and again.

"Why is he doing that?" I asked Tim.

"I'm sure he doesn't see us, just try to sleep," Tim reassured. I turned my focus to the castle wall, where divots along its base were caked in old soot. Probably where peasants, or whoever, built little fires to keep themselves warm. Who knows how many bones or other ancient objects were buried beneath us.

No one hassled us throughout the night or morning. We had only seven miles to go to reach Bratislava, where we would stay for two nights. I woke up next to the ancient wall and buried my face in my sleeping bag to pretend the sun wasn't out yet. I could hear cars driving past and the whirring of the Eurail trains making their way through town. Yes, in Europe even rural towns have some form of train available to the locals. I packed up quick, determined to get us hot coffee from a local restaurant who would hopefully also let us use their bathroom. About a block away from us along the Danube river was the quaint café busy for the morning breakfast rush. Across from the restaurant was a trailhead full of joggers and hikers stretching in preparation for exercising along a dirt trail beside the river.

I ordered Tim and I coffee to go, and took full advantage of the single bathroom while customers waited in line outside of the door. Washing the bike dirt and castle plants off of my hands and splashing water on my face was my version of a satisfying shower. I went outside and handed Tim his coffee, who had managed to find a bit of free WIFI out near the trailhead. I sipped my drink next to the river with sunshine warming my face and was overcome by the feeling of summer that I had been longing for, and hoped would last. We packed our bikes and searched for a faucet to fill our empty water bottles but couldn't find one. I searched a park playground, house walls for spigots, the train station, the trailhead, another park along the water, and there was no water to be found. Not even a store.

I saw a couple walking through a parking lot, sweaty from hiking and held up my empty water bottles. "Do you know where I can find water?" I asked.

"No thank you," they responded, turning up their noses and walking past. My eyes followed them, puzzled. No one seemed to know what water was so we took our chances biking in summer weather being hydrated on coffee alone, hoping to find a store or spigot on the way to Bratislava.

Bratislava: Revenge from the Woods

Immediately after leaving Hainburg the trail took a turn up a steep hill along a small highway. I scanned every passing house for a hose or spigot, already panting and stopping to remove layers with the sun beating down on me. The ride to Bratislava was going to be much shorter than our ride the day before, and after that first hill it was already much smoother sailing. We rode along the highway through rural fields, past tiny farms and abandoned castles up in the hills. The bike path took a turn away from the highway and went through fields of wildflowers, past the backs of houses with lush green yards, then back to the highway again. I sang songs, changing the lyrics to be about riding into Slovakia, and nodded my head at passing cyclists. For the first time in months I could feel the sun baking my shoulders as I whizzed through the cool breeze. The sky was bright blue, and everything around me was green. Bugs buzzed around me as if to join in on the adventure and I spit them out of my mouth after accidentally inhaling a few.

The trail intersected a cobblestone road, and there was our spigot on the side of an old farm building. We filled our empty plastic water bottles and chugged as much of the cold water as we could before hitting the road again. As we rode closer to Bratislava we passed physical remnants of the Iron Curtain, an abandoned military bunker, and also what seemed to be a Syrian refugee camp.

Bratislava's symbolic Schloss Hrad castle and Novy Most suspension bridge emerged before us, and at last we had arrived. The graffitied bridge took us over the Danube river where we cycled through tourist crowds toward the castle, and right into a Segway tour in the center of town.

We biked through ancient archways into the more modern-looking city center. Unlike most of California, some European cities have castles and churches dating over a thousand years old right next to buildings that were put up just a year ago. One minute Tim and I were navigating down a windy alleyway from the dark ages, only to then find ourselves in the middle of a multilane paved road, which eventually took us to the art-themed hostel we had booked. We locked our bikes up on the hostel's back porch and threw our bags into the empty Salvador Dali themed room. We went back into the lobby where the staff greeted us once more, this time with free welcome shots of Borovicka. Borovicka is similar to Gin, but made out of Juniper berries. Its slogan is "revenge from the woods."

We had two days to explore Bratislava like tourists, eating cereal-coated fried cheese and vegan dumplings, all while simultaneously planning the rest of our bike trip which we had yet to do. We poked around the town gawking at the castle from afar and getting some restaurant time in, which we tried to reserve just for new countries with new food to experience. We went back to the hostel's bar to take advantage of our guest discounts and chatted with the bartenders and other guests. A young man named Nicholas became our temporary traveler friend who we spent the evening drinking and listen to 80's New Wave with at the bar.

The next day we dedicated to making breakfast in the kitchen and planning the rest of our bike trip. Tim was cooking and became frustrated when he realized we had no butter or oil to cook our eggs with, so I decided to run to the nearest market since he was already in the middle of preparing food. I speed walked quite a few blocks to the nearest small grocery store and flew inside straight to the butter. Staring at the butter selection, I sifted through each option inspecting the butter one by one. I could tell it was butter but some were different than others, and since I couldn't read the language I had no idea what the difference was. I picked the cheapest stick and decided just to grab it and go but this foreign word was sticking out to me as familiar, and I didn't know why. *Is it horse? Does that mean horse? Can they make butter from horses? I have no idea.* I put it back and grabbed the next one up in price. I'm pretty sure there is no such thing as horse butter, and that market definitely wasn't selling it, but sometimes not knowing the language had me second guessing myself. I mean, horse meat *was* legal in some European countries?

I glanced around the store quickly to see if there was anything else we needed, when I heard a crash down the aisle. A little old lady who was taking just as long shopping for wine as I was looking for butter dropped her bottle. The glass smashed on the ground, making it look like a bloody crime scene. She grabbed another bottle off the shelf then walked away as if nothing had happened. I booked it to the cash register as fast as I could from a different aisle to get back to Tim who was awaiting my butter, yet the elderly woman somehow made it before me, cutting me off right at the register. I stood there holding my one stick of butter as she slowly pulled each vegetable one by one out of her full cart and onto the counter. The checker scanned each item then handed it back. The woman appeared to be angry and complaining to the cashier, who seemed annoyed with the woman. I sat there bored, watching the elderly women break the tops of her carrots off to make more room in her overflowing rolling bag.

That evening we stayed up late enjoying one last night in the hostel bar then went back to our big empty room to sleep, except now we had a roommate. A last minute guest had arrived, a large, hairy, middle-aged man, who decided - of course - to take the closest bunk he could to ours in a completely empty room of beds. We had come in from drinking and he didn't even flinch. The man's snoring shook the room and we giggled and imitated him, again with the man having no clue of our existence.

When we woke up in the morning the man was already gone. We packed our bags and our bikes and rode to a large grocery store for water and snacks. From there we were on our way back to the trail as rain clouds moved in overhead. We rode through town back to the big bridge which was now decorated in white shirts splattered in fake blood and banners reading "Doctors are dead, who will treat in Syria" in Slovak.

Confused whether to take the trail on the North side of the Danube or the South (our vague map said North, our book said South), we stuck with the South side and headed to our next stop, a little town of castles and dentists.

Mosonmagyaróvár: Like a Dream

We reached the South side of the Danube river with the wind trying to beat my jacket apart and the sky growing darker. We had to get our mileage in as soon as possible, since we were already headed out somewhat late. The rain sprinkled us a bit, but after a few miles the sun came out and we were back to pedaling hard, with legs growing sore, down small highways next to endless open fields. Passing through small towns was my favorite. I loved the little Hungarian dogs, and I envied the never-ending front yard gardens. Hungary seemed like a dream.

We rode through the Hungarian countryside and stopped here and there to eat the rest of our snacks that we carried from Bratislava. An old train next to a fishing pond and picnic area made a nice break spot, where we each took a shot of Borovicka from Tim's pack and I ate more of my cold bologna tofu. The sign ahead of us said Mosonmagyaróvár, a difficult name to remember, was just ahead.

The road zigzagged through residential streets into the small town, right up to the castle walls. Óvári castle now belonged to the local University, but its history goes back to the Romans. Moson, as I was calling it, was known as a town of dentist offices, having the worldwide highest dentists to total population ratio, as we could see as we rode up.

Once more, we arrived in a new town on our bikes with no place to stay. These little towns had no hostels, and we couldn't afford to stay in one of the few nice hotels, so as usual we explored Mosonmagyaróvár while scouting out a sleeping spot. Another goal was to find a pub to spend a few hours warming ourselves in, while taking advantage of using a real bathroom, outlets to charge our phones, and possible free WIFI, all while trying the local beer.

We locked our bikes up outside of some church doors and walked the small cobblestone main street, poking our heads into a party store to laugh at "hen party" decorations, then we found our pub. It was an Irish pub, or so it said. Irish flags and green paper shamrocks were hung next to Guinness signs, though most of the few beers on tap were from Eastern Europe. Even more east of us, which was exciting because it meant being closer to somewhere new. It was just us in the bar with the bartender, who first looked at us funny yet seemed nice enough. We chatted with him using the few English words he knew while asking about the beer selection. After a couple hours Tim and I each used the bathroom one last time then went out to get our bikes as the sun began to set.

There weren't many decent sleeping spots hidden from passing people or cars, so we went back to the castle to sleep under the old moat bridge. What once was a drawbridge was now cemented and stationary. The deep moat held nothing but soft green grass, yet our spot under the bridge was just dirt and bugs. I drifted to sleep, then woke up early having strange dreams, unsure in my half-asleep state whether they were genuinely happening or not. I could hear someone mowing the grass around the castle, and in my dream the ground shook hard around us for minutes on end. I opened my eyes to see a man in the distance on a ride-on mower and assured myself the earth was not shaking.

I squeezed in a bit more sleep, not wanting to leave my warm sleeping bag, but the sun had been up for a while, so it was soon time to pack up and go. We walked with sleepy eyes past the man mowing the grass and past people jogging along the castle wall. The looks we received were as if some monster or troll had instead crawled out from the spooky stone moat's archway. We chugged the last of our water and walked across the street to our bikes which were locked outside of a restaurant. I glanced back and forth for a wall spigot or a drinking fountain, and of course, there were none. We still had the other half of the town to bike through before the bike path went rural again, so we hoped for good luck in spotting a store, since our food had mostly run out as well.

It's hard to be in a crappy mood once you hop on a bike in good weather. Wind in your hair, birds chirping, green trees as far as the eye can see. We spotted big stork nests on top of poles, and more castles older than anything man-made I had ever seen in California. Many castles were just left abandoned in the middle of small towns or turned into community churches.

Tree branches dangled over the bike path and I would pop off my seat to head-butt them out of having nothing else better to do. "I *thought* that's what you were trying to do." Tim yelled up to me, shaking his head. "At first I thought there was something wrong with your seat."

Right before we headed off again along the small two-lane highway into open fields, we spotted a store. We took turns going in to grab snacks and water so we wouldn't have to deal with locking up the bikes or bringing in our packs. I went first, grabbing sunflower seeds, unsure of which were the salted ones, some chips, and a big bottle of water. There were quite a few water bottles to choose from, and I did my best to inspect each one for carbonation. I studied the words on the bottle that I could not make out. I held the plastic up to the light, wondering if there were more bubbles than usual. I shook them. I compared labels. Eventually, I grabbed one that looked okay and went to check out. "No bubbles?" I asked the cashier. She looked back at me confused while nodding.

I handed the snacks and water to Tim, who twisted the top off hearing a burst of carbonation. He gave me a side-eye glance and went in to try for himself. I tried to chug the carbonated water, and the bubbles felt rough on my throat. I stood outside burping until Tim came out with a few more snacks and another bottle of water. He looked at me slyly, showing off his skills at buying non-carbonated water. Tim twisted the bottle open and it burst with carbonation as well. We just couldn't win. We hit the path with our spicy water, spitting unfortunately unsalted sunflower seeds into the plants beside us. I sat up to boop my head on a tree branch. Tim shook his head.

Györ: This is the Life

The pictures of Györ I had seen online looked beautiful, and I was excited to be staying in a hotel for the night. Not a hostel, not a shared apartment, an actual hotel. A place that sat next door to spas and had a white table clothed restaurant on the river. We weren't purposely meaning to stay somewhere fancy, it was just the cheapest lodging we found, costing not much more than a hostel. Again, there were no hostels in such a small town and now the weather forecast was showing rain for the next two days, which made sleeping outside sound unpleasant if not necessary.

We arrived in Györ early which left us time to explore the town, take showers for the first time since Bratislava, and wash our socks and underwear in the sink. Our hotel bed consisted of two stiff twin mattresses pushed together on the same bed frame, topped with towels folded into the shape of swans. I appreciated the hard mattresses. I loved the swans. I hung my clean underwear out on the balcony to dry and I felt like a million bucks. *Ah, this is the life.* I showered, put on clean clothes and inspected myself in the mirror. There is a certain look your face takes on when you've been living for weeks or months outdoors traveling slowly, one mile at a time. Whether it be by foot or by bike, or whatever. I looked unkempt. My eyebrow hairs stuck out in odd directions and the wind and sun had turned my skin pink. Nothing about it was bad or unfortunate. It actually felt free. I patted my pink face with a swan and put on free lotion I knew I was allergic to.

We hit the street on our bikes, flying as free as a leaf in the wind, with no bags or carbonated water to drag us down. We stocked up our food for the upcoming day from a grocery store and bought a bottle of wine named after Elizabeth Bathory to drink in the hotel later that night. Our bikes bounced up and down the cobblestone streets next to kids playing around a water fountain set to music. We wandered through a Hungarian version of a dollar store then went "home" for the night.

I put on the best clean outfit I could make out of my limited amount of clothes, and went to get dinner at the restaurant. I drank a Heineken and ate pasta watching the lights change colors on the bridge outside the window over the river. The front desk was kind enough to open our Bathory wine with an opener from the restaurant without charging a fee, and we spent the rest of the night resting in preparation of riding to Komárno in the morning.

I expected the rain but was still not happy to see it first thing as I woke up. We packed our bags and started to waterproof our gear with trash bags and tape. I shivered and jogged in place outside the hotel, hoping for the rain to die down. We went back inside for a few cappuccinos in the restaurant to allow some time for the rain clouds to pass; but the rain never let up, so it was now or never.

We rode through town and stopped to check our maps to figure out where the trailhead started again. We went up and down streets, following the description in our book, but kept getting turned around. The book was wrong, or we were in the wrong place. The map's pictures were vague and the streets we needed seemed to not exist. We paused to look at the map again and try another direction, but it started to pour. We sheltered ourselves from the rain under a canopied bike rack and hoped the rain would die down.

I was not happy. I was nervous. The sky was dark, and between our two bikes we had one dim light and no reflectors. We both were wearing black and were about to be riding on small highway roads in pouring rain for most of the day. We would be doing hard work in miserable conditions, invisible to traffic, for what? To say we did it? I was done for the day. From the pit of my stomach, just the thought of trying to make it out there gave me a horrible feeling. I told Tim how I felt, knowing he would be disappointed, and he was. We were right across from the train station, and Komárno and Komárom were only a few stops up. We had a pension room above a café booked and we could be out of the rain as soon as we wanted.

I didn't care anymore about the mileage, I didn't care about "cheating" if it meant being safe. After checking out the train prices, which were roughly three dollars a person including bike fare, we came to an agreement to flip-flop our miles. We had a day off planned a few days ahead in our schedule and would move it to this day instead. We would ride the train to Komárom, check into our room, explore the town and rest, then take the train back to Györ the next morning to finish the miles we'd skipped. I was down. I was happy, Tim was happy. We jumped on the train and soon arrived in Komárom.

Komárom/Komárno: American Culture Shock

We flip-flopped our EBO Eurovelo section for a day due to taking a bad weather zero the day before, and so we could slack pack instead. Had to camel up first. Skies out thighs out!

That was hiker lingo for: we left Györ eastbound for Komárom and Komárno (what was once one small town, eventually divided into two, separated by the Danube river. Although Komárno is in Slovakia, while Komárom is in Hungary), yet due to pouring rain I felt compelled to not bike in such rough weather and low visibility. We skipped ahead on the train from Györ to Komárom, then took a day off in order to take the train back the next day to finish the miles we had skipped. This way we would have better weather and less weight due to leaving our gear in our rented room on the Komárno side of the river and train tracks.

We spent our unplanned day off relaxing in our creepy empty pension room, then exploring the small town on foot. A pension is normally just a guesthouse or house with guest rooms similar to a bed and breakfast. Our pension room was one of six bedrooms with a small bathroom tucked up a staircase over a small café and bar. A café in a small town which tourists don't really come to, where we were staying right in the historic center down a cobblestone alley between the town hall and an office building. For both of the two nights we stayed, I swore no one was there except for us. At night the workers went home, and it was just us in a creaky old building with cathedral bells chiming through the night. Even though I was sure we were alone, there was this odd feeling someone else might be watching from the shadows. Sleeping next to castles across Hungary and Slovakia wasn't as eerie as the pension in Komárno. Komárno, by the way, translates to "a place with many mosquitos." Thankfully, it did not live up to its name

Komárno was sleepy and quiet with dark grey skies. We wandered little markets where I bought ketchup flavored Cheetos, then ended the night at a pizza place for dinner. We woke up early to the sound of bells from Saint Andrew's Cathedral and got ready to bike to the train station. It was nice riding without our bags, which also allowed us to make better time. I was happy things worked out the way they did, since what started as a nice, comfortable, sunny, paved ride through fields outside of Györ turned into riding muddy dirt roads uphill through residential neighborhoods. We waved to people working in their gardens, kept our eye out for an old abandoned church the size of a hut we had read about in our guidebook, and stopped to pet cats.

We were on a rural road through forest trying not to let our wheels become stuck in the mud, when a giant dog in a front yard started to snarl and bark at Tim as he rode past. The fence that held the dog was dilapidated, missing most of its wooden planks. Terrified the dog would bolt at me as I went past, I hid behind some bushes and tried my hardest to see if the dog was chained. I had no way of defending myself if it wasn't and decided to come after me. I couldn't tell, and I had to go either way, so I hopped back on my bike and took my chance. The dog snarled and growled, barking at us wheeled intruders, yanking at the end of the chain it fortunately had.

After a long day of biking small highways and towns with no bike lanes, interrupted once by pouring rain, we rode back into Komárom. Right up to a big box grocery and household item store similar to a Target. Something we hadn't seen since being home in the US, one and a half months prior. Walking into the store practically knocked us off our feet. We were officially experiencing our first culture shock. Except it was reverse culture shock, I guess; the shock of our own culture. I felt overstimulated. The fluorescent lights were bright overhead. Shopping carts darted back and forth. Even though I immediately wanted to escape back to the Hungarian countryside, my eyes widened as I realized in front of me was everything I could ever need to buy right at my immediate disposal. I walked the camping aisle touching everything on the shelves. Most things were fairly cheap, but there wasn't much gear we needed that would be worth carrying. We grabbed snacks and a couple of small items we had been needing, then crossed the bridge into Komárno on the Slovakia side of the river to end our easy thirty-five-mile day.

We turned right off of the main street and onto the bumpy cobblestones leading to our room, when a sign caught Tim's eye. "Viking bar. Should we?"

"Why not?"

We grabbed our grocery bag and threw a lock around the bikes then followed the signs. The entire historic center of town was quiet and empty. That seemed to be typical for our stay in Komárno. Apparently all of the town's residents must have been hanging out at the Target-like superstore.

We walked down an alley between closed stores to a large outside patio, presumably belonging to the Viking bar. A heavy closed door on a brick wall had to be the only option for where the bar could reside. Inside the door was a steep stone staircase with a low, curved brick ceiling overhead. It went down into what looked like some sort of medieval dungeon. At the bottom of the stairs were two long dungeonesque rooms connected to each other, with a large opening in between, and the arched brick ceiling connecting one to the next. In the front room was a large wood bar with stools spanning the length of the wall, and in the second was tables, chairs, and a small stage. The place was empty except for a woman working the bar. Tim and I ended our day with two large steins of beer each, then retreated back to the creepy room next to ancient ringing bells. In three days, we would be in Budapest.

Esztergom: Light Bikes and Wet Shoes

It was sprinkling as we left our pension room and walked into the town center to unlock our bikes. Before starting our journey toward Esztergom, we drank two cappuccinos each at a café next to the bike racks, then bundled up to hit the road. We rode next to the river for a few miles, then into the fields along the dense forest which blocked the river view. The sprinkling let up for a while, and the road became flat and nicely paved. We passed houses and I was jealous of how these people lived such rural lives, yet still had a train to take them into the city whenever they pleased. Tim played a podcast on his phone as loud as it would go, perched in his bike basket. The path was littered in miniature snails. I felt bad crunching them under my bike tires, but I had no other choice.

We pulled onto the main strip of a small town on the Slovakia side of the Danube, consisting of just a grocery store and a restaurant, when it started to pour. We were hungry, and the restaurant seemed like a nice place to hang out in while letting the rain clouds pass. I scanned the menu taped to the restaurant's window, hoping to see any recognizable meatless food word. To my surprise, the menu was in both Slovak and German. I didn't know either of those languages, but from having spent more time in Germany and Austria, I was excited to see some familiarity. Pommes frittes, salat ohne fleich, I'll have both! Fresh food. Warm fries. I couldn't remember the last time I had eaten fresh vegetables. Tim ordered schnitzel, and we each got a local beer to sip on while the storm passed outside the window.

A steady stream of locals continued to enter the small family restaurant to get out of the rain. They all seemed to know each other, and all knew the family running the restaurant as well. They joked with each other and men chatted, sipping their beer. It was a wonderful crowd, and even though we couldn't understand what they were saying, their presence definitely uplifted the mood. The clouds parted and we said goodbye. We were more than halfway to our next stopping point and pressed on hard to beat the looming dark clouds.

After a while, we had run out of luck. We were pedaling uphill against a busy two-lane highway, trying our best to miss potholes in the crappy road, when the clouds decided to dump. My glasses fogged up and water droplets blocked my vision. We pulled off onto a muddy dirt driveway to quickly waterproof what we could, but most of our efforts were useless. Already our feet were swimming in our shoes. There was nothing else to do but keep heading towards Esztergom. I stashed my glasses in a plastic grocery bag and rode into the rain until it stopped, since I couldn't see a thing with them on anyway. We found a covered bus stop to duck into to ring out our clothes and pour out the inches of water standing in our shoes. It was smooth, although soggy, riding from there on out.

The rain clouds disappeared and we rode the highway delirious and wet, yelling at statues in fields and chugging along until we hit the bridge into Esztergom. Over the bridge was a castle on a cliffside towering over the Danube river. The sun had come out and the sky was blue. We rode over the pristine bridge, our jaws dropping open as we watched the castle pass us on our left side. It was all beautiful and unreal. We took a right at the first main road and rode less than a mile along the river until finding the campground where we had booked two beds in a small bunkhouse cabin.

We checked into our campsite still soaked from the rain. They only took cash so Tim and I emptied our pockets to see how many euros we had left, giving them every small bill we had minus about ten cents we still owed. We still had not even seen a bank or an ATM where we could get Hungarian forint. We had a few large bills left, but most places in Hungary couldn't make change in euro, and didn't want to figure out how to do the conversion of the change into forint.

We were put in our own little cabin of two bunk beds parallel to each other, since the rest of the cabins were, of course, shared with large groups of school children which the camp hosts figured we wouldn't want to be bunk buddies with.

We took over every bed with our clothes, stretching bungee cords from bunk to bunk as clotheslines. I walked to the campground bathroom with tween school kids staring confused and whispering to one another. Yeah, I'm just a 30-year-old tattooed American lady with hair past my butt, wearing what resembles pajamas in the daytime because the rest of my clothes are wet, walking into a public restroom barefoot. Nothing to see here. Maybe I should have charged admission to see what a freak show I was so I could make the ten cents I owed the camp hosts.

I was eager to head back to the end of the bridge because what looked like a fair was going on at the base of the castle. I could see rides, hear music, and spot food tents. Man, do I love fairs. I got my way and we rode on light bikes and wet shoes back to the center of town.

Techno blasted from carnival rides right on the riverbank, big pans of food similar to paella cooked under small food tents. Beer was everywhere. We still didn't have the right cash though. We ducked into a small bar with a big outdoor patio but they too didn't take euro or credit card. We found a small downtown area with intricate statues near old fountains. It looked like an old town square kings might have been crowned in. All of the stores were closed for the evening, and no ATMs were in sight. We walked past the back side of the fair, and found a café with a small outdoor patio looking toward the castle and main street. They welcomed us with Heineken and offered to take credit card, so we had a few beers as the sun went down and the castle up on the cliffs lit up.

A group of two men and a small boy were at a table across from ours and started trying to introduce themselves and ask us questions. The one doing most of the talking was a tall, scrawny, intoxicated man in baggy clothes who barely spoke any English. That didn't stop him from trying to start a conversation. He held his glass up to cheers us after his introduction, telling us he was proudly from Slovakia. We explained to him we had just been in Slovakia and liked it there. He seemed pleased. We tried to describe where we were from and that we were riding bikes but it was hard to get across. The man went back to his seat but every so often would yell out and motion with his beer to us for a distant, wobbly, cheers. I pointed out to Tim the man was wearing a Tupac shirt with *California* in large letters. It was colorful and sleeveless, with the letters and picture of Tupac's face covering the entire shirt. "Oh yeah," Tim said, he then motioned for the drunk man to come back over. He stumbled back, excited to talk to us again.

"Tupac," Tim said, pointing at the shirt.

"Yes!" he said back excited.

"California. That's where we're from. Not far from where Tupac was from." The man looked confused. Tim pulled out his driver's license and held it up to the man, pointing at the big *California* on top.

"Wow!" the man exclaimed. "You're from California. By Tupac? Wow!"

People in Europe couldn't really give a shit about which English speaking country you were from but being from California sometimes got us treated like celebrities, especially in small towns like Esztergom. The man tried to ask us why we would come to Hungary, which led to us again mention the bike trip which still got a little lost in the language barrier. Also riding bikes across Austria, Hungary, and Slovakia just didn't seem like a very touristy thing to do. The man went back to his seat and a few minutes later a group of young high school girls in skirts walked by with their backpacks on. He whistled at them, and one of the passing girls turned to flip him off. Tim and I looked at each other and laughed, applauding her in our heads.

On our way back toward the cabin we followed music through a dark alley lit only by a few street lamps and the castle on the hill. It sounded familiar. *What is this music? I've heard it before.* It echoed eerily, growing louder as we walked. Soon we were behind a big stage with flashing lights and a live band playing, right in the middle of the town fair. "Thank you, we are ABBA Slovakia," the woman on stage said in English with a thick Slovak accent. We watched a few ABBA songs and I let out a loud burp, turning heads around me. Ah Europe, where burps are offensive yet street urinals and audible farting are the norm.

We went back to cozy up in our bunkhouse cabin. We listened to music, and I drew in a notebook until falling asleep. The next morning, we put our wet clothes back on and found our way back to the bike trail. We didn't have the time or currency to stop for snacks or coffee, so I wasn't in the best mood. My period had also come, so I was crampy, hungry, and un-caffeinated, in soggy clothes.

We rode along the river all day except for a few miles of highway. We had two river crossings to Szentendre and hoped the ferries would take large bills in euro since we had still not seen a bank. Thankfully the campground was fine with us shorting them the ten cents. We reached our first river crossing and had an hour until the ferry would arrive to take us across.

There was a small house by the ferry dock with a café sign on it. It looked dark and empty, but we peered in and a woman told us to come in and sit at a small bar next to the door. The house was dark, but rustic and pretty. A small pit bull walked in and out of the house as he pleased. The woman was okay with us paying in the bills we had, so we ordered our two cappuccinos each as well as a bottle of peach juice and some candy for the road.

Cars were lining up outside as well as another man on his bike, so we knew it was time to get on the ferry. Thankfully the ferry operator was okay with taking euro. If he wasn't I'm not sure what our alternative for crossing the rushing Danube would have been. We watched him rope off the platform pulled by a small tugboat and secure it to the dock, load on two cars, then let the few of us with bikes on. It only took about fifteen minutes to slowly cross the water. The sky was grey, and the fresh air coming off of the Danube felt nice. The man secured the ferry platform to the dock on the other side of the river and all of a sudden we were in Slovakia again.

This became one of my favorite days on the bike trail. All day we passed small towns along the river. Beautiful secluded homes on the water, a winding highway along a cliffside, distant castles like usual, and green parks with forest paths.

We almost missed our second ferry of the day, trying to buy tickets from a ticket window as the cars and passengers were already being loaded onto the platform. We got our tickets and ran on making it just in time. The ferry took us back across the Danube river into Hungary again. We walked our bikes off of the ferry platform leading right to a crowded family restaurant at lunchtime. It was convenient since we were starving, and there were no other places around to get food. I went inside to check the menu and couldn't say no to more cereal coated fried cheese, salad, and beer. Tim got some soup he loaded with chili oil. It was the first time we had seen a hot condiment of any kind across Europe, so we were craving it. He put so much in his soup he started to sweat, and the waitress felt the need to ask him if he was okay. After a lovely lunch, we headed to our destination of Szentendre. Our last night on the Eurovelo 6.

Szentendre: Let's Play with Me

The sun came out as we rode into Szentendre. I was growing tired fast, but felt excited to get off my bike and explore the campground occupying a miniature island we would be ending our day at. We followed the trail along the sparkling Danube, passing parks and houses, then hit a street fair blocking the entire path. Food carts and restaurants lined both sides of the trail which had transformed from paved to dirt. Groups of couples walked with a child's hand in one hand and a cold beer in the other.

Our bikes slowly crawled through the crowd. We tried to get as close as we could to other cyclists and follow their paths through the sea of people, dinging our bells as we went. This went on for quite a while, which slowed us down immensely. We continued on, hoping we were still going the correct way. The dirt trail got rougher. My muscles were sore, but I powered through. Our book and maps did not show how to get to this private little island off of the trail, so we were relying on sight alone and a phone screenshot of what it should look like. The path split and took us to a major street, where we then had to turn and find our way back to the river's edge. Staying along the river was the only way we would be able to spot the island and the little bridge going to it, supposedly from the trail.

Pap-Sziget a sign read. "That's it!" We rode over the bridge onto the tiny island on the Danube, under a large *Welcome* sign arched over the road. An excited elderly couple popped out to greet us from a small store and check-in window surrounded by gardens and picnic tables.

"Hello!" they exclaimed. "Are you Tim and Bridget? How are you? Where did you come from? Where is your car? Bikes? Did you come on bikes? Where did you bike from? Put down your bikes. We will help you to your room!"

We answered the many questions the friendly couple had for us and talked about California and our bike trip while going through the check-in process. They handed us our key, pointed out our cabin, and gave us a tour of the property.

There was a small restaurant in what looked like a dusty log cabin, showers and bathrooms for the campers, a few bunkhouses, and stilted yellow bungalows with green roofs lining the water's edge. We locked our bikes to one of the wood stilts under our bungalow and went inside to set down our things. It was definitely rustic, but still something that would have cost around $100 a night in California. We were spending roughly $30. Inside was a kitchen covered in spider webs, a small bathroom, and a full-size bed filling the entire tiny living room. At the back of the living room was a door to another small dark room the size of a closet, only big enough for the two creaky old twin beds which inhabited it.

We opened the windows to let out the stuffy air, then headed back to the store window to drink a beer in the sun on the picnic benches and enjoy the wonderful weather and scenery. We picked a local beer and Tim ordered a shot of buffalo grass vodka, which the woman handed to us through the store window with a big smile. We were out of food and the store only had snacks, so we decided to try the restaurant as the sun began to set.

The restaurant's large porch was just as old and spidery as the bungalow, although I found it quaint. The inside looked like a 1970's living room. Wood-paneled walls and dark green carpet, with large boar heads mounted on every wall. The tables were family-style, set up for multiple guests to sit together instead of each group having a private table of their own. Just a few long wood tables lined the entire length of the restaurant, surrounded by cheap rickety chairs. The only guests there were us though, so we had the place to ourselves. I scanned the menu looking for any familiar sounding word indicating something I could eat. More fried cheese and fries. Fried mushrooms too. After chowing down our dinner, we went back to our private bedroom beside the river for a good night's sleep.

I pulled back the blanket and sheets to inspect the bed for spiders or any other kinds of creatures who could be snuggled up beneath. The bed was perfectly clean, but I noticed the pink and green comforter, sheets, and pillowcases all had the same cute-looking sentence and leaves printed across. The sentence said, "Let's play with me."

We packed our things in the morning and chomped on some restaurant leftovers on our private riverside porch. We checked out, then had our two cappuccinos each on the picnic benches outside of the store window which served them. The sun felt amazing on my skin, and a cool breeze kept it from feeling too hot. I wished Tim a happy birthday. A perfect occasion to end our Eurovelo adventure on. We threw our things on our bikes and took off, leaving our peaceful island to enjoy our last day on the bike trail. As we rode off of the island, the arched *Welcome* sign overhead now said *Goodbye* as we departed.

Budapest: Grinded on by Pukey Nineteen-Year-Olds

Our last day on the bike trail was supposed to be a short one. We only had twenty-six miles until reaching Budapest, where we had a hostel booked and would still have most of the day to celebrate Tim's thirty-fifth birthday. Unfortunately those last few miles turned us around quite a few times. It was a weekend, and the bike paths were filled with joggers and other cyclists. We were led on and off the bike path, having to stop often to check our vague map and read the trail description in our book to see how or where to get back on, instead of aimlessly riding in the direction we figured Budapest was.

We rode on and off the Danube, passing green fields then city streets. We sat at a red light letting a passenger train pass when another person biking Eurovelo 6 pulled up next to us. We looked each other up and down. He wore a blue cap which matched his blue cycling kit. His light-weight touring bike held a smartphone and GPS mounted on the handlebars, and his large panniers were packed to the brim with heavy cooking and camping gear. It looked like he was prepared to spend the rest of his life on his bike.

"You're doing the Eurovelo?" he asked Tim, who was next to him.

"Yes, we rode here from Vienna," Tim answered back.

The man did a double take, his eyes widening then darting back and forth between our two bikes. "You rode on those?! From Vienna?"

"Yes." we both laughed.

"How much further will you go?"

"Only to Budapest. We've almost made it."

"Okay, good luck!"

"You too!"

The train passed, and the light turned green. Tim and I, and the other cyclist, checked our phones to figure out which way we were supposed to be going, then simultaneously shrugged, taking a right onto the nearest bike lane, obviously confused about whether it was the correct way. We followed the main road until we could see the Danube again and its paved bike and walking paths.

Boats went up and down the river, and the beautiful Hungarian Parliament building appeared across the water in the distance. The picturesque Gothic building is both the largest and tallest in all of Hungary, looking even bigger as it sits on the water's edge with its mirrored reflection below. My jaw dropped as we approached it closer from across the river.

The bike lane became its own road with its own traffic lights. It had barriers attempting to block foot traffic from using the lane, which many tourists ignored. We flew with the breeze through green lights, parallel to the car traffic, until a clueless distracted tourist stopped their baby stroller right in the red-outlined bike lane, causing us to slam our brakes before creaming the young child with our overly packed metal rust buckets, whose brakes I'm surprised actually worked. I tried my best to give a warning *ding*, but my bell was so rusted it barely muttered a sound. Sometimes I would smack it with my hand while riding country roads out of boredom just to see if I could get it to make a noise. Entering Budapest got so ridiculous I just started yelling "DING" while rolling up to crowds of people standing in the bike lane.

We zigzagged through the crowd, right up to the bridge unifying Buda and Pest. We had made it! Vienna to Budapest unprepared, approximately 275 miles on shitty bikes. Right in time to celebrate Tim's birthday Budapest style.

We rode across the bridge and around the town, through more tourist crowds blocking bike lanes, to our hostel in the Jewish district. One block from our hostel was Dohány Street Synagogue, the largest Jewish synagogue in Europe and second largest in the world, with seating for at least three thousand. Its courtyard is a mass grave from the

Hungarian Holocaust and a memorial, sitting on the inside border of what once was the Budapest Ghetto. Our hostel was inside of what would have been these barbed wired walls, and over two thousand of the people forced to live inside where buried at the Synagogue. It was a sobering welcome to Budapest.

We checked into our so-called "Party Hostel" which worried me a bit since sharing a bedroom with drunk and rowdy roommates isn't exactly my thing, but for the price and proximity to the bars and tourist attractions, it couldn't be beat. The front desk gave us a quick tour and a stack of drink coupons for each night we had booked.

We headed out for a real meal across the street at an American themed restaurant decorated like a tacky diner. We were desperate for food, and I guess the novelty of it was appealing after being away from the US for so long. Tim ordered an American food sample plate complete with a burrito, cheeseburger, chicken wings, mashed potatoes, onion rings, corn on the cob, fries, and tortilla chips. Somehow a quick birthday dinner turned into a $60 splurge, since they didn't take credit cards and we still didn't have Hungarian forint. They let us pay in euro, but took their own steep exchange rate in return. So much for Hungary being cheap.

After eating the most expensive crappy American diner food we'd ever had, we hit up a bank for some forint then went back to catch happy hour at the hostel's bar and use our free drink coupons.

The hostel staff and guests were busy getting ready for a party boat night, which the hostel put on monthly. For a flat fee, the hostel would take guests out on a floating nightclub on the Danube river with all drinks included. It sounded like a fun adventure for Tim's birthday, but it was a little pricey, and the crowd wasn't really the type we wanted to party with. The hostel workers tried their hardest to convince us to go, yet warned it was geared more toward young single travelers. Most of them would be college students, with some even fresh out of high school. Being grinded on by pukey nineteen-year-olds while stuck out on open water didn't seem like the best option for our first night in a party city, so we skipped the boat party to wander the streets on our own.

After a few minutes of online research while sipping on a free welcome shot from the bar, I discovered Tim and I were right in the heart of Budapest's ruins pubs. These were once large abandoned warehouses left to decay after World War II, turned into some of the world's most imaginative, creative, and hippest nightclubs and bars. I created a basic map of the best ruins pubs, and we were off to explore them for the rest of the night.

First on our list was Szimpla. Only a few blocks from our hostel was the large two-story warehouse with broken windows next to a hip food truck lot. The double doors were wide open, with signs displaying events of the week and what rooms they took place in.

We wandered into the dark doorway where a store filled with local art and handmade items sat to the left side, and a dark stairwell leading to a basement venue sat to the right. In front of us was a large opening to an outdoor courtyard, with bars and spray-painted stairwells on each side. The courtyard was amazing. Each table, chair, couch, every piece of furniture in the whole place looked like a mismatched thrift store find. Colorful tapestries, chairs, random found items, and art pieces hung across the entire open-air second story of the building as shade for the courtyard below.

The closest bar was very modern, low-lit with neon lights and odd found items displayed on the walls. We ordered drinks then continued to wander the space. We took a staircase lit by one color-changing light bulb up to the second story, where we found a billiard room, a small café, more bars, and various other rooms filled with tables and old couches to lounge on. Music boomed through the entire warehouse, and a large screen had random movie scenes projected onto it. A balcony overlooking the first story was the pathway from room to room upstairs, although most also connected through random doors. We took a seat on a balcony to people watch and finish our drinks. I was utterly blown away. Szimpla looked like the artsiest squat I'd ever seen, yet it was filled with club hoppers and tourists who found it through Trip Advisor. Either way, I loved it so much I didn't care who else was there.

Techno clubs were huge in Europe, and Budapest was definitely on the map as a big club city. The ruins pubs may have been art galleries, casual bars, and show spaces during the day and evenings, but after midnight was when Budapest really came alive. People flooded the streets in their finest clubwear, sipping alcohol, snacking on street food, and drifting from club to club. Most clubs stayed open until four or even six in the morning.

Tim and I left Szimpla for the second biggest ruins pub, called Instant, then planned to make our way to multiple across town. Instant looked like a nice pub in an old building surrounded by other popular bars, but after walking in towards the middle of the building, we found ourselves on the bottom of another two-story courtyard decorated in large art pieces. A large herd of life-sized rabbit sculptures swirled overhead under the night sky. A giant owl figure with wings outstretched across another wall was dangling above. It felt like a fancy bar and a quirky art warehouse combined into one.

We ordered drinks and explored upstairs, following creepy staircases lined with weird artwork up to random rooms connecting to each other. Each room had old couches and furniture set up as private hang out spots. Some were large rooms, and some were the size of small closets with only two chairs and a table fitting inside. Some had views to one of the bars, while others were pushed back and impossible to see or find without doing some real exploring. Tim and I stayed out until nearly two in the morning, exploring every inch of each ruins pub we found, until deciding to head back to the hostel for one last drink before going to bed.

We showed up a little tipsy to an empty closed bar in a quiet sleeping hostel. "What?!" Tim slurred. "I thought this was a *party* hostel! How is the bar closed?"

"*Shhh!*" I laughed. "Don't wake people up!" I agreed though. Even the crazy kids who got drunk and grinded each other on the party boat were sound asleep, as Budapest's party scene was at its peak hours. Tim and I joined the hostel in slumber, sleeping well into the next morning.

After sleeping most of the morning away, we stopped by a food truck for loaded veggie dogs then wandered our way across downtown. The first interesting place we came across was a metal bar. A small, two-story corner building surrounded by banks and markets displaying band posters in every window. Motörhead and Judas Priest posters hung on the walls and ceilings, and old Metallica played on the speakers. The place was dead, and really not all that cool for a metal bar, but a perfect random place to come across for a quick drink. It was similar to the kind of metal bars we found often which were just regular bars with an ACDC poster hung on a wall. This one had noticeably better taste in music as well as a fantastic selection of beers themed after metal or rock bands. We ordered one of the Motörhead, Queen, and Iron Maiden bottles to split between us before leaving to explore more of downtown Budapest.

We walked across town and found a little street market to wander, then made our way to the water's edge on the Danube. Well known sculptors from Budapest, such as Raffay Dávid, had amazing statues scattered across the city, so we went from statue to statue next to the water admiring them. I tried to take a picture with one of the statues when a couple came out of nowhere, intercepting me with their selfie stick. We left and moved on to the next statue when, again, the same couple ran up and blocked us from the statue by placing themselves in front of it, their cell phone extended out to our faces. Annoyed, we saw what we could of the statues, while simultaneously racing the oblivious couple down the river walk.

"I don't get it," Tim said within obvious earshot of the couple. "What do they even do with them? Get back home to their friends and family and flip through a slideshow saying 'this is a picture of *me*, this is a picture of *me*, oh... here's another picture of *me*.'"

The couple turned their back on the glistening blue river and extended their phone out into the crowded walkway. "Here is a picture of *me*." Tim narrated as we walked past.

We walked a few blocks into the city center to see Saint Stephen's Basilica. At the cathedral's entrance was a large courtyard lined with small shops and quaint cafés with their tables, chairs, and umbrellas lining both sides in rows. Each with a podium and formally dressed waiter extending their menu out to passing tourists. We walked past the restaurants without giving them a second thought until one caught our eye. The outdoor tables with folded cloth napkins and a well-dressed waiter holding a leather-bound menu looked the same as all of the other cafés, but under the name, Café Montmartre, was another sign saying "Manowar Bar."

We blew past the menu in the waiter's extended hand and stepped inside the open doorway. Classical music played over the stereo, as expected for a café only a few yards from a well-known Neoclassical, eighteenth-century basilica, yet inside was a bar whose every inch was plastered with posters and memorabilia of the metal band Manowar. Our mouths hung open as we both looked to each other and laughed. Naturally, we each ordered a pint and took a seat at a table in a corner of the small room to stare at the walls. Framed posters, flags, drumsticks, and shirts, every wall was covered. It was the most hilariously random place we could have found, especially paired with the calm music and nicely dressed staff. After our drinks we drifted across downtown, then spent the rest of the night at the hostel, preparing to visit Szechenyi bath in the morning.

Besides clubs and bars, another iconic part of Budapest is its thermal baths. One of the reasons the Romans colonized Northern Budapest, was so they could take advantage of the area's medicinal thermal springs. During the middle ages the Turkish built bathhouses around these springs, some of whose ruins are still visible today. A few people recommended other baths, some of which did not allow women (they hosted events geared toward gay men), but we decided to go with the famous Szechenyi, even though it was said to be the more crowded tourist bath. It was about twenty dollars per person to get in for the day. We chose a weekday, hoping it would be less crowded, and walked all the way across town just for the hell of it.

Once we reached the outer edge of downtown, we took a seat to rest for a few seconds on a bench. A young man approached us, asking Tim if he could try on his sunglasses. Tim just kind of gave him a weird look. The man kept begging Tim, offering his glasses for Tim to try on in exchange. Tim continued to give the man a dirty look, mostly ignoring him, until the man came up and nervously took the glasses resting on Tim's head and handed him his glasses. Tim shrugged and put the dude's glasses on the top of his head. The man became happy and giddy, taunting Tim about having his glasses now for good. It was obvious this was some kind of scam, which the man was failing epically at. He must have thought that since we were tourists Tim's sunglasses were worth something, but they were some goofy plastic pieces of shit he found. They were probably worth no more than five dollars. The man's own glasses were probably worth more. Tim shrugged again and pulled his new glasses down over his eyes.

Szechenyi Baths sat inside of City Park, similar to Golden Gate Park or Central Park. City Park in Budapest is three hundred and two acres of space, filled with museums, a zoo, botanical gardens, restaurants, a lake, and even a castle. We walked through the statues lining the park's entrance, called Hero's Square, and down the grassy paths until we reached the bath's ticket window.

For twenty years Szechenyi Baths was just a stone-walled bath on a small island in the middle of City Park's lake. By the end of 1880, the bath was so popular, a new palace was built to hold all the bathers. The original building was opened in 1913, which was still too small for the popularity of the baths. Eventually additions were added, and by 1927, the outdoor pools. We walked inside and admired a fountain and centaur statue called *Fishing Triton* by Jozsef Rona in the main entrance, which the Internet describes as a "statue of centaur with Triton and pissing boy." A man took our tickets and led us to our locker and changing room.

Ready to enter the pools, we walked on wet floors from room to room, following doors and other half-naked people who looked like they knew where they were going. Each room was humid and smelled of chlorine, and had one pool or multiple small pools filled with either cold, warm, or hot medicinal thermal water. Elderly people would swim back and forth across the small pools, then hop from one to the other experiencing the different water temperatures. Although the hot water looked tempting, we kept walking from room to room, trying to figure out how to get outside. Famous pictures of Szechenyi Baths showed the picturesque outdoor pools and fountains surrounded by bright yellow walls, and that's what we wanted to find. Eventually, a door led us outside and the sight was just as amazing as the pictures we had seen.

The water outside was only slightly heated, but comfortable enough on a gloomy day. There were outdoor concession stands selling beer and snacks. Naturally, we bought both. We let a whirlpool pull our bodies in circles around curved tile walls between beer breaks. After a few hours of swimming, the sun began to set. We sat poolside watching two twenty-something women take pictures of themselves and each other with a selfie stick for close to three hours straight. Yes, three hours, with no breaks to relax in the water. We were perplexed. It became so ridiculous Tim and I felt we needed to do something about it. Obviously a few beers in, we started photobombing for close to an hour as breaching whales, whale song and all. *AAAAHHHRRRR??!!* We would moan, popping out of the water then splashing back under on our sides. Other tourists were having trouble keeping in their laughter. The next day I curiously searched Instagram hashtags for #szechenyibath and actually did find a picture of the women posing with us whaling around in the background.

It eventually started getting late, and most of the people had left. Tim and I wrapped ourselves in our towels and tried to head back inside, but the door was locked. A few others were exiting a door on the other side of the outdoor pools, so we followed. All entryways in the direction of our locker were locked. A security guard spotted us trying to open doors confused, and ran over.

"We've been looking for you! We closed the baths, but one locker still remained. It's you, yes? Where have you been?"

"We were in the outdoor pool, we had no idea the baths had closed."

"There's no way you wouldn't have known. You can't just stay late, after we close."

"We had no idea, there were still people in the pool with us."

"Yes, they have passes to leave out of this exit. You have a locker, you have to leave earlier."

"They didn't tell us that when we checked in!"

"They tell everyone!"

The man took us to our locker and waited for us to quickly change, then unlocked the front door to let us out.

"We're really sorry for making you wait. We really didn't know! Have a good night."

The man finally cracked a smile and said good night back.

We took a long way back, deciding to explore the dark park. We found Vajdahunyad Castle, now the Museum of

Hungarian Architecture, lighting up the dark park and followed a trail around it through bushes. We passed the statues in Hero's Square lit by the full moon, teenagers making out against one of them. Like the stubborn broke-asses we were, we walked the whole three and a half miles back to our hostel.

We only had a few days left in Budapest, so the next morning it was time to do the things you always hear adventurers brag about: laundry and errands. Down the street from the hostel was a laundromat with WIFI, a bar, and a kid's play area. Most of the parks we passed on our bike ride had rock climbing, hammocks, and trampolines in the playgrounds for kids. Not only the parks but the little riverside beer gardens as well. If not a full playground, they at least had a small plastic slide.

We did our laundry and used the WIFI to complete our other mission for the day. The inevitable had come, it was time for us to sell Pfeffy and Purple Badass. We had both bikes listed online and mine already had a few people interested. A college student wanted to meet up with me the next morning to buy it. Tim's bike wasn't getting any interest, so we kept lowering the price. It was our second to last night in town, and our last day with our bikes, so we decided to end the day with a bike ride along the Danube.

We waited until the sun had gone down and the partiers had come out, to people watch and find cheap food for dinner. Tim chose a burrito window, which was a brave choice. The images of the food on the outside of the window were part of a Taco Bell ad campaign, yet the burrito Tim received contained shredded chicken, iceberg lettuce, tortilla chips, corn, and vinaigrette in a flatbread-textured tortilla. We threw a few cold bottles of Arany Ászok into Pfeffy's basket and rode toward the river.

At the edge of the Danube was a small ferry boat with large windows. Inside were tables and chairs decorated with white tablecloths, wine glasses, and fancy dinnerware. We stopped to watch people board the boat while drinking a beer under a large tree under the moonlight. We were only a few blocks away from the Hungarian Parliament Building, which we still hadn't seen up close. It was our next destination. We could see it down the riverwalk glowing yellow against the water.

We got back on our bikes and rode up to the front of the incredible building. Right when we arrived in the center of the Parliament Building Pfeffy's tire blew. "Shit!" Tim yelled. "Why did this have to happen right now?" We sat down against the water's edge and shared another beer while discussing what to do.

"I cannot believe that happened just now. Think about it?? We rode here from Vienna with no real bike pump, no tire patches, no tubes. We're crazy. Through fields of nothing. This could have happened at any time and it just happened now." We both started laughing. It was unbelievable. "How am I going to fix this on our last day in town though?"

"Might as well just sell the bike as is. Even if we don't make our money back, we would still be out way less than if we had somehow rented bikes."

"We still have to get back to the hostel."

"I'll walk with you. We aren't *that* far."

We walked with our bikes around the building and then back toward the hostel. Tim picked up Pfeffy one last time and held him over his head in front of the Parliament Building, only his dark silhouette was visible in front of the bright yellow lights glowing around him.

We woke up stressed out. There was so much to do before we got on another Ryanair plane the next morning. I checked in for the flight online, I printed our tickets, I packed my bag, I unlocked Purple Badass and rode him to the nearest train station where I made the exchange for €60. Tim came with me, rolling Pfeffy along.

We still had no one committed to buying Pfeffy, so it was time to just give him up. We debated finding a homeless person to give it to, if we had no other options, although they would still have to fix the tire. While walking we passed a bike rental storefront with old bikes in the window. Tim went in to see if they wanted the bike, even if just for parts.

"Yes, we buy used bikes. This one is in pretty rough shape though." The man looked at Pfeffy and then looked at us.

"We paid €110 for it in Vienna, just to ride it here. The tire blew last night. We fly out tomorrow, so we have to get rid of it."

"You rode *this*, from Vienna?!"

"Yes," we laughed.

"The most I can do is €30," the man winced, thinking we would reject the offer.

"That's fine!" Tim said.

We made the exchange, and Tim cut off the knitted blue sleeve Pfeffy came with and stuffed it into his pocket as a keepsake. We walked from the bike shop back to the river, happy and sad our belongings were suddenly so much less. Our time with the rust buckets was officially no more. So was our time with Eastern Europe, which we fell in love with. We had one last night in town, and it was time to see the castle on the hill.

We arrived at the base of a hill on the other side of the Danube and paid the equivalent of roughly seven dollars each to take a round trip ride on a small tram, called a Funicular, up to Castle Hill. This was a steep cable car line originally opened in 1870 to bring passengers up the hill to Buda Castle. The first palace built on Castle Hill was built for King Béla IV between 1247 and 1265. The oldest portion of existing palace was built in the 14th century by the younger brother of Louis I of Hungary. The palace traded hands throughout the years and was added onto by most of its rulers. Eventually, it became one of the largest Gothic palaces existing during the Middle Ages. The palace was destroyed in the great siege of 1686, then rebuilt but accidentally partially burned down. In 1748 the palace was awarded grants to be finished, and the new Royal Palace became a symbol for peace and friendship between the Hungarian dynasty and the nation of Hungary. The palace was destroyed again during World War II, and not rebuilt until 1966. It took until the 1980's to finish the interiors. It is now a museum and gallery.

From up on Castle Hill, we could see the Danube, downtown, and the Parliament Building at sunset. It was beautiful. A cathedral sat behind us, whose stained glass windows glowed as the sun continued to disappear. I did a double take. I was surrounded by 14th century-old buildings, whose original structures dated back much further, but right inside of an arch in Fisherman's Bastion was a glowing ATM. Another example of modern life loudly clashing with ancient past.

We walked the little uneven stone roads and alleys into the night, with no destination in mind. Restaurants were filling up with dinner crowds. I could really go for a snack and a beer, but everything looked too fancy. We walked back up to the top of the hill, next to ruins which now belonged to sleeping feral cats. The full moon hung directly over the top of a statue of a man on a horse - right on top of his head, like a round glowing hat. From this hill, we could see all of Buda for the first time. It was much more residential looking. Rolling hills of nice houses and apartments. Down a paved walking path along the top of the hill was a gazebo lit by string lights. Under the gazebo were little white marble tables with red table runners and a small bar.

"Let's get a drink there!" I begged.

"It must be part of a restaurant though. Look how fancy the tables look."

"I'm sure we could just order a beer. Look how nice it is, a little gazebo looking over everything. Under the moonlight."

"Okay, but we have to hurry to make it back to the tram by ten for the last ride down."

"We can manage that."

We sat at a fancy little table, where the waitress lit a candle and brought us each a large glass stein of beer. We were both a little on edge, feeling stressed out about having to leave the next morning. But it couldn't have been a better place to enjoy a drink before going back to the hostel.

It was getting close to the time we had to get back to the tram, so we ran. We ran right up to the door of the ticket office, still having ten minutes before it shut down for the night. Just our luck, the lights were off and the door was locked. A man was inside the tram, and we knocked on the window.

He opened the door, "I was just about to leave you!"

"We thought we still had ten minutes. Thanks for letting us on!"

We talked with the tram operator as he closed everything up to ride it home himself. We stared out of the glass, taking in the last bit of Budapest we would see on our trip, from the top of the glowing buildings, down to the base of the river.

When we arrived at the hostel, I asked the front desk what the best way to get to the airport would be, trying to figure out how early we had to leave for our 11:35 AM flight.

"Oh yeah, you just walk six blocks to the subway station in Deák Ferenc Square, take the train east toward Köbanya-Kispest station, where you will transfer heading to Ferihegy vasútállomás station. From there, it's kind of hard to find, but there is an unmarked bus behind the station that goes straight to the airport. It all takes about forty-five minutes, as long as you make every train and bus on time.

Or you can just take a taxi. It only costs €15 and would be a lot less of a hassle. It's a twenty-minute drive."

"Really? Only €15?" I said while wiping the sweat off my forehead after trying to keep up with his directions.

"Yes, I just called a cab for a guest the other day and it was only that much."

"Wow, okay. We will just do that then. That seems like a lot less of a headache. So, I just ask the front desk to call a taxi in the morning?"

"Yeah. I'm working night shift so I'll still be here in the morning to call one for you," he laughed.

I walked into the room to tell Tim the news. "The front desk said we could take a train to another train to an un-marked bus in a lot, or we can just pay €15 to take a taxi, and they can call one for us in the morning before we leave."

"Only €15? The subway is even cheaper though, why don't we just take the subway and the bus."

"It sounds so complicated. And we would have to leave at least two hours earlier just to give us time to find where we are going and not miss any of them. The taxi would give me so much peace of mind. Plus we would be able to get a bit more sleep."

"Whatever you want to do."

In the morning we threw the last of our things into our backpacks, wiping the sleep out of our eyes, and wandered out into the lobby to wait for our taxi. A nice man picked us up right outside of the hostel doors, and we confirmed he took euro since we spent all of our forint. He drove us out of downtown, onto the freeway, passing houses and factories. The taxi meter ticking up and up. We were still on the freeway and the meter climbed to, and then passed €15. Tim's eyes met mine, obviously unhappy. I shrugged back. Up and up it went. I was panicking. Tim was sweating. I opened my wallet and started checking every pocket I had.

"Do you only take cash?" I asked the driver.

"Yes, cash only." he responded.

SHIT SHIT SHIT, I thought. Tim looked pissed. "Do you have *any* cash?" I asked him, whispering.

"None." he responded sternly. "What are we going to do? We should have taken the subway!"

"I only have €45." The meter was cents from €45. "I'm going to have to tell him." I was sweating and freaking out. *Will we have to walk? We're almost to €45. We're just gonna have to jump out of the damn cab at the next exit and walk the rest of the way. We'll miss our flight.* The driver exited the freeway at a sign marked *Airport*. "I'm sorry," I spoke up to the driver, "we only have €45 in cash. The hostel told me the ride would be less than that. If you could just get us as far as you can."

"No problem, the airport is right here." He stopped the meter at €45 right while we were pulling up to the terminal. I felt bad for not tipping, but obviously I had no choice.

The initial plan for traveling Europe was to start in the north west, seeing the UK and Ireland, then continuing in a counterclockwise direction around continental Europe, going from the Netherlands to Belgium to France, down to Portugal, Spain, Italy, etcetera. We would go down to Greece then circle back up into Eastern Europe, to Germany then Denmark and as far north as our time and budget would allow, before somehow finding our way back to London to fly back to Philadelphia. Because we decided on doing the bike trip, this took us far off course. We cut right through the center of Europe, from Belgium to Budapest. There was still more of Germany and Eastern Europe we wanted to see, but instead of zigzagging back and forth all over the continent, we decided to board a last minute, €50, three-hour flight from Budapest to Madrid. The plan was to circle from Madrid to Portugal to Seville, Barcelona, then continue the path counterclockwise passing back through France and into Italy.

We exited the taxi and threw our backpacks over our shoulders. "Why did we not take the subway?!" Tim demanded.

"How was I supposed to know the guy at the hostel would be so wrong about the price?! He told me he helped a guest get a cab to the airport just a few days ago, and they quoted the ride at €15." We walked into the airport, scrambling to find the passport stamping desk.

Madrid: Feels Like Home

After being so impressed with the pristine country of Hungary, we were really expecting Madrid to be like another Paris: dirty, crowded with tourists, flooded with pickpockets, and dog shit smeared as far as the eye can see. We boarded a metro train to the outskirts of the city where we would be staying with a local woman and her family in a spare room in their apartment. I kept my eyes peeled on the metro. After reading about the scams often performed in Madrid and Barcelona, busting a clipboard out of a hand was the least I was willing to do if someone tried to touch me.

We arrived at our stop with no issues, and emerged from the underground metro station to the warm sunny neighborhood of what would be considered the projects in America. There was trash blowing in the wind through dusty parks, and every tall brick structure had laundry hung off of the balconies. We found our apartment in one of these buildings. The woman took us in, and, with the little amount of English she knew, exclaimed her excitement for us to be there and offered whatever she had to us as guests. She even knocked on our bedroom door minutes after showing us to our room, to introduce us to a tiny chirping pet bird perched on the tip of her extended finger. We took a quick siesta in the warm breeze of the room's open window then hit the neighboring streets to explore.

Madrid at this point was so different than what we were expecting. It really felt like home. Literally, we felt like we were in South San Diego because of the familiar smells, warm air, dry parks, liquor stores, and Spanish signs. All it needed was the best burritos in the world on every corner. Or just any burritos in general would have been nice. We bought snacks and hot sauce to keep in our backpacks, and a glass quart of cold beer called Mahou to share while we walked. We ate falafel outside of a Kebab shop to people watch before sunset. We returned to our room past parks of children playing, and locals hanging out listening to music playing out of their parked cars. It was 10 PM, and the sun was still up.

In the morning we planned to take the metro into town to move to a hostel in the city center for two nights. It was Sunday afternoon, and before boarding the metro we stopped into one of the many corner store markets to buy some cheap groceries to bring into the city. The store we went into was run by an Asian family, who all had thick Spanish accents and spoke little English. I picked up a package of microwave mac 'n cheese. The brand was Chinese, the instructions and ingredients were in Spanish, yet the front read *World Tour USA* in English, with an image of the Statue of Liberty. Naturally, I bought the mac 'n cheese and stuffed it into my backpack with my hot sauce and tube of German mustard.

We rode the metro train into the center of Madrid, coming out of the underground back into what looked like more typical European sights: ancient architecture in every direction, tourists circling decorative fountains with maps in hand, sidewalk cafés lining cobblestone alleys serving steaming pans of paella. And cheering, lots of cheering. The city still had the familiar dry heat reminding us of San Diego. It's hard to not just lay down on the grass in a sunny park and submerge yourself in it.

The hostel was down one of these cobblestone alleys lined with restaurants. The bottom floor had a lobby, front desk, and a glass door leading to an outdoor courtyard. Up the large, old, wood staircase were floors of rooms. "At four we will have free sangria in the courtyard." Free sangria was tempting, but Tim and I were set on exploring the town. We packed our day bag and stepped back outside. We walked to a famous food market called Mercado San Miguel to browse the cases of tapas and sample sangria.

Outside we heard the cheering again and decided to follow it. We walked down the road and turned a corner where at least one hundred people dressed in burgundy and blue sung and chanted, holding a pint of beer to the sky or a lit flare. Beyond the crowd was a paddy wagon surrounded by riot cops, standing and waiting for the fútbol fans to get any more out of control. I didn't know anything about the sports teams, but I still found it all exciting and fun. Everyone was so ridiculously pumped and happy it was hard not to join in. There was a big group of high school kids and couples in their twenties drinking beer on steps in the sun across the street, so we decided to join them.

Tim looked up the game when we got back to the hostel. It was Barcelona versus Seville at the big stadium right in town. Tim decided he wanted to watch the game, and I was down to hang out with locals in a sports bar, so we went out and looked for somewhere to watch it on TV. The sun had gone down, but crowds wearing Seville and Barcelona team scarves, or holding them up over their heads like a flag, still flooded the streets. Most of the fans went to the actual game, while we entered an empty pub and cheered along with the bartenders. Barcelona won and the streets flooded with people chanting once more. We walked back to our room to catch some sleep.

In the morning we grabbed our day bag and headed to El Rastro, the largest flea market in Europe. A few blocks before reaching the market we came across a small square filled with tables. It was like a small zine fest. There were tables of zines, patches, pins, posters, stickers, shirts, and other things. I wanted to buy a cat keychain that doubled as brass knuckles, but figured I'd have to get rid of it before boarding another plane. When we reached El Rastro we hurried from booth to booth, trying to take it all in. Purses, clothes, souvenirs. Tim bought a small tin, the size of an Altoid tin that looked like it belonged to some teenage metal kid. It was all banged up and covered in band stickers. I bought a solitary black earring to stick in a spare ear hole that had been empty for quite a few years.

The flea market was lined with antique stores and small restaurants. We each bought a spinach empanada from one of their windows. When we had seen all of the stalls, we continued to follow the crowds of people in random directions. They led us to a park full of statues, surrounded by official-looking old buildings. A man handed us samples outside of a gelato shop. It was a flavor I had never tasted before. Well, it was familiar, just not in the form of gelato. It was amazing, but I couldn't place it.

"Let's go back and buy some of that," I recommended. We went back and stared into the glass at all the different flavors. "Which one was it?"

"Ah, yogurt! It was yogurt flavored gelato."

"Oh, it must have been. What an odd flavor."

We got a cup to share and passed it back and forth, wanting more. "It's so good!" It didn't taste like Greek yogurt. It didn't taste like vanilla yogurt. It tasted like plain yogurt, which I didn't realize had such a distinct taste. Now I had a new thing to love about Europe. I imagined in the future we would have conversations such as: "You saw the Louvre, the Parthenon, Pompeii, and ate pizza in Napoli, what stuck with you in such an inspiring and historical continent?"

"Uh...Yeah...You know... Yogurt flavored gelato, curry Cup-o-Noodles, ketchup flavored Cheetos, and ginormous grocery store veggie dogs."

After exploring, we made it back to the hostel in time for the free sangria. We were a little early, so we chatted with the hostel employee setting it up. They put out small plastic cups, which could be refilled as many times as the sangria lasted in the time it was supposed to be out. The sangria itself came in a twenty-liter space bag.

Our last day in Madrid was a lazy day. We went to wander a 350-acre park filled with sculptures and a lake, called Buen Retiro Park. After exploring the gardens, we took a seat on the grass under tall trees next to the lake. People circled the water in paddle boats, or ate snacks on picnic tables outside of concession stands. Tim and I both had sewing that needed to be done. We unpacked deteriorating clothing from our day bag in the shade and attempted to repair it. It was a nice way to enjoy the park and lovely weather while finishing errands at the same time.

While strolling back we tried our best to find the Oso y el Madroño statue, finally spotting it in Puerta del Sol in the center of a crowd. We went back toward the food market to try paella from a neighboring restaurant, then went back to spend the night showering and packing, preparing ourselves for Portugal.

Évora: We Bones That Here Are, For Yours Await

A bus took us on a long ride into Portugal, where the bus driver ended up passing our stop at four in the morning, leaving us to walk up sleepy-eyed asking "Évora?" She angrily flipped a U-turn and dumped us at our stop in a dark field outside of the town center. We set our things down in a spot where we could get some sleep, in a patch of grass under trees near the side of the road. We laid out a ground sheet and our sleeping bags, took off our shoes, blew up our mini pillows, tucked in and closed our eyes. Right at that moment, we shot up out of our sleeping bags at the *psst psst psst* sound of sprinklers turning on to water the opposite side of the grass patch we were trying to sleep on. The water just barely hit the edge of our sleeping bags.

Tim scooted our belongings to a better spot while I put on my shoes and looked for more sprinkler heads in the grass. I assumed that at some point the other side of the grass would have to be watered. We moved our things as far from all sprinkler heads as possible, which was hard to do. We were in dirt and pine needles, up against an old stone wall covered in spider webs and roly-poly bugs. The wind was still blowing mist from the sprinklers toward us, but I pulled our groundsheet out just enough to fold over the feet of our sleeping bags. At this point we figured we did all we could and tried our hardest just to fall asleep, not caring if a bit of mist was still drifting our way.

"I bet you the sprinklers will turn off after fifteen minutes," Tim said. "That's how long they seem to stay on for." Exactly fifteen minutes later the sprinklers turned off, and the other side turned on.

I dozed off to the sound of the sprinklers spraying for another fifteen minutes before turning off completely. We slept soundly in the small countryside town silence, with the occasional car passing down the two-lane road, as the cloud-covered sun slowly rose. The sky grew darker, and raindrops started falling through the trees and down onto us. "You've got to be joking," Tim said, without even opening his eyes. We slept through the sprinkles, burying our faces into our sleeping bags. The sprinkles quickly turned into pouring rain. I jumped out of my sleeping bag, half asleep, and started sloppily shoving it into my backpack. I threw on my rain jacket, pulled out my pack cover, and tried my best to pull my jeans over my wool leggings and shove my feet into my wet shoes all while being soaked. We were packed up and ready to go but had no idea where we were.

We took cover under a tree for a few minutes while I tried to see if I could pull up a map of the town on my phone. Our phone service was still off, yet if a map to a town had previously been loaded on WIFI, *sometimes* it would still work offline using just the phone's built-in GPS. The map showed me a glowing blue dot of where we were, and a red marker of where our hostel was in the town center. No map, streets, or anything else would load. Just a tan screen with two dots. I couldn't even tell how zoomed in or out I was on the map. We had no other ideas except to walk toward the dot hoping it would at least lead us in the direction of Évora's town square.

It was still only six in the morning. Check in time wasn't until 2:30 PM. The dot on my phone led us to a towering ancient stone wall half a block away. The town's center was somewhere on the other side. We walked the road alongside the wall until we found a large entrance, and followed the old cobblestone road toward our dot. The road was old and uneven. All of the buildings matched. They were white, some with yellow trim. Streets the size of small alleyways zigzagged back and forth, becoming steeper as we reached the center of town.

We passed cute little shops, all closed as the town still slept. When the steepness plateaued, we were in a small town square, surrounded by ancient architecture, breathtaking cathedrals, and a fountain right in the center. Besides Ghent in Belgium, it was definitely the most medieval town we had seen so far. But Ghent was also clean and modern as you walked away from the castle. Évora looked more untouched and lived in, surrounded by rural farmland. We didn't know anything about Évora when we chose to stop there. I was looking for somewhere to break up the bus ride from Madrid to Lisbon, and it seemed like the only real option. There wasn't a lot of tourist information about the city, but I did read there was a bone church you could visit for €2, and that was a good enough reason for us.

Évora makes the list as one of the ten cities listed in the Most Ancient European Towns Network. The town center we would be staying in was mostly preserved, and still partially enclosed by the medieval walls we had to find our way through. The city walls were built by the Romans in 57 BC, something we definitely didn't know until well after we had been staring frustrated at a dot on a phone screen against one of them.

We were staying next to the Church of Santo Antão in Giraldo Square, a beautiful church built in 1557. Giraldo Square, or Praça do Giraldo, is the main square of Évora and has been the heart of the city since the 13th century. In the center of the square was a fountain called The Fonte Henriquina which was surrounded by little buildings and cafés. Such a beautiful, relaxing place was once the setting for many bloody occasions, such as the beheading of the Duke of Braganza in 1484. During the Spanish Inquisition it was also the location of thousands of autos-da-fé, a ritual public penance as an act of faith. This included execution,

sometimes by burning at the stake. The regional court con-
demned 22,000 people within 200 years. Our hostel room's
balcony sat over this square and fountain.

It started to sprinkle again, so we took cover under a
restaurant's awning. The restaurant had steal-able WIFI,
which was a plus. I wanted so bad to sleep, but at this point
we had already practically pulled an all-nighter and there
was no chance of finding somewhere to doze off out of the
public eye or the rain. A few well-dressed men and women
walked past us and gave us weird looks. This wasn't exactly
a tourist town. I had a wet sleeping bag draped over me, my
shoes off next to me, and it looked like I had woken up in a
bush. Who knows how long it had been since I showered.

I turned my head to the restaurant's window to scan
the menu taped to the glass. Inside, the restaurant staff
made tables and set out pastries, prepping to open. This
was my first time trying to read Portuguese. All I needed
to find were a few magic words, and my shitty morning
would be made. Anything sounding along the lines of cappuccino or café was good enough. Some brood or pan or
crumpet or whatever would be fine as well. I didn't see
the word cappuccino or latte, but went inside to sit down
anyway. It was warm and comfortable, and we took a small
table by the window, far enough from the other restaurant
guests to make sure they didn't feel put off by our presence. We asked for a cappuccino, and the waitress nodded.
She brought us a pastry and kept the cappuccinos coming.

Quite a bit of time had passed and we figured we were
overstaying our welcome. The other customers were all
eating, while we sat on our phones only buying coffee. We

went back into the main square where the sun had finally decided to show itself. To appear even more like weirdos, we took out our bright red sleeping bags and draped them along the sides of the 445 year old fountain to dry them in the sun as we waited for the hostel to open. The hostel was a small white door right in the town center across from the fountain. A man unlocked the door and walked in and Tim followed, seeing if there was any way we could check in early in hopes of napping. Early check in was not an option. It was 7:30 and we still had seven hours to wait, but they nicely let us store our backpacks at the hostel so we could groggily explore the town as tourists without lugging around everything we owned.

I snuck back into the restaurant and walked straight back to the bathrooms to clean myself up a bit and use the facilities, then came out as ready as I would ever be to enjoy my first day in Évora. We walked the town trying to find another cathedral and some Roman ruins. Large packs of children and elderly moved past us, "going to our hostel," we joked, in reference to past hostels we had stayed at jam-packed full of children. We moved fast through small cobblestone alleys, trying to pass the slow herds. It was field trip day for the nursing homes and school children, I suppose. The castle was surrounded by more elderly, posing for pictures together and flooding in and out of its doors. They were the only other tourists in town, and I figured they were local to somewhere nearby.

We found the Roman Temple of Évora in the heart of the historical center of the town, which is just off to one side of the town center. The temple was first built by the

Romans around the 1st century, destroyed in the 5th century, becoming ruins. In the middle ages the ruins were integrated into a tower in the Castle of Évora, holding a butcher shop. In 1789 reconstruction was started to restore the temple, and by 1840 a whole archaeological excavation went underway around the entire area, including finishing the restoration of the temple columns. During the time the Romans had built the temple, it was a whole room, now it lies as just the iconic Roman columns standing on their own. It had been no more than forty-five minutes since leaving the hostel, and somehow we had seen the entire town center.

Stores were limited in Évora. We found a ninety-nine-cent type of store full of poorly translated toy titles, where we bought a very inappropriate lighter with a cartoon picture of a used condom on it. There was a vegetarian restaurant where we ate local vegan dishes. While wandering the small streets lined with shops, we stopped at a small local wine store. It looked way too fancy for our budget, but I thought it wouldn't hurt to pop in and see if they had anything cheap. The walls were lined with bottles from local wineries around Évora. Most were a bit pricey, but I did a double take, seeing two bottles priced at only €2 each. A woman saw us browsing and asked if we wanted to try any of the wines. I had already made enough of a fool of myself, so of course I had to keep it going by asking to try the two cheapest bottles. The woman poured us tasters while giving us an overview of the taste and styles of the wines. She described the history of the family wineries and where they were in location to Évora. I took a sip, and my eyes widened. It was some of the best wine I had ever tried. I had tasted bottles worth over a hundred dollars in Napa, and at a few other special occasions. To me, someone honestly not too experienced in wine tasting, it tasted on par. I was in love. We foolishly bought only one of each bottle.

We checked into our hostel overlooking the fountain and town square. It was adorable and small. There was a small kitchen and living room, then stairs leading up to a few small bunk rooms. Our room had a little balcony looking over the square and fountain where all of those innocent people were murdered. Another small staircase led up to a roof patio. From the roof you could see out to the medieval walls that surround the town, and the old church towered over the rooftop balcony. You could peer over the edge and watch people walking down the tiny cobblestone alleyways, or look straight ahead and see other roofs of matching buildings and homes touching each other in long rows. Many of these also had rooftop balconies, where clothes hung on white drying racks. We popped open a bottle of fancy Portuguese Two Buck Chuck and enjoyed the sun setting over us, painting the sky neon pink.

Tim and I had never been to a bone church before. We had heard tales of the Sedlec Ossuary in the Czech Republic, and the Paris Catacombs, and had hoped to visit at least one of them while traveling Europe. The next morning we walked from the hostel to the plain white church a few blocks away, called the Igreja Real de São Francisco, the Church of Saint Francis. Inside we purchased tickets, again, trying to squeeze in past a few groups of elderly people and school children. A path led us through a museum in the church. It was about thirty minutes of winding through rooms filled with cases of religious relics, including garments and ancient statues of saints, some even made of wood. While the museum was interesting, we found ourselves wondering if we had purchased the wrong tickets.

The path led us back past the entrance and ticket counter, then through another entrance, where we were beat by another pushy group of elderly folk trying to squeeze into the velvet-roped pathway before we could. This chapel connected to the church is called Capela dos Ossos, formed in the 16th century by Franciscan monks who decided to move the remains of overcrowded monastic cemeteries and display them in the chapel as a way to visually contemplate the inevitability of death. The skulls and bones of around five thousand dead decorated every inch of the chapel. To enter the chapel, one has to pass under an archway inscribed *"Nós ossos que aqui estamos pelos vossos esperamos,"* which translates to "We bones that here are, for yours await." Inside was also a poem by Fr. António da Ascenção, displayed in both Portuguese and English:

Where are you going in such a hurry traveler?
Stop ... do not proceed;
You have no greater concern,
Than this one: that on which you focus your sight.

Recall how many have passed from this world,
Reflect on your similar end,
There is good reason to reflect
If only all did the same.

Ponder, you so influenced by fate,

Among the many concerns of the world,
So little do you reflect on death;

If by chance you glance at this place,
Stop ... for the sake of your journey,
The more you pause, the further on your journey you will be.

I felt amazed and honored to see such an eerie yet holy site. The imagery of the skulls was cool, but looking at each one up close and acknowledging it was the actual physical body of a real person, and now their final resting place, was a feeling I couldn't place. I just tried to take it all in while quietly respecting the dead. Something that was easy to focus on until another small herd of people shoved into me so they could get a better view.

We spent one last night drinking wine over Évora, enjoying the sunset and chatting with other travelers passing through. In the morning we threw on our backpacks and walked to the only train station just outside of town. There was little information online about tickets or train times, but we were told there should be some way we could head toward Lisbon from the station.

After leaving the castle walls, the town started to look more modern and industrial, while still remaining fairly rural and without big shopping centers or even a large grocery store to be seen. The train station was a small square building against train tracks next to a field. Instead of a ticket window there were only automated ticket machines next to a few benches to wait on. According to the ticket machine, we had three hours to wait before a train would come heading west. This was frustrating. An entire day would he wasted waiting and then riding on this train. We were unsure of what to do. There were no lockers to leave our backpacks in at the station, and hauling them back into town didn't sound fun. Even if we did go back, what would we do in town? We didn't have access to the hostel anymore, we had seen the sights, we really just wanted to get on our way.

Inside the station was a tiny coffee shop with a small deli. We sat down and took off our backpacks and ordered cappuccinos. Tim read a book while I worked on my writing. Every now and then one of us would walk outside and circle the building, poking at grass and kicking rocks. Cappuccinos turned into beers. We spent the entire time waiting in the coffee shop until finally, our train arrived.

Cascais: Estoril Smelled Like Home

Our train pulled into an underground station outside of Lisbon's city center where we got off to transfer. We stood inside the mostly empty station staring at a train map for close to ten minutes, pacing and arguing like obvious, clueless tourists. We were pretty confident in subway stations, but this transfer point had us stumped. We took a cross-country train into the city, where we were planning on transferring to a local subway train that could take us back out of town going west. We wanted to visit more of Portugal than just Lisbon and Évora, so after searching the

Internet, Tim picked the small beach town Cascais, just outside of Lisbon.

The station was dark, and a few men glared at us from the shadows. Neither of us were in a good mood, and we glared back. I know I'm a tourist, but I try my damnedest to show people who might take advantage of me that I see them and I'm not willing to play games or take any shit. We followed the labyrinth of station hallways like lab mice sniffing out cheese, searching for the logo of the train company we needed. There were at least three different train companies in this station, and multiple underground floors heading in various directions.

We found the ticket machine for the train we needed and made an attempt to purchase the correct ticket. The machine wouldn't take our cards, so we were stuck paying with the limited amount of change we could put together. We were running out of time to catch the train we needed and panicking. To make things even worse, we bought the wrong tickets. We tried holding our tickets to the sensor pad, and the large plastic turnstile doors would not budge, giving us a big red "X" on the screen. We looked at each other and gasped. That was the last of our cash. Tim threw his hands in the air, "We're screwed."

If you think Tim and Bridget remained Portuguese subway labyrinth urchins forever, turn to page 456. If you think Bridget looked back and forth, up and down for cameras, then squeezed closely behind a law-abiding woman passing legally through the turnstiles, please continue on with the rest of the chapter.

I passed through successfully, even though the big turn-stile doors hit me hard in the backpack. I did a little victory wiggle dance then looked over to Tim, straight-faced, thinking he was still damned to the subway for life. I knew Tim had been skilled at illegal turnstile crossing in his youth, squatting around New York City and Philadelphia. He was much more experienced than I. In fact, this was only one of my first times illegally crossing a turnstile. He looked back and forth, letting out a large sigh. There was no way of hopping over these doors. Tim was quite a bit larger than I. This was going to be tricky, especially with his backpack. Another person came walking with a ticket in hand and Tim squeezed behind, the doors slamming right onto the sides of his body. He pushed forward hard, forcing himself and then his backpack the rest of the way through the half-clamped doors. I'm sure this either broke the machine or set off some sort of silent alarm some-where, but we made our way through a few more winding hallways and onto our train without another issue.

Our train passed through the city, past large buildings with scattered graffiti, on a large bridge over water, then along the beach with the sun setting over the waves. We got off at a small stop on the beach. We stepped out of the subway car and onto an outdoor platform covered in white beach sand. We walked to the main road and knew we were near the hostel we booked, just not sure where. There is a real sense of freedom traveling unscheduled and un-plugged, but that also means often not knowing what the hell you're doing. One minute you think you're doomed to a train station for life, and the next you are on a secluded beach not knowing which way is north. At least you don't have to worry about being late for anything. We took a left on the main road and walked for a few blocks, hoping one of our cell phone maps would give us a floating dot. The dot appeared, moving further away as we walked, so we turned back the other way and walked about a mile before finding the street names we were searching for.

The town was beautiful, and actually just a few miles outside of Cascais. It was called Estoril, and Estoril smelled like home. Ocean air filled our nostrils, giving a comforting feeling of familiarity and nostalgia for San Diego. It was quiet except for the sound of the crashing waves.

We walked past a small castle right on the beach. Houses lining the main road along the shore ranged from big and beautiful to graffitied and abandoned. They were all beautiful, and the town was clean and quaint. It looked like if one of the wealthiest beach communities in Southern California belonged to the middle class. I admired the sun setting over a graffitied oceanfront house that I later found out was a busted squat which once hosted punk shows. A block up from the house was a cute three-story Victorian house turned into a hostel. Our home for the next three nights.

The temperature and environment in Estoril is so relaxing, almost its entire history is made up of different people moving in to enjoy it. The Phoenicians, Romans, and Arabs left remains dating back to the first millennium. It traded hands through different kings throughout the Reconquista and Portuguese Empire. At the end of the monarchy, Estoril became known as the place aristocrats and nobles came to vacation, as well as fled to escape Republican forces. You can see this in the many little mansions that sit against the beaches in between castle forts which were once used for protection.

Our room was big and clean, with wood floors and flowing white curtains over French doors leading out to a balcony. The hostel itself had a wraparound balcony with hammocks and a nicely decorated basement living room, which was usually empty. After settling in and taking much-needed showers, we joined the few other guests in the small bar area near the entryway. We each had a beer but were concerned about saving money, so we wandered the town once more in the dark searching for a store for cheaper drinks and better food to eat than the ramen in our backpacks. It took us a while to spot a grocery store, but we found it dark and closed. Nothing else was nearby and open except for a few fancy-looking restaurants. We went back to the hostel hungry and settled on another bar beer and backpack ramen.

First thing in the morning we booked it to the grocery store for supplies to cook ourselves a real breakfast. Estoril was very small and un-touristy, and even Cascais was not much of a tourist destination. A man of about eighteen years of age working at the hostel was adamant about asking us many questions about California and what we were doing in Estoril while we cooked. He barely spoke any English. We asked him if he was from Estoril and how he liked working at the hostel. He was from Cape Verde, and excited to be out on his own.

It was time to hit the beach. We packed our day bag with sunscreen, water, and snacks, then walked back toward the train station, to the beach under the old castle. Tim dove into the water as I explored the tide pools, finding a pristine mermaid's purse washed ashore. It was in perfect condition, yet whoever occupied it had already hatched. I later learned it was the egg sack of an Undulate Ray. I napped in the sunshine in my sports bra and running shorts I was using as a bathing suit, and dipped in the water from time to time. When we arrived back to our room, I noticed splotchy neon red sunburns all over my legs. We enjoyed the sunset from the porch of the hostel, then got a good night's rest to prepare for a day exploring Cascais.

Cascais was only two miles away, so we decided to walk there to enjoy the coast, then take the train back. The houses we passed became larger and more beautiful as we headed west. The road went from blacktop to cobblestone and the streets became smaller alleys. The little town was still fairly upscale. The shops were touristy and sold the expensive beach souvenirs people think look pretty at the time, then just become junk once they try to find a spot for it in their house. And it's all the same thing. Shells that say the city's name, oil paintings of waves, a thirty dollar scarf that they probably sell at Target for twenty-five dollars less.

Underneath and around these tourist shops and cafés sat the burial grounds of Neolithic settlements. Hundreds of ancient dead people, buried with pots, jewelry, and other offerings.

We passed a corner building with a store at the bottom and a bar on top. The bar's windows opened up completely, turning the dark bar more into a roofed patio with walls on only two sides. People sipped drinks, peering down to the street below. Operation Ivy was pumping out of the speakers, calling us up for a drink. When hearing the music, I was hoping for a random little beach punk bar, but it was more like a regular sports bar with a good taste in music. I bought the first IPA I had drank in months. After, we wandered again until the sun went down, then rode the train back to the stop by the castle on the beach and walked from there to the hostel.

In the morning we ordered coffee from the bar and spent one last time sitting at the wood tables chatting with the staff and other guests. American pop music played on the TV, which it had been since we arrived. We said goodbye to our temporary friends, and to Taylor Swift, and walked back to the train which would take us to the city of Lisboa.

Lisbon: I Don't Want Your Drugs

We stepped out of the dark train station and into the bright sunshine of downtown Lisbon. Tourists walked quickly up and down the sidewalks. To our right was a steep hill of crisscrossing streets lined with houses and corner stores. An old tram slowly made its way up and down the hill on a cable, for those who would rather pay a small fee than climb a mountain of stairs. Up this hill was our hostel. We were always the type to skip the trams and buses and trains if the destination was walkable, and this was no exception. We were only going a few blocks anyway. Up the steep staircases we went, from one street up to the next. We found our hostel and pushed the doorbell, waiting and sweating in the sun.

Click, BZZZZ. The buzzer sounded and the door unlocked. Inside the door was another long set of stairs. We climbed the stairs and entered the main entrance, where a hostel worker greeted us and led us to the front desk in a large common room. Travelers were splayed out all over the couches and floors, waiting for their turn to check in, or for their rooms to be ready. We took a seat against a wall and browsed the Internet while we waited for our turn.

Usually when it came to booking a hostel, we picked the best available option based on price, room size (the smaller the room, the fewer the roommates), amenities, and location to town or transportation. This Lisbon hostel had a full kitchen, which was a plus, beer for guests (at a price, of course), and lots of seating areas. The location wasn't horrible except for the dreaded hill, but the biggest negative was being stuck in a giant dorm room filled with other travelers who had obviously made their way to Lisbon for the nightlife. We were shown to our room, which, on top of that, was back down the stairs to the street and in a separate door.

The room was like a giant garage, or small warehouse. It was completely concrete with high ceilings, and a few private loft rooms up above. There were seven bunks, sleeping fourteen at max capacity. It had one toilet for everyone in the room to share, and two showers. The concrete floors inside the bathroom were always wet, and the door between the bathroom area and bedroom was only a plastic shower curtain. Thankfully the toilet itself had a real door.

Tim and I took an empty bunk on the wall opposite the bathroom. Since there weren't many windows, it was nice and dark inside. We took some time to relax on our beds before exploring the city. Our roommates consisted of a few quiet couples and groups of traveling friends, who mostly kept to themselves and only came to the room to sleep or go through their things. There was another group of about six young French men, between the ages of eighteen and twenty, who were definitely there to party.

Tim and I went to explore the neighborhood and stopped into a tiny hole in the wall sports bar to watch a soccer game, then came back to the room for an early night in after buying a large plastic bottle of sangria from the market down the street. I had some sewing to do, and we had future plans to book online. I stripped down to my leggings and climbed my bunk with a coffee mug of sangria in one hand, my cell phone and sewing supplies in the other. I got one knee up onto the mattress, right onto my hair, instantly stopping me dead in my tracks. I was sure I was going to dump the entire cup, but I was somehow able to free myself from... myself, and make it up without spilling a drop on the white sheets. Having low maintenance hair past your butt is nice in terms of the lack of grooming involved, but it can definitely get in the way.

In the bunk next to mine was a young woman already trying to sleep. I shimmied into the blankets, carefully leaning my sangria against me since I had nothing to use as a table or night stand. Every time I moved, the two-story bunk would sway and shake, sometimes banging against the wall. I tried my best to be courteous to my sleeping neighbor, yet being quiet was almost impossible.

The next day we set off to explore Lisbon like tourists. We walked the winding streets up and down the hills, poking into stores and looking for snacks we could bring back to the hostel. We walked forever trying to find a grocery store, even looking it up online before setting out. Every market we were led to was similar to a small liquor store. Our other food options were mostly upscale restaurants.

On our first day out we bought snacks from one of the liquor stores and settled on McDonald's for a veggie burger and fries. I found it funny how I had gone nearly fifteen years without eating at a McDonalds, but once I came to Europe, I was settling on eating there about once every five countries we wandered across.

We walked past the expensive clothing stores and through a craft fair, following tourist crowds down the busiest streets. On almost every corner Tim would be targeted by men selling drugs.

"*Hash? Hash? Hash? Pills?*" they would whisper loudly, blocking Tim on the sidewalk while half-pulling out a baggie from their pockets.

"No thank you." he would respond while stepping around them. It was happening so often I was starting to giggle every time we approached a busy corner. They never asked me, or many of the other tourists. They just saw the big tattooed bearded American and thought *here we go*.

Dinner time was approaching, and we were becoming hungry again. We peered down each street, most of them deserted with closed stores or restaurants with tables lining the sidewalks we knew we couldn't afford. We stood on an empty street corner looking into a closed shop window as a man in a business suit and briefcase walked past. The man turned down one of the streets, and while crossing just a few yards away from us, came to a complete stop to let out the loudest fart. I chuckled, as Tim threw his hands in the air and yelled "YES!" We laughed the whole way back to our hostel, where we had another early night in and broke out our last stash of ramen.

After eating, I got into bed to read a bit and sip on my sangria before going to sleep. It was close to midnight and the group of young French men were getting ready for a big night out at the clubs. Half of them were getting into their nicest sequined button-ups and slacks, while the others paraded around in colorful tiny underwear. I could see through the bathroom's plastic shower curtain door, where two of the men helped each other do their hair. They were each taking turns straightening and hair spraying each other's hair into tall, sculpted, for lack of a better term, blowouts. It was all very *Jersey Shore*, except these men were much more comfortable with their masculinity. Young, tanned, hairless men doing each other's hair in their tight underwear, in hopes of going out to hook up with women. I loved and hated them at the same time. The hate was mostly out of fear they were going to come back completely obliterated at three in the morning, fist-pumping, cheering, and bringing back half of the club to after party in our warehouse sleeping space. By the looks of them, they were not the type to be courteous to their bunkmates.

The bathroom had become their space; dance remixes of American pop music blasted from their cell phone speakers and multiple hair straighteners and blow dryers were plugged into every bathroom outlet. The corner of bunks they had chosen were covered in every inch by their possessions. Tacky embroidered button-up shirts from the night before hanging from the bunk's railings, used underwear, combs, more hairspray, body spray, and big rolling luggage bags open and half empty on the floors. Thankfully there was enough available sleeping space that no one had to bunk with them.

The men threw their clothes on, checked each other out, and took off. The room became dark and quiet. I covered my eyes, put my earplugs in, and drifted off to sleep. I woke in the morning surprised the men had been courteous after all. They were all back in their underwear again, snoring and splayed out across their beds. I had heard them sneak in at around six in the morning. They slept for most of the day while we and the rest of the tourist went out to explore, then continued their routine the next night.

Tim and I packed our day bag and took off toward Lisbon's castle overlooking the city. We walked through the crowded tourist streets, where already men were offering drugs to Tim. They usually wouldn't take no for an answer, trying hard to pester us into stopping. Tim was getting annoyed enough he started to pester them back.

"Hash?"

"*Hash!?*" Tim would yell back sarcastically. An odd look would come across their faces. I couldn't stop laughing.

We waited at a crosswalk for the light to turn green and one of the dealers would just not let up. "Hash? Pills? Coke?"

"I'm good."

"I can get anything you want."

"NO."

"Come on. It's good stuff."

"I DON'T WANT YOUR DRUGS," Tim yelled, turning heads in the crowd.

"Come on, don't do that," the man begged, looking pissed. He backed off immediately, staring us down as we crossed the street and I continued to laugh.

In the US we are taught as children this would happen to us one day. Once you're older, at some point you will be pressured into taking drugs. In reality people usually keep it to themselves unless they are offering at a party or social setting to be polite. And usually one would have to go out of their way to find a dealer. It's definitely a good thing we warn our youth about dangers that come with taking illegal substances, but in terms of being pressured, maybe the real focus should be on warning young ones about being coerced into buying parsley while traveling abroad.

We turned down a street we thought might lead up to the castle, stumbling upon a farmer's market before the ascent. They were selling mostly handmade goods and artwork. We wandered the aisles sampling local beer, then popped out the other side to continue our journey. Across the street sat a Doner and Kebab shop. Quite a step up from McDonald's, and most likely our only chance of grabbing cheap food. After inhaling some falafel, I felt content. Full and buzzed by noon, ready to explore.

We scaled the hill and found some steps leading through buildings and gardens, the walls decked out in beautiful murals. At the top of the hill we stopped to enjoy the views. Children played in a fountain, and a dog walked up to sniff our pants. We looked over the edge and could see all of the tightly packed houses with winding cobblestone walkways, rooftop porches with hammocks, and cruise ships on the ocean docked at the water's edge. The weather was perfect, and Lisbon was gorgeous.

We continued up the hill, into the tiny streets of tightly packed houses painted all different radiant colors. Almost every other house had a birdcage mounted outside of the front door with a parakeet or other small bird chirping inside. Clotheslines with drying shirts in varying vibrant hues also lined the outsides of houses. We walked up through the homes decorated in clothes and birds, past crappy nu-metal music blasting through one of the open doors. It was so oddly out of place, it was almost wonderful.

We reached the top where São Jorge Castle sat, excited to see the best views of the city from inside its walls. Instead of walking right in and up to the top we were stopped by a ticket window. Another tourist attraction outside of our budget. We were disappointed. The rows of houses were blocking the view of the city, so we had walked all that way for nothing. I peered through a fence next to a picnic bench and could see into the castle. After stopping for a breather on the bench in the shade, we decided to find our way back down, determined to find a good spot to see the city from above along the way.

We walked down the winding roads, right into a construction site. About a square block of space was surrounded by plywood, like a wooden warehouse with a detour path leading through the inside. Inside and along the path were information placards explaining the Roman ruins the plywood walls were protecting. What an interesting thing to accidentally come across! It was a Roman theater accidentally unearthed during construction, and now sat sectioned off for people to see. We made our way back down the hill, finding the nice view we were looking for. Through two open doors entering an art gallery, we could see a balcony on the other side overlooking the city. We quickly took a peek and left before the gallery workers could question us.

We went back down the hill as the wind started to pick up and the clouds grew gray. We made it back to our hostel right as it started to rain, and began to pack our things for Seville the next morning.

Seville: Are You a Chef?

We took a bus from Lisbon to Seville, and were dumped at a covered bus station next to a skate park as the sun was setting. The two of us were feeling tired and run down. On top of that we, again, had no idea where we were in relation to the hostel we booked.

We stepped out of the train station into a neighborhood that didn't look great. Not exactly the place I wanted to be with our backpacks on, oh yeah... and lost. There was a river to our right, and we honestly didn't even know which side of the river we needed to be on, or whether we were looking north or south. A dot appeared on one of our cell phones and we walked toward it, hoping we were heading in the right direction.

The sun disappeared, and street lights came on. As we walked more restaurants started to appear. Tapas restaurants lined every street and alley, with tables covering the sidewalks and large chalkboards advertising the food and drink specials. Some of them said, "We Speak English." Now that the sun was down, people were slowly coming out onto the streets to browse the restaurant menus. We followed the dot through ancient-looking alleyways. Little bars in alleys connected to stone cathedrals. In one of these alleys attached to a cathedral was an open bedroom window with a priest inside watching TV. I couldn't help but take a peek while walking past, my eyes scanning the religious art covering the walls.

The dot led us past more and more restaurants, "€2 Beer" a chalkboard sign read. I wanted a sidewalk café beer. I wanted off my feet. Instead we kept walking until we reached a small empty parking lot with a plain-looking three-story building. Next to the door was a small placard with the name of our hostel and an intercom. We were buzzed in and walked the tight, dark stairway to the third story, where a plain door had another placard with the hostel's name. A twenty-year-old blonde woman with a Southern accent greeted us at the door.

The hostel looked like a large apartment. There was a living room with a small balcony, a kitchen, one large bathroom with separate toilet stalls and showers, and three small bedrooms crammed with bunk beds. One room belonged to the two young women running the hostel and the other two rooms were for guests. In the small hallway near the front door was a desk where the blonde woman checked us in.

"Where in the South are you from?" Tim asked.

The woman laughed. "Georgia. Is it *that* obvious?"

"After rarely hearing any American accents for the last two months, it's very obvious!"

She went on to tell us about how her parents gifted her a trip to Europe for her college graduation. She kept pushing her flight back later and later, then eventually decided to just stay after the hostel staff offered her a part-time job. Free lodging and a bit of cash for checking people in and cleaning up. There was another woman working the hostel a few years younger who had the same story, except her trip to Europe was a gift for her high school graduation.

A few of the hostel guests seemed to have similar stories. I was envious of the fact they had paid college, free vacations, and degrees, all before the age of twenty-one. And that's why they all loved Europe. They could legally drink and club hop until six in the morning here, with a never-ending supply of new travelers to party with.

We were led to one of the cramped, dark rooms and picked two beds in the corner, closest to the rickety air-conditioner struggling its hardest to put out a little bit of cool air. There were no lockers, so we put our valuables in our day bag, draped a blanket over our backpacks, then headed out to explore.

We walked back down the same winding alleyways we took to find the hostel. Again past the priest watching TV in his room. We were back to one of the many stretches of café lined sidewalks and decided we should pick one, to splurge on a few appetizers and a drink before going back and getting some sleep. Most of the restaurants looked snooty and expensive. Some advertised odd, trendy things that didn't make sense, such as "low gluten tapas" or "paleo ice cream." I noticed one offering a few veggie options and decided it was the one.

This was our first time trying tapas. I figured we would pay an outrageous amount of money to have a small plate brought out with a sample of that style dish, needing to buy at least ten to get full. They weren't as expensive as I was expecting, only a few euros each, so we picked three tapas to share. Local cheese drizzled in honey, Brussels sprouts, artichoke hearts, and fresh bread which was free. Each dish came out larger than I expected, and was some of the most delicious food I had ever tasted. Tim and I left full and satisfied, ready to crawl into our beds next to strangers.

We each had one more beer before going to bed, where we got to meet the rest of the travelers in the living room of our hostel. The two women running the hostel joined us, giggling with two men their age who had also recently checked in. Across the living room was a young woman traveling on her own, pulling out her sleeping bag and laying it across an empty couch. The hostel's owner advised his employees to rent out a couch in the living room for a discount when the hostel was completely booked. I felt bad this woman wanted to sleep, so I decided to go to bed myself and soon everyone else did as well.

In the morning it was time to get shit done. We needed to get in some sightseeing and exploring, but first things first - find a grocery store and wash our clothes. While sitting on the balcony, watching the street below, we could see a grocery store just a few blocks from our building. Tim and I took a trip over, buying dinner supplies, fresh vegetables, and wine.

We did our laundry, wearing the little we had that could be considered clean so the rest of our clothes could be washed. We sipped cold beer in the heat of the patio with bare feet, since all socks were in the wash. On the roof where the drying rack was, we tried to stand in little strips of shade the roof's short ledge created so the hot ground wouldn't burn our skin. We showered, used WIFI, then once the evening came made ourselves a big pot of pasta paired with wine. Days like these seemed wasted in terms of seeing the city, but when you're constantly moving a fresh pair of clothes and option to cook with fresh vegetables almost felt as luxurious as a day at the spa.

It had been a while since we had fresh vegetables and a place to cook them. Tim whipped us up a quick marinara. Sautéed onion, garlic, bell pepper, and mushrooms stirred into tomato sauce. The women popped their heads into the kitchen, like cats do when you pull a can opener out of a drawer.

"What are you making?" they asked.

"Spaghetti," Tim responded.

"But what's *in* it? Vegetables?"

"Yes. Just a few vegetables and some garlic we found at the grocery store down the street, in canned tomato sauce."

"Wow, I've never seen anyone make their own spaghetti sauce like this. Are you a chef?"

"Nope," Tim laughed. "I just like to cook. This is a pretty basic dinner we like to make when we can."

"I wish I could cook like that!" The women then disappeared again.

It was Friday night, so most of the hostel was getting ready to go out to the clubs. The women got all dressed up, doing their hair in the bathroom while talking to the men about where they should all go. After eating our dinner, Tim and I strolled around town again to get out of the hostel before returning to hang out in the living room.

Before we went to bed our hostel-mates stopped back in to have a few drinks before going out to another club. All four of them were completely wasted. The brunette flirted with one of the guys, too drunk to make a move, but at least hinting, until the Georgian grabbed him, sticking her tongue down his throat whether he liked it or not. Tim and I met eyes, holding back laughter. I decided to call it a night while he stayed up with them and the other guests a little longer.

The next morning he filled me in on *Real Nineteen Year Olds of Seville Hostel*, which mostly just involved more awkward drunken flirting. I woke up, brushed my teeth, threw on my clean clothes and was ready to explore more of Seville than its €2 café beers and grocery store. We left late in the afternoon, while our housemates were still sleeping off their hangovers, and booked it across town by foot to Plaza De España and Catedral de Sevilla.

Catedral de Sevilla is the world's largest Gothic cathedral and third largest church in the world. It also holds Columbus' grave, a fact we didn't know at the time or else we could have entered to at least flip it off. The cathedral is located in the center of town, and is adjacent to many plazas and Alcazár Palace. We took our time exploring, then wandered back toward the hostel, since we really had nowhere to be.

We passed a Mexican food restaurant and thought we'd give it a try. We sat on the patio as the sun went down, holding the menus in front of our faces. At the bottom of one of the pages was a paragraph called *Our Beginnings*, which caught my eye. "The first *Iguanas Ranas* was founded in the ancient city of Tenochtitlan, in 1521, during its inauguration Hernán Cortes and his troops 'got all fucked up' with pure tequila [sic]." This was silly and incredibly random, yet obviously glossed over a lot of destruction and death, to say the least.

A large group of elderly men and women passed us by, led by a tour guide. "I don't know how they are all going to fit inside our hostel, but I'm sure that's where they're going," Tim said. I laughed.

After eating we still had time to kill around the city before getting ready to leave the next day. We bought a few beers from a store and decided to go drink them in the park. Plaza De España was attached to a large park called Parque de Maria Luisa, almost like a smaller version of Golden Gate Park in San Francisco, or Central Park in New York. We wandered past statues, fountains, and gardens, with bats swooping overhead.

"I can hear them," I said to Tim. "That noise, it's like their echolocation, or something."

"No you can't. People can't hear echolocation."

"Well I'm hearing it. You don't hear it?"

"Nope."

"Listen, there it is! Wait... Yeah there it goes again!"

Tim and I found some ruins in an unkempt corner of the park to sit at, across from an empty pond with broken statues. The bats circled overhead, swooping back and forth in every direction. "I can't believe you can't hear them."

"You're crazy," said Tim.

Barcelona: Honeymooning

It was a five hour drive from Seville to Barcelona. It took even longer on a bus. Tim and I searched the internet for a cheap, fast option, but rideshare, bus, and train were all expensive and slow. Out of curiosity, I tried Ryanair and there we had it. A last minute ticket was nearly €60, about $67, to get to Barcelona in under an hour. "Flying in Europe is ridiculous," I said, shaking my head.

After emerging from Barcelona Airport, we took a metro train toward La Rambla, where we wandered into the dark city streets heading south into the heart of the tourist area toward a hostel we had booked. I read about this area being the worst in Europe for pickpockets. I walked fast, knowing every valuable I carried was tightly packed away at the bottom of my backpack. Even my wallet. I was still worried though, since the articles I read mentioned not just pickpocketing but regular muggings as well. We would be instant targets here either way, but with our backpacks on at night, not really knowing where we were going made everything worse. We missed the left turn we were supposed to take toward our hostel, walking a few extra blocks until realizing we were going the wrong way. There were a few shady-looking characters out, peering at us from the shadows down dirty alleys, but since the bulk of the tourists weren't out at this time it seemed like the pickpockets weren't either. It was too late for the markets and beach yet too early for the clubs and restaurants.

We found our hostel where we were given a half-assed verbal tour and lecture on the rules, then went upstairs to find our room. The interior was hot and dingy. There was a full kitchen and a small bar for guests only. We took the one elevator up a few floors to our room. The room was small and stuffy, with a few rickety bunk beds and a small open window for a slight hope of a whisper of fresh air. It wasn't great, but it wasn't the worst either. And I didn't come to Barcelona for the hostels anyway.

We weren't sure what there was to wander to nearby, but we took our chance. The first step was grabbing a snack and beer to drink on the street. We sat on a curb across the street from the hostel, struggling to connect to the free WIFI to view a map of the area, passing a beer back and forth, when a couple came up and introduced themselves. The man instantly sat down and put his hand on my thigh. He leaned in close to drunkenly talk to me an inch away from my face. In America I would have been completely offended, but I gave the French man the benefit of the doubt, thinking his touchy-feely-ness might be cultural (and alcohol influenced) instead of sexual. He then leaned into Tim to talk to him, placing his hand on Tim's thigh as well, so I figured I was correct in my assumption. The man was with a woman as well, and they went on to tell us about how they were going to a Greek island, and if we were to find ourselves out that way to seek them out via a dog rescue the woman worked for. We said goodbye, and slid out from under their grips to explore the nearby alleys of Barcelona.

Most of La Rambla's streets were still dead, but we followed winding alleys where we found small crowds of people wandering them as well. Lines from pizza shops led out into the alleys and most people walked with plastic cups of beer in their hands, sold to-go from the pizza shops. We joined the crowd in satisfying pizza slices and beer, and continued to wander. A plaza was filled with more tourists, fancier restaurants, and people selling souvenirs on the streets. After a few hours we had made it to the ocean, and decided to start heading back to the stuffy room for some sleep.

The next morning we packed our bag to see as much of Barcelona in walking distance as we could on our way to the beach. We roamed La Rambla, packed our bag full of snacks and drinks from nearby stores, and found a thrift store to buy towels we could lay out on. They were fairly small bath towels, not much bigger than hand towels. We picked the nicest ones the thrift store had to offer, Tim picking a brown towel and I a yellow one.

We walked along the water, past knock off designer purses, scarves, shoes, sunglasses, and watches laid out on blankets as far as the eye could see down the winding park-lined sidewalk. Permanent signs on posts overhead warned not to buy from the sellers, who had no permits. The items were secured to the blankets, so if the men selling were caught they could grab the items up in one swoop and take off before getting ticketed, leaving the buyer with the fine.

Most of the men were African immigrants, and nearby sat women who were with them offering hair braiding. We reached Sant Sebastià beach and laid out our hand towels. I ran in for a quick dip then was content enough laying in the sun as Tim swam. I could fit my shoulders down to butt on my towel, then used our small day bag as a pillow with my arms wrapped around each side. I closed my eyes and listened to the sound of the tide whooshing in and out, nearby people chatting, and more people walking up and down the beach selling items to tourists. Most were men from Pakistan selling cold drinks, water, snacks, and beach blankets, and a few women offered massages.

"Mojito-mojito," the men passed by. "Cold beer, fresh beer."

"No thanks."

"Wat-agua?"

"Nope." I closed my eyes and ignored the sea of passing men as Tim came back to lay beside me.

"A duh duh duh?" said a nearby man. I raised my head. "Dur duh duh?"

"What is *that*?" I asked Tim.

"No idea. But he's selling fresh coconut?"

"A duh duh duh duh duh?"

We held back from giggling. Everyone on the crowded beach was quietly giggling. Some not so quietly. I'm not sure if his word for coconut was in another language or if he was trying to get our attention. If so he was doing a great job.

Tim continued to swim as I relaxed on the beach. I denied a man trying to sell me a blanket, but we ended up chatting. "Where are you visiting from?" he asked.

"California. What about you, where are you from?"

"I'm from Pakistan. You must be rich to travel here?"

"No, not really. It's definitely a privilege for me to travel Europe, but I tried to save money for seven years to take this trip across Europe."

"Oh I see. Have a good day."

"You too!"

We left the beach toasty and drained from the sun, but it was still somewhat early. It was evening but the sun was still high in the sky. We took a different way back to the hostel, following winding shop-lined alleys, leaving a trail of sand from our bodies and water from our hair.

We passed a dive bar painted black, plastered in large fliers for punk shows and DJ nights. A metal bar! We were still wet, sandy, and not wearing our best outfits for going to a bar, but I couldn't pass up a drink in a new punk or metal dive bar. And we had nothing else to do anyway. We stopped in for two beers, chatting with each other about the posters on the walls and listening to Iron Maiden on the jukebox.

We were still exhausted from the sun, so we returned to the hostel to shower and stay in for the rest of the night, preparing to check out in the morning. We had planned on staying one more night in Barcelona, but the next night was booked at our hostel as well as all of the other hostels we could find. Even our bus tickets were for one day later than we had a room booked for. We went down to our hostel's bar to use the WIFI, searching once more for any open hostels or nearby squats we could visit. We even searched the map for a deserted area on the city's edge where we could throw our sleeping bags down for the night. Our bus left early in the morning, so we would have to stay extremely close to town or near transportation that would take us there at five in the morning or earlier.

While making our plans, a hippy-looking older man sitting across from us heard our American accents and chimed in to ask where we were from. We talked about California, and he mentioned he was from Montana. He had a few weeks to travel and was seeing what he could on his own, and we talked about how we were halfway into our four-month journey. What started as nice chit chat quickly turned into him lecturing us on wine, and then asking if we were offended by a Nazi's right to march in the streets. Maybe he saw us as someone he could confide in with his hatred, I don't know. But now we were two months into a Europe trip, hadn't seen many Americans in quite some time, since we were still traveling offseason, and all of a sudden were sitting across the table from an old hippy from Montana who wanted us to know he was white pride and anti-immigrant.

We were tired, buzzed, and ready for bed, but Tim started schooling this guy left and right with facts. The man would say one meaningless buzzword he heard from *Fox News* and Tim would come back with a rebuttal debunking the false claim before the man could finish his sentence. I looked down at my phone and had a message from an old acquaintance who just so happened to be in Barcelona on her honeymoon. I planned for us to meet her the next day for lunch at a nearby vegan burrito spot she had picked out, then turned off my phone and waved good night to racist dude and Tim, then took the elevator up to bed.

I woke up the next morning and did the same old routine of packing my backpack ready to take off to someplace new, or in this case a destination unknown. We threw our backpacks on, with our new used towels hanging out of each side from under the top buckles. We walked up to the closed vegan restaurant only a few blocks from the hostel, where Ashton and her new husband Tony appeared from around a corner to greet us. We quickly caught up while the restaurant started to open. It was more of a food counter in a small natural food bakery than a restaurant. We ordered burritos and ate them standing against a wall with open windows facing the alley, then wandered outside to a fountain to talk a bit longer. The plan was to only hang out for an early lunch then go on our way, but we were having fun and none of us had other plans, so we grabbed a few beers and walked down to the water to chat more on a park bench under a shady tree.

"We are just going to take the subway out a ways and find an area outside of the city where we could crash," Tim explained our plans, or lack thereof, due to the hostels being booked.

"No, don't do that!" Ashton responded. "We have a... a really fancy honeymoon suite. It came with a package deal with our flights. It's honestly too fancy for me. We are never in the room except to sleep, and we come back to the room every night at around five in the morning because that's what time the bands stop playing at the festival we are here for. Why don't we sneak you guys into our hotel and you can stay there for the night since we won't be there anyway?"

"Are you sure?" I asked.

"You don't want us imposing on your honeymoon," Tim said.

"No, really! We won't even be there!"

We decided to take Ashton and Tony up on their offer and hopped in a cab with them back to their hotel.

We stepped out of the cab and looked up at the big blue glass skyscraper towering over us. "I told you it was fancy," Ashton said.

All four of us walked as fast as we could through the lobby and past the front desk. "Checking in? the concierge asked, seeing our backpacks.

"Oh no, we're already checked in!" Ashton answered back, holding up her room key and continuing to walk quickly to the elevator, with us following closely behind. She swiped her room key at the elevator and we jumped in quick, before any other questions could be asked.

We put our backpacks down in a corner of the pristine room covered in Ashton and Tony's things, then took the elevator up to see the rooftop pool and bar. The elevator dinged and we stepped out onto the roof. A waist-high glass wall was the only thing separating us from downtown Barcelona below. We could see the entire beach from one side, and The Basilica Sagrada Família in the distance on the other. Even though it was a little pricey, we ordered drinks from the rooftop bar and drank them poolside, enjoying the views of the ocean and the city surrounding us. After one beer the newlyweds decided to go back to nap before going back out to their festival again for the night.

Tim and I grabbed a spare key and went off to explore the new area to give them space.

The whole time we had been in Barcelona we could not find even a small grocery store. Now that we were in more of a downtown area out of the tourist destinations of La Rambla and the Gothic Quarter, we figured we would have better luck. We wandered block after block, winding down random streets in the general direction of the beach. When we reached the water, we found an entire permanent market filled with stalls of goods, as well as bars and restaurants spanning about a block. We passed it to sit on a secluded part of the beach next to resorts and clubs. I had my sweatshirt hood pulled up over my head since the sky had slowly started turning grey and the wind started to pick up. We decided to turn back, and on the way to the hotel we found a real grocery store where we were able to buy snacks and drinks for the next day's ten-hour bus ride to Nice.

We spent forever walking the aisles, trying to plan some sort of meal that could be made on a bus. After shopping, we were hungry, and wandered the streets looking for cheap cooked food. The sun was down and most of this part of the city was deserted. As we approached the hotel we saw a sushi restaurant's lights shining from across the street. I tried my best to read if they had any fishless sushi with the small amount of Spanish I could recognize off of the menu. "Pepino, zanahoria y aguacate," that'll do. It was still early, but I was falling asleep in my miso.

We finished up and quickly booked it to the elevator in the hotel then straight into the room. We picked a corner furthest from the bed, which was hard to do. I slept against the floor length window and Tim against the dresser and mini fridge. I put in my earplugs, covered my eyes with my bandana, and slipped into sleep. At around four thirty in the morning Tony and Ashton returned and fell into bed. Thirty minutes later our alarm vibrated us awake. We shoved our sleeping bags into our backpacks and headed out into the dark.

The bus station was maybe a mile away, close to the Basilica Sagrada Família. The sun was rising fast as we walked past a busy street with trash cluttered around the sidewalk. A suitcase laid open with its contents scattered across the street. Women's shoes, women's toiletries, women's clothes. I wondered what exactly had happened in this situation. She must have been robbed. Maybe her car was broken into and her bag was stolen, valuables taken then the rest thrown into the street. Seemed plausible, for any city really.

Nice: Don't You Hate it when You Wake up Next to an Abandoned Building in the French Riviera Because it's Sprinkling and Have to Hurry to Pick the Spiders out of Your Shoes?

It was already warm in the sun as we waited for the ten-hour bus ride ahead of us. I slept as much of the ride as I could on the freezing cold bus; waking to see my second glance of France. "Here we go France, this is your second chance!" Tim said as we crossed the border.

We didn't have a room booked for the night, but did have one booked for the following two days. We figured since we got in during the evening we could find a place near the beach to sleep and then check into our room in the morning. This plan worried us though, since our summer sunshine suddenly turned into pouring rain as the bus pulled into town.

According to the weather report the rain would clear up, so when our bus pulled into the Nice airport we decided to walk to a nearby mall to use WIFI, get snacks, and wait out the weather. We found the mall on our phone's map, right beside the airport on the other side of a small river. It was only sprinkling by this time, and we figured the walk should be short and sweet, except for the unfortunate fact airports aren't really designed to walk out of. We strolled the labyrinth of paths to baggage claims and rental car terminals. Finally we found a way out of the airport, then out of the parking lots, but the only way to cross the rushing river was a highway bridge towering over our heads with no sight of a sidewalk, or even a hill up to it. Seeing a jogger up on the bridge gave us hope, knowing at least there was a pedestrian path we could use if we could make it up there.

We tried another road, hoping it would cross paths with a way up to the bridge but our road just veered back to the airport. Right before we gave up and accepted our fate bound to the airport forever, there was an opening in a fence that went right to the path we needed, after also hopping a short wall. Onward to the mall! Except again it started to rain.

We looked down on the road we had been on before and saw another man leaving the airport on foot.

"Turn back now, you can never leave the airport. It now owns you forever!" I jokingly taunted from the bridge above.

We made it to the mall and successfully found a Starbucks, that was for some reason twice the price of any other Starbucks. I was just happy for the chance to charge our phones, relax, and use the bathrooms. Some local girls were snickering about me, whispering into each other's ears while blatantly staring through the bathroom mirror. I gave a cold blank stare back without blinking and they got the hint to continue on with their evening. I don't know what they were snickering about, but seeing as I was thirty with tattoos, body hair, and dreadlocks past my ass, I'm sure it could have been a number of things.

After an hour or two the Starbucks started to close down, but not before we met a fellow American now living in Nice. She was a woman in her fifties telling us about her adventures living all over Europe. I'm not sure how she had so much money, but she went on to tell us how she sold her enormous house to move into a smaller one so she could afford to put her two kids through college in and around New York. One at $60k a year and the other $50k. She was now living in Nice with her twenty-six-year-old boyfriend. I almost started to think her life story was bullshit, until here he came. A French man in his twenties wearing khaki shorts, a pink sweater tied around his shoulders, and a poofy white dog in one arm. "Now that's a sugar mama," Tim whispered as we grabbed our things to go.

We wandered the beach boardwalk beyond the mall into the night, passing fancy restaurant after fancy restaurant. Everything we found was either closed or too expensive. After about an hour of walking we decided on a Japanese place that had a few cheap sushi rolls on the menu, then hit the road back, looking for a place to crash. We walked on a dark busy road, when to the left appeared an empty field with a large abandoned house off in one corner. After about twenty minutes of investigating the field we settled on a spot under a tree not too far from the house.

The house was covered in graffiti and surrounded by stacks of wood pallets on one side. The basement window was missing, but the inside was filled from floor to ceiling with more pallets. And probably thousands of critters. We laid out our tarp, sleeping bags, and camp pillows then took a few shots of some rum Tim had bought in a grocery store attached to the mall.

Fireflies flickered in the field here and there, yells of young bar-goers echoed now and again through the streets, and eventually we fell asleep on our tarp under a tree next to the towering graffiti painted building in the French Riviera. We woke in the morning to sprinkling rain, of course, and quickly packed our bags to head toward downtown Nice after first picking the spiders from our shoes.

First we went back to the mall but everything was closed. Sunday, of course! On top of that the trains and buses were few and far between since the workers were on strike. We made it in time to catch one of the only trains of the day. The place we were staying at was a hostel situated right smack in between an African and Middle Eastern area of Nice, the Notre Dame of Nice – Notre-Dame de l'Assomption, and what seemed to be an upscale fashion district. Pretty random, but the location was only a ten or fifteen minute walk to the beach and the price was right.

We clicked the buzzer on the old unmarked building then walked up two flights of stairs, past families with children hanging out in the stairwell, and to the hostel's door. We were trying so hard to give France a second chance, but this hostel wasn't bringing France in any points. In fact, it ended up somehow being worse than anywhere we had stayed in Europe.

Immediately at check in we had to deal with their credit card machine breaking, using the last of our precious cash on two nights lodging plus a €30 deposit for the one key we both had to share. The kitchen smelled, and only fit about one person at a time comfortably. The silverware basically consisted of two plastic spoons, one of which we broke while washing it. Our bedroom's one shared toilet wasn't bolted down so sometimes you, and the toilet, would slide into the wall heater like a sideways drifting bumper car you can't quite get to go in the right direction. The one common room closed at 10:30 PM, forcing all guests to spend the rest of their night awake in a room where other people were trying to sleep. A cockroach greeted me while I was brushing my teeth, and the staff seemed to be having a different billing issue with every customer. The front desk woman actually came into our room close to midnight to tell the elderly roommate of ours they accidentally gave her an extra €10 in change and needed it back immediately.

Even though France was off to a rough start again, we admired how beautiful the town and beaches were. For our first full day in Nice we were excited to enjoy the clear blue ocean water with snacks and drinks. Unfortunately grocery stores were almost impossible to find, and the waves were littered with the bodies of an organism related to the Portuguese man-o-war.

It was time to move on to our thirteenth country, Italy! We didn't have much time to spend in Italy so we passed up Florence, Venice, and Milan to head straight to Rome, then planned on traveling to Naples then Bari to catch a ferry to Greece. We splurged on a taxi to the Nice airport bus terminal since the train and bus workers were still on strike. It was early, and we had barely slept due to our cute little old British lady roommate snoring like a chainsaw. Instead of hopping right onto our bus, we had almost a two-hour wait due to it arriving late. I kept wanting to run into the airport to find coffee, but I couldn't risk the bus coming and leaving without me while I was gone. At least we met some other Americans to become temporary bus friends with for most of the long eleven-hour ride.

Trains in Europe are very expensive. Flying, especially if you get your ticket in advance, is usually much cheaper than a few hours on a bus or train. The cheapest flight we found from one European country to another was under twenty dollars per person. The most expensive, last minute flight we bought was still only around sixty dollars per person. Sometimes while traveling Europe we needed to get to the next destination within the week but the only option that wouldn't completely empty our wallets was a long-distance bus. These buses are usually large and comfy, yet you could still be spending fifty euros sitting on a bus for an entire day, or night, for what would have normally been a few hour's drive.

We ended up traveling by bus quite a bit. At first you're excited, *I could sneak on a few beers and listen to music. I could catch up on the book I have stored on my phone. I could blog, draw, brainstorm ideas, read articles...* but it rarely works out that way. The winding roads and jerking motions ruin any chance of reading or writing, the lack of a strong "Free WIFI" signal means no articles or blogging, and the buses with one euro coin bathroom fees (which you are never prepared for) would make for an extremely uncomfortable, panicky, and possibly soggy ride if a few beers were had.

Let's also not forget issues that may arise with the driver. Although bus drivers are usually nice people just doing their job, they can sometimes be difficult to deal with as well. There was the woman who announced our stop at 4 AM in Évora, did a quick yield as if rolling a stop sign, then kept going. Leaving us confused, Tim standing in the aisle holding on as the bus zoomed through the tiny town we had already paid to stay in, and me bundled and groggy, holding my daypack to my chest wondering what was going on. After a few minutes of us trying to make sense of the situation we asked the driver, who didn't speak English, if she was planning on stopping in the town we had just past. She furiously made a U-turn and headed back to drop us off, asking why we didn't get off when she passed the first time.

"We tried, but you just kept going," Tim answered.

A month or so previous to that situation, a bus in Germany stopped for a break at a big station with lots of fast food options. Half of the passengers got off, leaving their belongings strewn across their seats. As we got up to follow, the door slammed shut and the driver sped the bus out of the parking lot, onto the Main Street with us still holding on in the aisle. We sat back down, thinking maybe the bus had to move to a different part of the station, but no, we sped through the town, onto the freeway, and on towards the next destination hours away. We still have no idea if some of the other passengers had been left behind or if the things strewn about belonged to the passengers who remained. After that experience, taking breaks made me incredibly nervous.

A bus in Portugal stopped for a break at a gas station and I bolted like a 90's game show contestant being timed to throw free shit into a grocery cart. First one in the bathroom, I peed, ran my hands under some water for a second, then dashed to the food line trying to beat the mostly elderly bus crowd while wiping my hands on my pants. The only decent vegetarian meal I could find that was real food and not just candy or chips was a plain vinaigrette and iceberg salad. I sat on a curb, where I could keep an eye on the bus, eating my plain vinegar salad, puckering my face from the sourness, and came to the resourceful conclusion I should go back into the store and get packets of ketchup and mayonnaise to mix together as Thousand

Island dressing. I even added potato chips as croutons. My plan worked, but as I was coming back outside the bus was boarding again.

I ran on with my salad concoction and finished eating it in my seat. A few minutes later the driver made his rounds and made it perfectly clear (well, clear if I spoke Portuguese) that I was not supposed to be eating on the bus. I guess it was okay though, for the man across the seat from me to be eating a huge sub-sandwich. Maybe he was just offended by my food preparation skills. Who knows.

I'm surprised I didn't spew my secret sauce once we hit the road. Sometimes a bus will take so many roundabouts in a row I think they are purposefully trying to make us sick. They might as well just load the bus onto one of those things that rotate train cars and let it spin. This same Portuguese driver must have had it out for me from the beginning. When initially boarding the bus, I got in line holding out my ticket and was instantly cut off by an elderly couple. The elderly man handed his ticket and boarded, while another passenger who was waiting behind me yelled "excuzi, excuzi!" to the couple for cutting. I handed my ticket, since it was my turn, and the driver went over it, waved on the elderly woman, then motioned for the next person in line's ticket. I stood there confused, then just boarded since he did in fact take my bus ticket. Before I could take my seat toward the middle of the bus, he came looking for me.

"I already gave you my ticket, you have it in your hand. Here... Bridget McGee." I said while shuffling through the papers in his hand. He seemed confused, but okay with it, and let me continue to take my seat.

We dealt with a lot when it came to that specific bus company, but some of the others were better. Drama seemed to continue to unfold even with companies where we had fewer issues though. Such as the time we were crossing the border from France into Italy and our bus driver got into a heated verbal fight with some Italian military men. I'm still not sure what that was about, but rumor on the bus had it that the driver was refusing to pay the highway toll.

Rome: Catholic Disneyland

We passed crashing waves and blue skies on the bus ride along the Mediterranean Sea, from Southern France into Italy. We arrived in Rome around 10 PM and took their confusing metro system to the central station, which wasn't far from the room we would be renting. The air in Rome was much more humid than anywhere we had been in Europe thus far. We walked through the night time heat, bought an absolutely horrid bottle of wine from a liquor store, then climbed the three flights of hot stairs to our very temporary home. They say you can't buy a bad bottle of wine in Europe, and that is a straight up lie. Bottom shelf liquor store wine in Europe is just as bad as it is in the US.

The room was comfortable, and we were so excited to have a nice private space with a large window, TV, private bathroom, and shared full kitchen. Even though this was a shared two bedroom, two bathroom apartment, we lucked out and had it to ourselves. We spent the night sipping our shitty wine, going through our things, and stretching out on the big bed.

The next morning we took off on foot to explore Rome, starting with the Colosseum. It was about a two mile walk but we made it there fairly quick. We circled the breathtaking ruins, trying to snap pictures in between moving herds of tourists. Since we specifically saved our money for only a few of Europe's sightseeing activities, the Colosseum and surrounding museums unfortunately didn't make it into the budget. Although we did have it in our plans to visit the Vatican museum and Sistine Chapel before leaving. We spent over an hour walking the perimeter of the building and nearby ruins, peeking into fences and seeing what we could from neighboring sidewalks. A tourist map led us from one destination to another, stopping in between to eat gelato topped with Stroopwafels in the sunshine.

While admiring some Roman ruins, a man stopped us to try to give us bracelets. He tried to take each of our hands to put the bracelet on, but we pulled away and nicely refused.

"We have no money," we pleaded. I also knew of this as one of the scams I had read about. A man ties a bracelet to your wrist and demands money for it, not accepting "returns."

The man begged and begged us to take the bracelets and we continued to walk on, nicely refusing over and over again. "It's yours for free. I want you to have it." he said.

"For free? I don't want to take your bracelet you could be selling to another person," said Tim.

"No, no. It's no big deal. You seem like nice people, I want you to have it."

Tim and I looked at each other confused. "I mean... Um, okay."

We each took a bracelet from the man as he continued to ask us where we were from, and we did the same. He was from Africa, and went on to tell us about how his wife gave birth to twins just the other day.

"Congratulations! We hope you can get home to your babies soon."

"Thank you, enjoy your bracelets!"

The next day we explored the Trevi Fountain, eating arancini in restaurants down cobblestone alleys and tasting free limoncello. Although we were warned Rome was one of the worst cities for pickpockets and scammers, we didn't have any issues. Here and there a pushy woman would try to sell us something, which did get annoying. Ideas ran through my head of how to deter these people, and I thought about how funny it would be to pretend to bless them in the name of Satan and see them go running. Is that messed up? I don't know. My computer autocorrected that to Sagan, which could have also been fitting.

Our third day was spent at Catholic Disneyland. The metro took us to Vatican City, where we paid only to go into the Vatican museum which was connected to the Sistine Chapel. The line to get in stretched half a city block, and inside the museum wasn't any less crowded. I was happy to get another famous museum in, although I was definitely burnt out on religious art. Pushy seas of tourists also made the museum difficult to enjoy.

We followed the crowd to the entrance of the Sistine Chapel, where we were instructed to cover our shoulders and put our cameras and phones away. I didn't realize there was a dress code and was dressed for walking in the summer heat. A tan tank top and my ripped black denim skirt with bike shorts underneath. I did what I could to make myself look modest, which only meant putting on my sweatshirt I fortunately brought, and walked inside hoping I wouldn't be spotted. I think they realized some of us weren't prepared to cover ourselves up. I was allowed to buy a ticket, so they had better let me in.

The chapel was kept completely silent. Only whispers were permitted. Whispers and the sound of security telling people "no pictures!" Tim slid his cell phone out of his pocket and slyly got a blurry picture of Michelangelo's *The Last Judgment* on the ceiling. I felt it was odd we couldn't take pictures, but I guess if the lack of accidental camera flashes going off keeps the frescos from deteriorating then it makes sense.

We went back for an early night in, looking up what we should do for our last two nights in Rome, and spent some time booking our next bus and ferry rides. I woke in the morning wrapped in soft blankets with a breeze flowing through the window, to a young woman throwing open the door, bursting right into our room. Tim and I sat up fast, as she yelled "Oh, sorry!" and slammed the door shut.

"Our roommates have arrived," I said, unimpressed. I got out of bed and headed down the hall to the bathroom that was designated for our room. Next door to the bathroom was the second bathroom, which shared a wall with the second bedroom. The bedroom door was opened and filled with four or five fashionable women in their early twenties, who were way too giddy for how early it was. I fiddled with the bathroom door lock, which was apparently non-existent. *Please, please, don't let them burst in on me in the bathroom, too.* I sat on the toilet as the door swung open. "Oh! Sorry!" a voice yelled in. I finished up, brushed my teeth, then went back into the hall and poked my head into their bedroom door.

"Hello! So, the bedroom over there is ours, and the bathroom closest to it as well. This bedroom and the bathroom next to it are yours. Okay, thanks!"

The women looked back at me wide-eyed and didn't say a word. I went to my room to change when my phone started ringing. It was the woman who owned the apartment.

"Are you still there? Have you checked out?" she asked.

"Yes, I'm here. We check out tomorrow."

"No, you check out today. Are the other guests there now? They needed to check in early."

"Yes, they are here. There has definitely been some sort of confusion. We asked to stay for four nights."

"Oh, well you only paid for three and your room is already booked for tonight."

"Oh, *great!* Okay, we will pack up and leave now."

"If you need to check out a bit late, that's okay."

"It's okay, it will only take us a few minutes to pack our things."

I got off the phone, explained what happened to Tim, who sighed and jumped out of bed, then checked the clock. We still had half an hour until check out time, which confused me even more because technically we had still paid to be in the room. I threw my things in my backpack and grabbed our stuff from the fridge, which the new roommates were already going through. We awkwardly left them to the bedroom that was now theirs. Dirty sheets and all.

Tim and I wandered aimlessly until finding a coffee shop next to the metro station with a big WIFI sign in the window. "Two cappuccinos and the WIFI password, please." We both stared deep into our phones with groggy eyes. Slurping down one cappuccino, and then another. We each tried to book one hostel after another.

"This one is close, but only the expensive rooms are left."

"This one is cheap and has availability, but it's far away." After an hour we found a decent place to book for a night that was cheap and only a few blocks away. A short walk later we found the stairs up to the hostel which led to the front desk. The woman was nice and asked us if it was our first time in Rome, which led us to explain our room situation. At least it was the first time we had messed up booking, and not too serious of a mess-up. The hostel was empty and dark. A narrow, windowless path led through a long, winding hallway of closed doors. Some of the doors were open to dimly lit bathrooms.

"You know, we have a big room you two might like. There are only two beds so you could have it to yourselves."

"Oh that's okay, we'll just take whatever's cheapest."

"No, we can upgrade you, you can have it at the same price. No one has booked it anyway."

"Really? Thank you!" She showed us to our room where we could finally relax once more. The room was huge, the size of an average living room, with one tall skinny window looking out to a brick wall, and two hard twin beds placed apart from each other. There was a table and a few chairs where we could sit and shuffle through our backpacks. Across the room was another door. I figured it went to a closet or something, but my curiosity got the best of me and I decided to try it. I opened the door, and inside was another room the same size as the room we were in. It was completely empty except for a few chairs, and the wall was lined with breezy open windows overlooking the street down below.

"This is amazing! Come and see this." I called out to Tim while sticking my head out the window. "How weird this room is unused."

We left the door open to fill our room with sunlight and fresh air, then left to experience our last night in Rome.

At this point we really needed our laundry done. The woman at the front desk recommended a laundromat some ten or so blocks away. I put on my puffy jacket and denim skirt with running shorts, and shoes with no socks, so everything else could be washed. It was night time, and the neighborhood became a little sketchy looking, but we found our laundromat and wandered the neighboring streets to waste time.

We stopped to admire a nose. Nasoni, which translates to big noses, are clean water fountains placed all over Rome and other parts of Italy, that run day and night. A three-foot-tall, rusty-looking cast iron pipe drips clean, cold water 24/7. The water is piped from an aqueduct originally built by the Romans. Some of them are a little fancier looking and called fontanelles. There is one that is even shaped like a wolf. Now you know all about the running street noses of Rome.

We passed an unmarked bar under a restaurant. A small staircase went down from the street to an open door below, where people loudly laughed inside. I peered down the stairs to see what was going on, and an entire room full of people looked up from their games to give me an evil look. It was definitely more of a family affair. We sat on a curb in the dark, under a large tree until our laundry was finished, then went back to our spacious room. First thing the next morning we thanked the woman once more for our room, then jumped on a bus to Napoli.

Naples: Drinking Rare Beer Out of a Vase in a Library Down a Dark Alley in the Tijuana of Italy

Naples was another city picked by Tim, which I knew nothing about. Nothing whatsoever. All I could assume was that it was probably a beautiful Italian city like Milan or Florence. I mean, we *did* skip Milan *and* Florence *for* Naples. I assumed there would be wine and cheese and limoncello and pizza. I knew it was along the ocean and that it was near Pompeii, which I *did* research as a destination I wanted to visit.

We emerged from the metro station at the top of a hill with tall, old buildings surrounding us. There were murals and graffiti, and mopeds zipping down the steep hill into town. We walked down the road until we came to an alley on our left in between two tall buildings. The alley came to a dead-end at a large, dilapidated old church, with a private green iron gate between brick pillars beside it. Instead of being a flat alley, the entire thing was more of a gradual stairway entrance to the baroque style church.

The church, Chiesa della Santissima Trinità alla Cesarea, was built in the 17th century but had been abandoned since 1980. Its stairs were made of piperno, a magmatic rock. The door looked cemented closed. The front looked like it was originally painted red, but the paint had mostly chipped off. The brick walls around the double staircases looked like some of the oldest brick I had ever seen. Deteriorating decorative columns framed what was once the doorway. On the left side of the church was a connected building that had been entirely restored and modernized, while on the right side, the paint was chipping off of the stone walls and the windows were closed and barred. The left side we learned was our hostel. The reason why the hostel sat touching this old church was because it was the nicely renovated and modernized former monastery and garden courtyard. The gardens had also been restored.

The green gate had a bell, which buzzed us into the large front yard of the hostel. The place was huge. It had sizeable grassy front, back, and side yards which were all connected. Each room and common room had large floor to ceiling windows looking out into the green yards. We were shown to our room where we picked a corner bunk and lockers. There were quite a few bunks, and one bathroom inside of the room for everyone to share. With how modern the hostel looked, you would have never known it was part of the creepy church.

We headed back downstairs for our complimentary shots of limoncello and talked to the hostel staff about getting around town.

"You can walk back up to the metro and take that three stops into downtown, or you can just walk down the hill. It's not far... if you don't mind walking, and hills."

"Walking is kinda our thing," we responded.

I went back into our room to pack a bag for town and glanced over to see that a new roommate had completely taken over the room's one table, and an entire corner. Every inch of the big round table was covered in belongings. Her clothes were even draped across the chair. In that corner were four lockers, one of which we took since the few on our side of the room were taken, and you couldn't even walk up to them. Every item from her backpack was on the floor or the table, no matter how big or how small. Some of it had even rolled across the room, off to somewhere she'd probably never find it again. I was hoping she was just looking for something in a panic, and not a total asshole. I shrugged, grabbed my things, and headed downtown.

We left the hostel, walked back out of the alley and onto the main road. The walk to town was very steep and longer than I expected. In fact, the more we walked, the more my expectations seemed off. Vehicles sped by, leaving fumes and smog behind them. Graffiti and murals covered most of the buildings the further we walked. *What is this place?* I thought.

When we reached the bottom of the hill, there was a dusty old park with dry grass, a larger street with more cars, and people waiting at a bus bench. To our right, the buildings got taller, older, and denser. The cobblestone alleys between buildings were tight, ancient, dark, and grimy, and they were in the direction we needed to go.

The deeper we ventured in, the more people we started to see, and the more kitchens, called friggitoria, meaning a place selling fried food, offering arancini, potato croquettes, and limoncello shots on tables in the streets. We took advantage of the street food, then kept on wandering, eventually grabbing a plastic shot of limoncello to go as well.

The alleys were amazing. I felt like a kid seeing Disneyland for the first time. My eyes couldn't take in enough. Old deteriorating stone archway tunnels connected alleys together. Stores with tables of used books in the walkways. Apartment balconies held trailing green plants overhead. Bright murals on crumbling walls.

This was a place your average American tourist would deem dirty and dangerous. I would later read an article stating that after being asked, many travelers chose Naples as the worst place they had ever traveled to. Only a small thirteen percent of travelers visiting Italy even decide to visit Naples at all. Years later, after looking back at having camped on beaches in Hawaii, swam with enormous

304 Bridget McGee Houchins

stingrays in the Out Islands of the Exumas, and summited snowy mountain peaks and desert island cliffs, I would still look back on Napoli as one of the most beautiful places I had ever been.

The graffiti became more prevalent around a large stone building. This building neighbored a small alley and was attached to an old, grey, stone church on its other side. The building was five stories tall, and at its base was wheat-pasted art, flyers, layers of graffiti and chipped yellow paint exposing the grey brick underneath. A squatter's rights flag hung out of a window, and an Antifa flag out of another.

The sun went down, and we kept walking and eating and drinking. The narrow streets opened up into a small park around a fenced off area of ancient ruins. Every inch of the park was packed full of people of all kinds and all ages drinking on curbs, benches, or just standing in the grass under the street lamps. Along the small park was a row of nice restaurants, one of them being a vegan restaurant, and a larger street meant for cars and not just mopeds and people drinking limoncello. I loved this place. Tim and I were smitten.

We headed back to a friggitoria for another shot of limoncello before exploring the dark winding alleys in a new direction. We walked with our little plastic shot glasses down an alley lit only by a large store window, belonging to a pet store that was closed for the day. The window was one wall of a small white-walled kennel holding a chihuahua puppy and two kittens. The kittens wobbled back and forth, batting at the torn newspaper used as their bedding. The puppy bounded quickly across the kennel, back and forth, speeding up and bouncing over the kittens as he ran. Tim and I laughed, trying to get the puppy's attention in an attempt to play with him from behind the glass. The puppy ignored us and became increasingly infatuated with one of the kittens. He toppled over it and started biting its ear. At first it still seemed like puppy fun and games, but the puppy started becoming more and more violent toward the kitten. They were about the same size, but the kittens had to be much younger, and couldn't stick up for themselves well. We banged on the glass, and eventually, the puppy started sifting through the litter box instead of torturing the kitten. We left before anything got any more depressing.

We picked another path, walking through the different narrow alleys. We stopped to admire a large mural when I noticed in the alley behind us was what seemed to be a library-pub. It had one large storefront window, shining a bright red light into the dark alley. Inside the window were rows and walls of books with nice furniture placed throughout. Two chairs sat right at the window with a coffee table in between and a bar behind them. It looked like a small upscale bookstore. The library-pub was dimly lit except for the red light, a few table lamps, and a light over the bar.

"Take a seat," we were instructed after entering. We picked the two large armchairs next to the window. There were no real tables, only chairs with side tables, and a small bar with three stools. The floor was cement but glowed red under the lights, as did the bookshelves. The full bar was lined with bookshelves, which even hung over it like an arch. There was not one wall or pillar that was not lined with the spines of books, as if the entire interior could have been made out of books. I definitely felt like I needed a robe and a cigar. Instead, I was brought a drink menu and a small bowl filled with peanuts and pretzels.

"They have Kwak!" Tim exclaimed. It was one of the beers we tried in Belgium, which was to be poured in a tall, thin, hourglass-shaped beer glass. Almost like something you would find in a science lab. The Kwak glass didn't even stand up on its own. It had a wooden stand and base to hold the glass upright. You could either pick up the entire glass in its stand and tip it back to your mouth to take a sip or take the glass out of the wooden stand to drink out of it. I'm not sure which way was correct. After returning back to the states from Europe I looked into this important question, and the Internet gave me wonderful advice, such as "You're supposed to eat the wooden handle first. Then drink your beer the usual way." Or "Leave the glass and holder on the bar. Lean forward and try to put your mouth over the top of the entire glass. Lean back with glass in mouth and let it all pour down your throat. When finished, use the wooden holder as firewood. I thought this was common knowledge."

"I wonder if it actually comes in the glass?" I whispered to Tim.

"Are you ready to order?"

"Yes, we'll both have the Kwak, thank you."

A few minutes later out comes the large oblong beaker held in a wooden stand. I sipped my delicious science experiment, blanketed in a soft red light, my back pressed against the armchair, surrounded by pristine wood bookshelves, admiring the graffiti murals in the alley our armchairs faced. I'm sure to anyone else this story sounds like I might have been on hallucinogens. "No, I'm telling you. I was drinking rare beer out of a vase in a library down a dark alley in the Tijuana of Italy."

After the one, large, high percentage Belgian beer at the library-pub, we zig-zagged once more through the dark alleys. Each alley led to a bigger street or square, with people drinking around statues of ancient figures, lined in each direction with little hole-in-the-wall-restaurants. We passed the restaurants and bars to keep walking, finding new sculptures, murals, or cathedrals with every turn. Some of the bars and restaurants had a worker outside trying to convince passersby to come in.

We passed a pizza shop when a man called to us "Come in! Our-a pizza, izzza da *BEST-a* pizza!" Tim and I glared at each other, wide-eyed and holding in laughter.

"Sorry, not this time!" We walked on and then burst out laughing once the man was far enough away. "Oh my God! Day five in Italy and that was our first experience with a living Italian stereotype."

We kept walking until a bar actually did catch our eye. The bar itself looked unappealing. Small, sterile, empty, too bright, with TVs too loud. But outside its door was a chalkboard sign saying "€1 BEER" then underneath in smaller writing was "Deal is for to go only." *€1 beer? To go only?* We stared, talking to ourselves aloud. "So, the beer is €1, but only if you drink it in the street?"

"Yeah," Tim confirmed. Without saying another word, we both turned toward the door and walked inside. Three minutes later we were back in the alley again but with ice cold glass bottles of Peroni in hand.

After drinking a €1 street beer, and after plenty of €1 street shots, we made it safely back to our hostel, up, up, up, the treacherous hill.

I quietly opened the door to our room and tiptoed across the wood floors, through rows of sleeping strangers. I used my phone as a flashlight to wade through the messy roommate's belongings to my locker, which still covered an entire corner of the room. I was pretty drunk, and it was obvious this woman wasn't going through her things in a panic, this is just how she lives. Communally, at that. Every so often in hostels you have one of these jerks. She had so much stuff. I joked about wanting to know what was in one of those enormous backpacking packs and now I could see what one example held. I knew I was starting my period within the next week or two, so I drunkenly grabbed one of the tampons out of an entire box of them strewn across the table, as if someone was chucking bird seed into a lake at swimming ducks. I pocketed it in my things, then climbed into bed and dozed off.

We woke up late, sleeping off the alcohol for as long as we could, then went down to breakfast before walking back into downtown to really explore Napoli during the day. Our outlet adaptor for our chargers had decided to crap out only two and a half months into our trip, so one of the errands of the day was to find a new one for cheap which would hopefully last the rest of our journey. Another goal was to try the vegan restaurant we had passed the night before.

We walked back down the steep hill, mopeds and buses flying past. We approached the bottom of the hill and veered off to the right. The restaurant was at the edge of the first small park we found full of drinking Italians the night before. In the center of the small grassy area was a nonchalant little fenced off area with dirt and stone walls below it. People sat and smoked and drank around these like it was nothing, but this fenced off area was there to protect ancient Greek ruins. An old wall that used to go around the city. This was mind-blowing, being from California.

I was starving when we entered the vegan restaurant and sat down at a small table near the window. My hunger made it difficult to be choosy and stay within our budget. But eventually my hunger won out and I ordered an appetizer. *Ceci Fritti - Deep fried spicy chickpeas* €2.50 sounded like a good choice. Those are words I like, "deep fried" and "spicy." You can't go wrong. The alternatives for an appetizer were olives or vegetables, at a higher price. I'll have "deep fried" and "spicy" anything, please.

"I think it's just chickpeas," Tim said.

"It can't be just chickpeas. That's not what it says. And it's only €2.50." I don't know what I was picturing. Just anything deep fried made out of chickpeas. Even just chickpeas themselves, maybe battered, or something. The rest of the menu was vegan cheese plates, potato dishes, bean soups, sautéed vegetables, and seitan skewers. We chose salad, skewers, and seitan in tomato sauce to split as a main course, to nurse our sluggish bodies after a night out in the alleys.

Out comes the appetizer. The plate was placed before us. Chickpeas. *Huh*, I thought. It was literally just a plate of chickpeas. Naked chickpeas. No batter, no fry. *He couldn't have been right. It can't be just chickpeas. Well, it's a restaurant appetizer, I'm sure they taste good.* I went in to take a bite, struggling to roll a chickpea onto my fork. I put one in my mouth, chewed, swallowed, then instantly started laughing.

"What??" Tim asked, confused.

"I guess you're right. It's just chickpeas. That's all. Just... plain... chickpeas."

"I told you!"

"This is literally what people who don't understand vegan food think vegan food is."

We both looked down at the plate of hard, tasteless legumes and laughed. I grabbed my fork and pushed more on using my finger, and then shoveled them into my mouth.

"You're actually going to eat it?"

"We paid for it, and I'm hungry. It's food?"

"I guess so."

"Do you want some?"

"No." Tim laughed. "The rabbit food is all yours."

The rest of the meal came and made up for the bland appetizer. We inhaled our soup and then trekked on deeper into downtown, toward the ocean. We took the same route as the night before, except stayed more on the main road instead of winding through alleys. We did veer off up a hill to check out a street market, finding the cheap outlet adaptor we were hoping for.

The stores and restaurants got much fancier as we walked on. The street food and alley limoncello shots disappeared; instead, downtown had sidewalk cafés with podiums holding neatly piled leather-bound menus next to buttoned-up greeters wearing slacks. The crowds grew larger. The main street ended in a cul-de-sac of restaurants and tourist shops just before the water's edge. We ignored the knickknacks, sped through the crowds, almost losing one another, and took a path toward the castle on the Tyrrhenian sea. I became more uncomfortable the longer I walked. It wasn't walking itself that was bothering me. That I was used to, even with tendonitis creeping in here and there. I had began to suspect I was starting my period. *It's too early though, isn't it?* I pressed on. *Ouch!* My abdomen constricted and throbbed. *Maybe not.*

Castel dell'Ovo was named after a legend where a Roman poet, sorcerer, and predictor of the future named Virgil buried a magical egg in the foundation of the castle while it was being built for protection. If the egg broke, it meant the castle, and Naples, would be destroyed in a disastrous event. This is why it is called the castle of the egg. The castle sits on its own little island, now a peninsula thanks to modern-day humans connecting the two. The island was first settled by Greeks in the 6th century BC, who called it Megaris. The legend stated the heartbroken siren Partenope washed onto the island after failing to seduce Ulysses. In the 5th century AD, the ancient Romans took over (what a surprise), building a villa for one of their generals. After the Romans, it became a monastery that was later destroyed. The castle was completed in the 15th century, and a small fishing village joined its base in the 19th century. The fishing village technically still stands and is called Borgo Marinaro. The castle now contains a museum, with restaurants and a marina below in the fishing village.

We took the steep staircase up to Castel dell'Ovo, taking in the views while I tried to ignore the cramps. From the castle, we could see all of downtown Napoli and Mount Vesuvius towering in the distance. The sun was shining, the weather was perfect and breezy, Napoli was glittering in all its glory, sun shining on hills of windows literally making the city sparkle. I could hear the waves crash against the cliffs below us, and kids laughing, chasing each other around old canons. I sat down and read a lone message scribbled on the stone wall: *I hate you, please love me.*

"I need to find a bathroom," I told Tim. "Now."

The indoor areas of the castle had been locked up or turned into museum displays and offices. Thankfully, there was a public bathroom. I ran in and waited my turn in a panic. The elderly woman in front of me was taking so long. Finally, the stall was mine, yet any form of toilet paper was nonexistent. I turned and walked back out with my head down, the elderly woman and her husband looking toward me confused.

"What's wrong?" Tim asked.

"I can't possibly open the floodgates and not have toilet paper. There aren't even paper towels. I'll have to just deal with it and find another bathroom somewhere else." *If only I had brought that tampon I stole,* I thought. This was like a sick joke. It was all too ironic. The period karma fairy had come for me.

We finished exploring the castle then walked back into downtown. A man working at our hostel had told us we could buy cheap tickets to Pompeii from any newsstand or tourist shop, but that we should get them early to get the good deal. We hadn't seen a newsstand or a tourist shop the night before, so our mission walking back through downtown was to find these tickets. We went from store to store, Tim asking about the tickets and me about a bathroom. Of course, newsstands and tourist shops didn't have bathrooms, but they also had no clue what tickets we were talking about. Hell, we didn't even know.

We kept walking and exploring. Well, Tim was walking, I was waddling. I had on my torn up black denim skirt, sewn from old jeans, with short black bike shorts underneath. Whatever mess was happening had so far thankfully not escaped my clothes, but it was making me chafe horribly, which is debatably almost worse when you're walking multiple miles. I was thirsty and frustrated and hurting.

We passed a long decorative hallway with benches away from crowds, the perfect place to sit for a minute before carrying on. I was afraid to sit, but I did it anyway, sitting on my foot instead of directly on the white bench, to lessen the probability of leaving a red butt stamp. Tim felt bad for me but was also growing frustrated. We were both sick of the crowds, far from our hostel, and tired of trying to find these nonexistent tickets.

At the end of the long hallway was a post office and another tourist shop. Tim left to inquire about the tickets while I slowly got up to follow behind. He tried the store with no luck, then tried the post office as a last-ditch effort. While he waited to be helped I browsed the store next door, and realized they had a bathroom. A single stall, private bathroom. I ran into the bathroom without asking, did some damage control, and stuffed my underwear full of neatly folded paper towels. I came out with a big smile and bought some water. The post office didn't have tickets to Pompeii either. We were told to just take the metro and buy them at the front gate, so that's what we would do. We tried. I was still hurting and chaffed, but now hydrated and a little more sure of myself than before.

"Do you need to go back to the hostel?" Tim asked.

"We're already down here. I don't want to ruin the day by going back already. It's already evening, and if we go back I won't want to come back downtown again tonight. It's our last night in town."

I still had so much love for Naples. I wanted to go back to the area we were the night before. Tim did too. I couldn't waste experiencing the town one last time, even if it meant I was bloody and my inner thighs were rubbed raw. Two days were not enough, I wanted to live here.

We reached the edge of the alleys filled with food and liquor and sat down next to a metro station to watch the people go by. Most of them were young. Coming out to party, I assumed. Small groups formed of teenagers giggling to each other, or hip couples in their twenties walking past holding hands. They were all incredibly fashionable, in a weird futuristic way. Crop tops, platform shoes, bright hair. It was the epitome of late 2010's fashion before it had really hit stores in America. It was very entertaining. I kept wondering what interesting looks I would see next, and I was never disappointed. I even got to see some nonsensical English sentences printed on shirts, a favorite European find for Tim and me. Some favorites were "Don't mess with the matter, get straight to the point," "Big Star - Live like your dying [sic]," "Fast Run," and "If you can carry the game you can carry the bag."

The sun was setting, so we said screw it and pretty much repeated our first night in Naples. The alcohol helped me forget about my physical situation, but it started getting late, and we still had to prepare for Pompeii, pack, and be out by check-out time. We both wobbled back towards the hill, but this is where I decided walking was not going to "kind of be my thing." At least not tonight. My thighs and legs could take no more. They definitely couldn't take no hill at one in the morning. Instead, we walked back to the metro station and were in our beds before we knew it.

The next morning we were going to Pompeii. The hostel offered its own transportation, but it was cheaper and less limited to just jump back on the metro and go there on our own. And of course, we didn't pay for a tour or even an audio tour. We read up on Pompeii and what to see before getting there and explored on our own, which was much cheaper, although I'm sure we missed out on quite a bit of information.

A rickety metal subway car zoomed through Naples toward Mount Vesuvius and Pompeii. Out of the window, we could see passing houses and neighborhoods, completely surrounded by greenery. In the distance was the ocean glistening in the sunlight, and ahead of us was the mountain. Naples was like a dream. A dream of green mountains, adorable ancient houses, empty oceanfront castles, and €1 to-go beers. The metro train stopped to let people on or off, and a group of men with instruments came on to play music for change. I was familiar with subway busking from spending time in New York, San Francisco, any large city with some sort of subway system really. Normally you don't make eye contact then say sorry when they come around to collect change unless, I guess, you have some to spare. I stared at the window watching the scenery quickly pass, looking in all of the little green yards that backed up against the tracks. The upbeat music paired flawlessly with the passing scene. It was like a movie. I couldn't help but smile. The men put out their hats while passing to the next car and Tim gave them a €1 coin.

We stepped off at the stop for Pompeii and walked a dirt road where men herded us to a ticket window. The men didn't work for Pompeii though, they worked for a private tour company. And the window wasn't for tickets to enter Pompeii, it was for tickets to the private tour. I spotted this and waved Tim on to follow me past, while everyone else lined up. Eventually, some other tourists got the hint and started breaking off as well. We found the *real* line into Pompeii. One line for people going solo, one line for private group tours. In walked half of our metro train buying their second ticket of the day in the private group tour line, with a peppy group leader directing the way. I was eyeing an audio tour poster while in line, and eventually got out and walked up to a window to see how much they were. An €8 extra fee. Times two is too much. We got our regular no-tour tickets for $22 each, and walked through the gates.

Pompeii is the site of an incredibly well preserved ancient Roman town wiped out by one of Mount Vesuvius' volcanic eruptions in 79 AD. The eruption killed thousands, leaving the town abandoned for nearly fifteen hundred years, covered in thirteen to twenty feet of volcanic ash and pumice, and continuing to be buried by multiple layers of various substances for years after. This ash protected and preserved the town, and even its inhabitants, due to the lack of air and moisture reaching it for more than a millennium. The site was rediscovered in 1599 but archaeologists didn't start excavating until 1748. Pompeii's artifacts provide detailed insight into the life of a town existing from 7th or 6th century BC until its demise in 79 AD.

Archaeologists found people and animals frozen in ash just how they had died, many crouching or covering their faces, babies lying helpless on their backs. Belongings still remained where they had been left, including uncovered jars of preserved fruit and loaves of bread. In today's Pompeii you can see remnants of religious temples, bars, bakeries, ornate bathhouses, vacation homes, restaurants, a gymnasium, a hotel, swimming pools, an extensive aqueduct, one of the oldest existing Roman amphitheaters of its kind, brothels, and even the ancient Roman equivalent of a fast food joint. The existing buildings still hold paintings, pottery, kitchen counters, decorative tile, ancient graffiti, and signs.

Wine labels were even found containing the world's earliest known marketing pun "Vesuvinum," its name being a mix of Vesuvius and "vinum," Latin for wine. Pornographic frescoes were removed from early tourism in Pompeii (who's tourism started over two hundred and fifty years prior to our visit), then were moved to and locked up in a "secret museum" in 1821. Existing obscene frescos that didn't get hauled away were locked in cabinets on premises and shown to men, but not women, for an additional fee until the 1960's. Now most of Pompeii's porn sits in the Naples National Archaeological Museum.

I didn't know what to expect. I wanted to see someplace old and ancient, and I definitely got what I wanted here. Fog was rolling over grassy hills, and the still active Vesuvius stood eerily beside us. We made our way through Pompeii's little alleys, were you could peek into someone's house from almost two thousand years before. I looked down at the mosaic floor tiles inside of a doorway, which pictured a wild boar being taken down by dogs, from at the very least 1,937 years ago. It was surreal. I wanted to touch it. I couldn't comprehend what these people were like, how they thought, what the world was like back then. Some of this was during the time Jesus would have lived. The volcano is still there. The grass and the plants. I'm sure the scenery has changed, but not by much, I assume? I was back in time.

"And this on the ground is... well... just take a look. Yes, it's what you think it is," a tour group leader said while walking past. Tim and I eavesdropped, stepping in closer to listen, trying to see what was on the ground. There were *oohs, ahhs,* and laughing. The group passed, and we walked over to where they had been standing. There was a penis carved into the stone alley. Ancient dick graffiti. A man... carved a penis... into the sidewalk... during one of the same years parts of the Bible were still being written. More than sixteen years before the Gospel of John and the Book of Revelations existed. Less than fifty-two years after Jesus was baptized. And that is just if the penis was carved toward the end of Pompeii's existence. Some Pompeii frescos dated back to 1 – 45 AD. The penis could have been only a few years younger than Jesus. At the same time Jesus was turning water into wine, some dude was carving a dick into the sidewalk in Pompeii. And I got to see it.

Flowers were blooming, and the clouds started to mist. We took shelter from the sprinkling under some trees by the amphitheater until the clouds passed, which didn't take long. I pulled some chips from my bag then walked across a small field to the only trash can I could see. Tim followed, and we chatted and shared the snack. The only few other people around were still hiding from the light rain, far from where we were. Or so we thought. Tim turned his back on the trash can and ripped a boisterous, thundering fart. *THHHHRRRRRRPP.* Directly behind him was a hunched over elderly man putting something into the trash can. The man turned and walked back toward the amphitheater without a word or a second glance, while Tim and I couldn't help but buckle over with laughter until tears poured down our cheeks. We continued to cry our way to a little indoor museum, the direction others seemed to go.

We regained our composure just in time to see Pompeii's people frozen in time.

Pliny the Younger had a first-hand account of the eruption from across a nearby bay, writing "A dense black cloud was coming up behind us, spreading over the Earth like a flood. 'Let us leave the road while we can still see,' I said, 'or we shall be knocked down and trampled underfoot in the dark by the crowd behind.' We had scarcely sat down to rest when darkness fell, not the dark of a moonless or cloudy night, but as if the lamp had been put out in a closed room. You could hear the shrieks of women, the wailing of infants, and the shouting of men; some were calling their parents, others their children or their wives, trying to recognize them by their voices. People bewailed their own fate or that of their relatives, and there were some who prayed for death in their terror of dying. Many besought the aid of the gods, but still more imagined there were no gods left, and that the universe was plunged into eternal darkness forevermore." His uncle, Pliny the Elder, died while trying to help stranded victims.

It started to rain by the time we reached the exit. People were piling into a room, which once was the house of Vettii. Most of it was roped off so we couldn't get close enough to touch the walls. In this room hung twelve different panels of mythological scenes in various styles found throughout Pompeii's history. The house of Vettii is believed to have belonged to two former slaves, possibly brothers. Other famous frescos still resided in Pompeii, such as *Venus in the Shell* and *Flora*. Once the rain died down we made a run for it, past some postcard stands, back down the road, and onto the metro.

The hostel nicely let us keep our bags in the lobby for the day, so we returned back to retrieve them. I was kind of disappointed we weren't staying for another night. I loved being in Naples, and even just lounging around the hostel's gardens to relax sounded wonderful. We had to leave though, on to the next city. And the next city, and the next city, and the one after that. Fourteen countries in, five to go. On top of that, we would be revisiting a few new parts of countries we had already passed through.

We hopped right back on the metro with our bags, to the central station where we would take a bus down Italy to a city called Bari. Not to hang out, but to get on a ferry. As I sat waiting for our bus, I noticed a dick scribbled across a wall of graffiti. I chuckled. Some things never change.

Bari: Seventeen Hours at Sea

Forget Bari... we were going to Greece! Greece was a big one for me. Any time someone asked me what I was looking forward to most, I would say Greece. I didn't even know exactly what Greece would be like, but it was exciting as an art history nerd, it looks beautiful in pictures, I hear they have an awesome punk scene, and I know they have great food. To get to Greece, we first spent one night and less than a day in Bari so we could take a seventeen-hour ferry to Patras, Greece. The plan was to spend a few days relaxing and exploring Patras before taking a three-hour bus ride to Athens, where we would spend another week.

When we stepped off the bus in Bari the sun had already gone down and we had no place booked to stay. The first thing we found while walking aimlessly in a random direction was a castle. The castle had a deep moat which now held a neatly trimmed grass lawn. There was no bridge to sleep under, and every part of the grass was exposed if viewed from the right angle. Getting into the moat also meant lowering ourselves down a large wall. We were still in the town center and I didn't like the look of it as a sleeping spot. It was too early to go to sleep, and too many lone wandering people were circling the castle after dark. I wanted to be hidden, so we decided to keep walking.

We were right on the ocean and a paved boardwalk led down the coast for miles. Between the boardwalk and the water was a stone half-wall and large jagged rocks. We hoped that if we just kept walking, maybe at some point there would be a secluded beach area to sleep on. The sidewalk winded through a hip-looking neighborhood. Trash cans lined the streets for trash day and the smell filled the air. We sat down on a bench to rest and see if maybe we could get some WIFI to check a map to see where we were and what was around. A couple sat on the bench next to us and asked us where we were from.

"We're from California," I answered back.

"Oh, so you smoke weed?" he asked, in broken English. I laughed.

"Actually, I don't, but plenty of people in California do."

"Yes, there is supposed to be good weed," the man smiled. His partner remained silent, I assume she didn't speak English. We said goodbye and kept walking aimlessly along the water, toward a hopeful sleeping spot.

The sidewalk rounded a corner and we heard echoing live music. As we walked toward the music, we started to recognize the songs. It was Guns n Roses, but it didn't sound like Axl Rose singing.

"Woah, it sounds like the singer of ACDC. Which is who is singing for Guns n Roses now, and aren't they touring Europe??" I thought aloud. Up on the hill in front of us were stadium lights filling the night sky. "I bet they're playing right there."

"Maybe," Tim responded. We walked on silently, bored, and tired. I just wanted somewhere comfortable to go. Anywhere. "It does sound like the singer of ACDC," Tim thought aloud after a while had passed. "I wonder if you're right."

"It has to be. Let's follow the music. Maybe we can sneak in. That will give us something to do!"

We stayed on the path, as it continued to weave along the coast. We rounded another corner and right in front of us was a small waterfront bar. The bar had one open wall, with people drinking and dancing both inside and outside of the small square building. And there they were. The Guns n Roses cover band.

When Tim and I first started dating, we went out to the local fair where we ended up seeing who we decided to call "Not Journey." It was a Journey cover band, who we watched while taking full $10 drinks off of tables, abandoned by dancing soccer moms who already had one too many. The stumbling couples and bad dancers would pay for a full beer, take a sip, and then fifteen minutes later buy another forgetting they already had one. One man's waste is our free beers. And now, we had officially seen "Not Guns n Roses."

We stood across the street watching for a few minutes, then continued our aimless walk. Instead of walking away from the city life, toward somewhere quiet and empty to sleep, we walked right into the downtown area. The sharp rocks along the water turned into boat docks and on the other side was another huge castle turned into a museum, with a small park along the water below it. We scoped out around the castle, looking for a hidden nook to sleep in. The park was pretty open in terms of visibility from the street, but it was mostly empty and had a few dark spots against the castle wall. It would have to do if we couldn't find anything better. We wandered into the downtown area and sat on a bench to watch people coming in and out of bars. After an hour or two we retreated to the park to pull out our sleeping bags and drift off to sleep.

"GO! GO! Get out of here!" Tim yelled. I shot up out of my sleeping bag to see a dog holding a ball over us. Across the park stood its owner, scared to death. He had thrown the ball to our sleeping area, scaring the crap out of Tim, who woke up being hit by the ball and then opened his eyes to see a huge dog running toward him. This in turn scared the man who didn't see us sleeping in the park. The man called his dog, who clumsily bounded back across the grass, as he still stood there confused by our presence.

It was too early. The sun was out and the weather was nice, but we were shaded by a tree and I wanted badly to pull my sleeping bag over my head and go back to sleep. People were starting to stare though, and I was worried one of them might call the cops. We packed up our things and found a new spot in the sun, away from playing dogs, leaning against our backpacks to nap in the park like normal people for a few more minutes. We still had most of the day before we had to board our ferry. We had no food or drinks, so the goal of the day was to find supplies to stock our bags with.

We walked all over downtown, which was mostly nice restaurants and designer clothes stores. Even the coffee shops were all fancy cafés. We went in one anyway to use the bathrooms and compose ourselves, and mow down pastries and drinks. Our day was spent reading books in a large park, where one of us could watch the bags while the other could leave to wander in search of a grocery store, or any cheap food. We even stopped to ask people on the street, and no one knew of a nearby grocery store. Eventually, we wandered upon a little market where I bought mass amounts of mixed crackers and nuts, a cheap bottle of wine, and sandwich supplies. I ended up settling on a veggie burger from Burger King for lunch, where I pocketed mustard packets for our sandwiches. I walked back toward Tim, down a street of pristine designer stores on either side, shoving the veggie burger into my face with ketchup and mustard juices running in a stream down my hands and arms.

I had done plenty of sailing in recent years, and a few ferries, speedboats, and a fishing boat or two throughout my life, but at this point I had never been out to sea for seventeen hours straight. Out at sea doesn't bother me, what does is the increasing amount of motion sickness I get as I age. To make things worse, my anxiety tends to make me feel or assume I am getting nauseous even if I'm not. The thought of being on a seventeen-hour passenger-boat ride sounded hideous. The Internet wasn't offering me any advice on what to expect, so I went in hoping for the best.

We boarded the ferry alongside couples with dogs, families with campers, a few twenty-something American, Canadian, and British backpackers, and semi-trucks – one even filled with cows. The ship's decks had awesome views, there was enough room to not feel much motion, and the common rooms were exquisite. There was anything you could have wanted on board, if you could afford it, and honestly the prices weren't much higher than those at a restaurant. Some of the families, backpackers, and truck drivers settled into their private rooms, while the rest claimed seating in the common areas to later sleep on. This was the cheapest ticket option, which we took advantage of.

Instead of running inside to battle families of ten over cushions to later slumber on, we headed to the bar and ordered a round of expensive beer (when in... or near Rome?). We then relaxed outside on the upper deck with some young travelers from Michigan, waiting for the last of the passengers and trucks to board. Two hours later our ship took off and we moved inside, where our cozy common room quickly turned into something more along the lines of a Chuck E Cheese's.

Families scattered their bags across every couch-like seat to claim it for hours, without even being in the room. I kneeled between two luggage bags used to reserve a sleeping spot on the empty padded bench spanning the length of the entire room to plug my tablet into the only empty outlet I could see, then went back to my chair. Just by doing this, one of the parents glared at me and a small child ran to tattle on me to their mother. Babies screamed blood-curdling shrieks, and older children threw tantrums around us. After an hour of trying to read and write in Daycare Land, Tim and I scooted over to the "bar," which was really just the same thing as the front lobby we had been in, except bigger and with alcohol, food, more adults, and almost no children. We reunited with our Michigan travelers who were with another group of backpackers on board, and went back to drinking our wine.

Rain had been pouring since we left the dock at Bari so hanging out in the moonlight outside wasn't really an option. There was a dark room with movie theater style seating designated for couch sleepers to squeeze into for a slightly more comfortable night at first come first serve. After spending most of the night drinking my wine, I decided to do the responsible thing of squeezing into a corner in the dark room to attempt a few hours of sleep.

People were sprawled out over every seat, leaving no piece of cloth uncovered in an attempt to claim as much as they could as their own. I found an area of floor behind the very back row of seats next to a shelving area for luggage. I took off my skirt and shoes and crawled into my sleeping bag in the rest of my clothes and leggings, pulled out my inflatable pack pillow, and tied a bandana around my eyes. I got a lot of weird looks for some reason, being the only person on the floor, but it was comfortable for the time being. Comfortable for about thirty minutes until a loud *BANG* launched me out of my sleep. We were in a lightning storm, in the middle of the ocean, in some sea I wasn't familiar with. I'm fairly confident in the vessels humanity has engineered, which have been getting people where they need to go every minute of every day across all parts of the world with little issue compared to the vast number of successful voyages, flights, train rides, or whatever else. But I had to admit that my anxiety went through the roof. I pulled my bandana back over my eyes and tried to fall back to sleep without thinking about what drowning in a cold sea might feel like.

Two hours later the lights came on and a voice came over the ship's speakers telling us to prepare for departure. *What?* I thought, while peering out of my bandana and waking my phone to check the time. We weren't supposed to arrive at four in the morning. I jumped up along with the other sleeping passengers and started shoving my things back into my backpack. I walked up, backpack on, eyes puffy and half closed, to Tim who was sleeping in the bar area and poked him awake.

"Are we here?" I asked.

"No, go back to sleep. There is one other stop before ours."

Great, I thought. I got up for nothing. Although I guess I had no other choice. It was either get up or be trampled, since my sleeping floor was against the baggage shelf. At least when returning back to the room which was now dark again, there were plenty of seats to choose from. I followed the other passengers' example by taking an entire row of seats to myself.

Patras: Efcharistó

We had a nice place to ourselves in Patras for a few days, so in true siesta form, we'd relax throughout the heat of the day then go out to explore around 9 PM, when the city came alive. Not long after arriving in town, I had heard of a candlelight vigil for the Orlando nightclub shooting which had happened two days prior. An unfortunate event where a man opened fire in a gay nightclub in Orlando, Florida, killing forty-nine people and leaving another fifty-eight wounded. It seemed we had received quite a bit of bad news taking place in both America and various European countries while we were traveling. Some form of terrorism was fairly rampant on both continents. We were usually alone in our feelings of sorrow for those who had passed in these recent events, so I felt the vigil would be a good way to meet other people who had similar feelings. Even if we didn't chat with any locals about Orlando, it couldn't hurt to go light a candle in support. We decided we would relax for a bit and shower, then go to the vigil once it started.

Our apartment was owned by a tall, blond, Greek woman in her early 40's named Nina. It was supposed to be a shared apartment, but since no one else would be in the other room we had the place to ourselves for almost a week. She left snacks out and local white wine in the fridge. The place was so nice it was like a fancy hotel, yet extremely affordable since we weren't in much of a tourist destination. Everything was white and there was a balcony on each side of the apartment. The balcony off of the living room looked down onto a main street, with the downtown shopping area to the right and an old cathedral to the left. A brightly colored mural of a woman's face stared up at us from the side of a building across the street. Our place was relaxing and felt like home. We immediately started referring to it as our home. Our apartment.

We got ready to go out at 7 PM and walked the streets, watching stores close and restaurants set up to open. We found the main square, where young people chatted on benches and little kiosks sold snacks, drinks, and magazines. We drifted over to a group of twenty-somethings lighting tea lights and placing them on a rainbow flag inscribed with *ORLANDO* in large letters. A man came up and greeted us, offering us candles to place on the flag. We talked with him for a few minutes then went on to people watch in the square, after lighting and placing our candles.

The more the sun disappeared, the more people would start to come out. Groups of laughing teens, single elderly folk, couples with children, and those surrounding the rainbow flag in the center of the square. I followed my tradition of researching local punk or metal bars, and according to the Internet, there was one about two blocks from the square. We headed over even though it was early for Greece, and of course it was closed. Not only closed but it looked possibly abandoned. Of course the things I find online could always be outdated, but this supposed "rock bar" had posted an event for a music night just a week prior. I really doubt the place went out of business in the last week, and we were there during the listed business hours. We explored and walked a few streets, peeking in closed store windows and talking about the neighborhood gardens and murals. I knew the rock bar had to be open by this time, but we checked once more and it still looked as closed as ever.

Just because the name was ridiculous, we decided to grab a drink at a place we randomly came across called *Cafe "Must" Pub*. It was a tiny building, the only open business on the block, with a glowing white sign and a small closed door. It didn't look inviting at all but I felt I had to see what this place was about. We opened the door and entered the stuffy, hot, dark, candle-lit bar the size of a small room. Three older chain-smoking women turned their heads to look at us, and I swear the record screeched to a stop. Trying not to make anything more awkward, we took a seat at a small table and ordered two of the cheapest types of beer they had available, which they charged us a ridiculously high price for. "Well that backfired," our eyes said to each other from across the table. Smiles peeked through as we tried not to laugh at the situation we had put ourselves in. We then politely left after we had finished our drinks.

We woke the next morning in our lovely apartment, sipped coffee on our balcony, washed our disgusting sleeping bags and hung them out to dry in the hot Patras sun. The drying rack was on the balcony off the kitchen, which hung over other little layered balconies and apartment courtyards, with a background of picturesque mountains in the distance. Our morning ritual became sipping coffee while watching the mountains turn gold in the sunlight. Below us cats on balconies would bat at bugs or fallen leaves.

After lazing the day away watching important Greek documentaries such as Disney's *Hercules* on my tablet, we hit the streets at 9 PM to explore. Again, the retail side of Patras had gone to sleep, yet the sidewalk-lined restaurants were packed to the brim with families watching a soccer game on outdoor TVs. Adults would chat with drinks in hand, cheering for their team from time to time over tables covered in Greek food. Children ran the sidewalks playing tag.

I was determined to try the rock bar again, so we took a dark side street back toward the main square. It was just as deserted-looking as the night before. I tried to peek into the window but the glass was blocked by black paper. There were no open signs. Nothing lit up whatsoever.

We stopped by a little beer and snack tent in the square where a stern elderly woman handed Tim his change. "Efcharistó," he said, to thank the woman. We had heard the Greeks especially appreciate if you try to speak their language, and boy was that right. The woman loudly gasped, and her face lit up as if Tim had just gifted her a free car.

"Wow!" she exclaimed. "Efcharistó," she said back, blushing.

We aimlessly wandered into the darkness, searching for whatever else nighttime Patras had to offer. Flyers for shows and protests started appearing and becoming ever more prevalent as we walked. Then, from down the street we could see the oh-so-familiar sight of a huge black warehouse covered in squatter's rights graffiti. The large steel door was shut, and unfortunately the only Greek word we knew was thank you, so there was no way we could read what the flyers said. We wandered back and decided to try the rock bar one last time. The dark windows and lack of signs sat in front of us at rock bar. *How is this possible?* I thought. Then we did the one thing we probably should have done two nights ago: open the door.

The door swung open and we peeked in through the dark entryway to see a large open space and a lit up bar across the room. No one was there except for the bartender and DJ, who welcomed us in for a drink. The DJ spun Iron Maiden, Judas Priest, Dio, and other similar tunes. Tim was verbally excited for every song, throwing his fist in the air then drumming on the bar to the music, and the DJ kept 'em coming. After our first round he even put on accompanying music videos on a TV mounted on the wall. After finishing two rounds of beer we got up off of our seats to return "home," when the bartender brought over a third round on the house.

We left rock bar buzzed and happy. When we arrived home, we listened to more music and stayed up talking, sipping on our free white wine, playing song after song until 5 AM. We woke up late and packed our things in the heat of the morning, ready for Athens.

Athens: Every Kind of Person, Except Cops

After spending the last few weeks in friendly small towns, we made the mistake of walking into Athens like we owned the place. Typically, when I entered a new big-city metro I had my guard up, side-eyeing every stranger. It wasn't just in new countries, as a woman you learn to act like this in even in your own hometown. Wearing my backpack in public in a tourist city was like wearing a big red target on my back with a neon sign reading "tourist," so I prepared myself by having a constant mental bubble of awareness of my surroundings.

While transferring metro trains midday in Athens, we were suddenly bombarded by a group of five or six men crowding into our subway car. I tried to keep my wits about me but nothing seemed too out of the ordinary, until one man in the back of the car started screaming either "NO" or "GO," and the whole group jumped off of the train before the doors slammed shut and the train sped down the tracks. Tim and I looked at each other and I had a bad feeling in the pit of my stomach. Something was wrong, but I couldn't figure out what. A minute or two later Tim started checking his things. When the men crowded in they shoved into Tim, opening a zipper then minutes later fishing out his wallet before yelling and jumping off the train. They didn't get much cash, and thankfully didn't take his passport, but they got all three of our credit cards and Tim's debit card. This left us with only the few hundred bucks on my debit card as a limited way to pay for things until who knows when. Some of that money in my account was set aside for when we returned back to the states without jobs.

We were renting an apartment from a family for the week, so we departed the metro still feeling confused and mentally shaken while walking over to the man we were meeting, Christos, and his two young boys. I told Christos what had happened then followed him and his sons back to the apartment, while Tim went back to the train station the men jumped off at to search the trash cans for any unwanted things from his wallet they might have ditched.

The apartment was a tiny one-bedroom with a balcony. It was so hot outside that the doors, windows, and blinds had to continuously be kept closed to keep the heat out. There was one stand-alone fan to shuffle the hot air around the apartment. Christos apologized for our situation, offering to loan us money which I thanked him for, yet denied. He showed me how to turn the water heater on if we needed to use it, as his youngest son picked up breakables in the kitchen prompting the older son to tattle on him. The boys were very polite, but barely spoke any English. The elder son, who was about six, asked me in broken English if I spoke Greek and I apologized no. Christos and his boys prepared to leave, opening the sliding glass door and letting the 100-degree breeze into the apartment, which I later closed. When leaving, the six-year-old poked his small round face with thick black-framed glasses back inside to yell "Good noon!" back to me with a smile.

I imagined the city of Athens would be one big ancient tourist destination. I know the country has had its rough times, but I still imagined clean streets and wealthy families eating gelato in the heat, under awe-inspiring ruins along the clear blue ocean. Athens was not like this at all, but again, it had that homey feeling Madrid seemed to have, minus familiar similarities to San Diego.

Our neighborhood was mostly people from the Middle East. The ground was dry, the streets were scattered here and there with trash blowing in the wind, and the heat and sun were relentless. Clotheslines hung from every balcony, including our own. Men smoked cigarettes outside of Middle Eastern markets. Graffiti was everywhere. I walked the potholed alley past the ruins of half of an abandoned building, avoiding a gawking catcaller, to wait outside of the metro station for Tim to emerge. Hopefully with some contents of his wallet. I stole some weak WIFI from Everest Café next to the station to check my credit card out of curiosity. Our cards barely worked in Europe as it was, so I wasn't too concerned about someone trying to get money out of them as long as we could get them suspended within the hour.

Tim found me outside the café, approaching with a disappointed look on his face. I showed him the way to our new home for the next week, as we discussed what we would do about money. The WIFI in our place was slow, and was also our only way of making phone calls. We sat on the phone calling banks and arranging for Tim's credit cards to be sent to Bratislava in a week, and for mine to be sent to San Diego since it was maxed out anyway.

After a few hours of phone calls and hiding from the midday heat, we were somewhat ready to hit the town and see some of Athens at the cooler 4 PM temperature of 102 degrees. While researching things to see in Athens, I noticed a lot of the big squats and sites of protests just so happened to be within blocks of our apartment. We walked down the closest large street towards downtown, past the National Technical University of Athens (Athens Polytechnic), which was also covered in graffiti depicting anarchy signs and random tags. Black anarchist banners hung from windows with messages in Greek. I figured the school must have been abandoned, but in fact it was still an active college and one of the oldest colleges in Greece. It was also known for the Athens Polytechnic uprising of 1973, where students barricaded themselves inside of the school and broadcasted from a pirate radio transmission calling for Athens to rebel against Greece's military dictatorship. Eventually the military broke through the college's gates with a tank, killing twenty-three people. November 17th is a holiday in Greece to commemorate the death of these students.

I had heard through friends who have visited Athens that there are streets you might walk down that will be blocked off by riot cops. This neighborhood was also a few blocks from our place, and its border lands right against the backside of Athens Polytechnic. Exarchia, the neighborhood without police. A community of punks, anarchists, Greek families, immigrants, students, stray dogs, and cats. You can find just about any kind of person in Exarchia, except cops. Exarchia was vibrant. Buildings and alleyways were entirely coated in political graffiti and colorful murals of everything from beautiful artwork to Nazis being stomped. Empty lots were turned into people's parks, complete with protesters' memorials and makeshift coffee shops.

We wandered the alleyways looking for a small park where locals gathered to lounge and drink beer in the evenings. We noticed as we searched for the park that some cross streets bordering Exarchia did have a few riot cops stationed on corners. They weren't there to keep people out, but to keep protesters in. We found our reclaimed park surrounded by bookstores, cafés, and dive bars. The sun set over young people smoking cigarettes, dogs rolling in dry plants, and little old ladies chatting on benches. Tim and I counted our change and bought Greek beer from a snack cart at the corner of the park. The park was just dirt, lined with bushes on one side. Mosquitos buzzed here and there but weren't too obnoxious. The park was dimly lit with the orange glow of street lamps. After a few cold beers in the heat of the night, we walked back to our place to rest.

The next morning I ran to the nearest corner store to buy a few snacks for the kitchen. Juice, breakfast foods, oven pizza, veggies, beer, and gelato. Gelato was all over Europe, but we still yearned for the true secret to gelato we first experienced in Madrid. The yogurt flavored gelato. We craved it. Our eyes scanned for it while passing any gelato cart. It was everywhere before we had fallen in love with it, and of course after we had tasted its glory we couldn't find it anymore. But there it was, in a tub next to the ice cream in an Athenian corner store. I walked back to the apartment and showed Tim the gold I had found. He praised me for my find, yet questioned it as well, since we did not have a freezer. We had a mini-fridge with one of those little iced-over top shelves that are supposed to act as one. The tub of gelato was too tall for the small ice shelf, so I sat it in the fridge surrounded by ice packs. Every day I would switch out the melted ice packs surrounding my gelato with frozen ones, but of course from day one it remained half-melted with a blob of frozen gelato still floating at its core.

Mornings in Athens became a ritual. The radio in the kitchen was set to a pop station which I would turn on after getting out of bed every morning when the heat became too unbearable to continue sleeping. Radio on, pot of coffee brewing, fan moved to the living room, doors and windows shut until the sun went down again. The entire first half of the day was spent hiding from the heat, lazing about the apartment half dressed, with wet washcloths cooled by the fridge draped around our shoulders as an alternative to air conditioning. I'd pour two mugs of coffee topped with a heaping plop of half-melted yogurt flavored gelato. Starbucks had *nothing* on this shit.

The kitchen was brightly colored with orange walls and little bugs would sometimes pop their antennaed heads out of cracks if I didn't clean up after myself fast enough.

The news channel on TV would show stories around the world. Donald Trump, fires ravaging Southern California, Brexit polls, and riots following a gay pride parade in Turkey.

Every day around 3 PM we would pack our day bag with frozen water bottles that sat on the freezer shelf overnight and wander the tourist destinations or recommended city districts before spending our spare coins on beer in Exarchia.

In downtown we found a flea market alongside ancient ruins, scammers trying to tie bracelets on tourists' wrists outside of the train station, and a few punk/metal stores selling records, patches, Hot-Topic-looking clothes, and knock off band shirts. We walked to the top of the Acropolis to enjoy the city views and ancient ruins from the side of the hill, since the entry fee was out of our budget. Later we pet friendly Exarchian stray cats and enticed them with sticks.

One particular day, we emerged from our sweaty lair at 3 PM ready to hit the town and found everything closed. Sunday. Sundays always got us. At least it would give us a good excuse to finally try real Greek food, if we could find on open restaurant. We wandered back into Exarchia to see which cafés remained open and browsed a few menus. A Cretan restaurant caught our eye, and we sat down at a table on the patio under a shady awning. A waitress arrived, setting down two menus, two shot glasses filled with clear alcohol, and a basket of bread, then walked back inside. We stared at the liquor then stared at each other. Was it free? What was it? Was this a local digestif to go with the meal, or a scam where if you breathe on it an extra €100 would be added to the bill? We decided to take our chances and drink our pre-lunch shots. The alcohol ended up being Tsikoudia, or Raki, a Cretan grape-based pomace brandy similar to moonshine, often homemade on the island. And yes, it was free.

We ordered a Greek salad and mixed plate with samples of the different local foods to share. All of the cheese came unpasteurized from local sheep, and it was apparent the vegetables had not yet been tainted by refrigeration. It was the freshest food I think I've ever tasted from a restaurant. The Greek salad was on an entirely different level than what I'd had back home, and I wished it would never end.

We ate our meal then wandered "home," passing closed record stores, and another punk store. A fancy-looking wine store was open, so I popped in to see what they had. Normally fancy wine was out of our budget, but since we got lucky in Portugal, I figured we could try Greece. Bottles of wine covered every wall of the store, with prices at €20 and up, but there were also plastic two-liter bottles of wine for much less. Neither of us had ever seen a plastic two-liter bottle of wine, especially in a fancy wine shop, so we had to try it. We paid a few euros for a bottle, and went home to relax. I sipped on my fairly disgusting two liters of wine as the sun set. Men screamed outside. A lot of them. It made me jump at first, but I figured there must be a soccer game on.

Our last day in Athens was set aside for the beach. We got up at a reasonable hour, borrowed some towels from our temporary home, and walked across town to the above-ground metro. We went past the first beach, second, we just kept on going. If you head out further than other tourists you usually find a better, less crowded spot. A great beach passed with ocean-front bars and we jumped out. There were two beach recliners in front of the water available, so I grabbed them. Tim and I took turns inquiring about drinks and dipping into the warm water.

I bought us beer at the beach bar, but for Tim's round he walked to the snack cart on the street and bought the same beer for half the price. I knew I kept him around for something. I continually drenched myself in the sea just for enough time to soak then slowly dry out in the sun on my chair. One of us had to stay with our stuff, and Tim was hell-bent on being in the ocean so I didn't mind just consuming the breeze, sunshine, and cold bottle of Mythos from my chair.

A little girl wearing only bathing suit bottoms gave the older boys stink-eye, then held up a water-gun, peering through its plastic scope with one eye. *What a little badass*, I thought. Two women dressed like *Jersey Shore's* Snookie and Jwoww sauntered across the beach dragging a small Chihuahua behind them. A waiter followed closely behind, his arm outstretched with a tray carrying their drinks. I watched the children from time to time and I watched the women, slathering themselves in tanning oil then each taking turns photographing each other posing sexy in the waves. They were the most glamourous-looking people on the beach, although also the most awkwardly tipsy. I stared at my pale hairy legs, which were actually a bit tanned, and turned onto my stomach, closing my eyes. It was refreshing to see so many variances in femininity and woman-hood just in the last five minutes. The glamorous LGBT women, the little badass with the squirt gun dominating the boys, and then me - the hairy, tattooed, beer drinker.

I got up to float in the ocean one more time before leaving. Parents threw their laughing children into the air and they splashed down into the water. An old man stared at me as if his life depended on it. I stared back, hoping he would let up but it only made him smile. I tried to ignore him and sink further down into the water, hiding whatever it was he had to stare at, but he continued moving closer and then spoke.

"Why?" he pointed to parts on his body where I had tattoos.

"Ah, tattoos?" I asked.

"Yes, why?"

I rolled my eyes. "Because I wanted to." I let myself float towards shore, avoiding any more awkward conversation. He continued to stare and smile. I went back to my chair and we packed our bag and towels to return "home."

The next morning was a race in 100-degree weather to find a place to print our boarding passes with the leftover change we had. We also had to clean up, pack, and figure out the metro train to the airport. The original plan was to bus, hitchhike, or ride-share our way to Istanbul and then Croatia but it just wasn't a good time politically to visit Turkey, and Croatia was going to be a hard one to reach, taking days to get to by bus. We just didn't have the time. One and a half months was all we had left to cram in as many countries as we possibly could and somehow make it back to London for our flight back to Philadelphia.

We got back on the underground train for the first time since getting robbed, and the crowd packed in. I took off my backpack and smooshed it into a corner, practically sitting on it while I held onto a bar. I told Tim to do the same, which he did from the center of the train, surrounded by people on all sides.

A man in his twenties shoved in through the subway door and into a man next to Tim. The man was shifting around uncomfortably, and I tried to watch what he was doing from the reflection in a window. Another man standing next to Tim had the top pocket of his backpack open, but I had no idea if the shifty twenty-something did it while shoving into him, or if the man had left it a few inches un-zipped. If I saw anything I was going to yell, but there was no way I wanted to falsely accuse anyone or put myself in danger.

The young man kept making eye contact with a tall man next to him, I figured they were together. The tall man seemed to be peeking into the backpack and the twenty-something pushed a thick plastic shopping bag against the backpack and was then digging into it. Was he digging into his own bag or using it as a mask to dig into the open backpack? I couldn't tell and I was shaking. I watched as closely as I could and I couldn't see anything being retrieved. The hand came up with nothing in it, from what I could tell. I knew for a fact something sketchy was going down, but they were being so sly I had no way to prove it or even know for sure what was going on. The doors slid open and it was our stop. Thankfully the man with the backpack was getting off as well and we left the pickpockets behind.

We arrived at the airport barely making it there in time. Our tickets were scanned, then we followed the maze of duty-free-lined paths to our gate, speed walking and out of breath. *Where is security? Is there no security??* I thought. *There is no way. Right? An airport can't just not have security.* I was freaking out. I'm pretty rational when it comes to flying fears, but there had been multiple terrorist attacks since we had been in Europe and we were neighboring a war zone.

I know all airports are different, I had been to at least thirty in the last three years alone, but no security would be a new one for me. We followed the signs to our gate number and there it was. Security! I never in my wildest dreams thought I would be happy to see any form of security. We somehow made it past security and into our gate in time to relax and enjoy an overpriced beer to calm our nerves. I didn't finish mine in time to board, but carried in onto the Ryanair plane anyway.

Bratislava and Cachtice: The Bones of Virgins

Bratislava, our old friend. It was nice to be back somewhere we had been months earlier for a second time. I walked Bratislava like it was my old neighborhood. I knew where the best Lidl grocery store was that carried chili-pepper-infused tofu, I knew where all the hip vegan joints were, yet we still managed to get lost finding downtown from the new hostel we chose.

"I'm BAAACKK. I'm BAACK in Bratislava agaiin," I sang as Tim looked back at me and shook his head.

We were finally back in wonderful weather with cool and refreshing air. We checked into our hostel, then went out for fried cheese and veggie burgers then came back to the hostel for happy hour. There was a lush green porch with water misters and wandering baby kittens. It was open for coffee and beer during the day, then an underground cave bar would open for drinks at night. The cave bar was small, but nice and had that earthy wet-dirt smell to it. There was a "fight racism" sticker on one of the draft beer handles and all of the hostel workers who worked the bar were friendly.

We listened to a conversation between a young Irish woman who had already had too many shots and some young American nerds trying hard to woo her with facts about California. It's always awkward for that to happen around us because we want to butt in, but don't want to be weird. It's also hard to not butt in and be weird when you've rarely heard an American accent, or even any kind of English accent, in months. Tim ended up joining the awkward conversation. I took a Borovicka shot while *Pump Up the Jam* came over the stereo, then went off to bed.

The bedroom was full and stuffy. I scaled the massive windowsill in the dark, trying to yank the window open for some air without slipping to my death or kicking a sleeping person in the face. After accomplishing the task, I threw my things in a locker and snuggled up under my cheap sheet as the smell of feet drifted out of the newly cracked window at the foot of my bunk.

I woke in the morning to a room full of people. Stinky shoes, messy beds, a slight breeze from the window, and an angry stranger in the corner complaining to a friend about losing her towel. I hadn't showered since first arriving in Athens, almost a week prior, and couldn't bear going another day with multiple days of sweat and sunscreen caked to my body. Showering in Greece was pointless since it was over 100 degrees in the day, and only slightly cooler at night. Even if I did shower I would be a sweaty mess the minute my body left the cold water. Thankfully, Bratislava was nice and cool. I could shower and probably even stay clean for another week, if I wanted to.

I grabbed my towel, clean clothes, and toiletries and booked it to the only bathroom I knew of in the hostel. For some reason the whole ground floor seemed to have only one bathroom. Not the typical hostel bathroom with multiple separate toilet and shower stalls, but one bathroom equipped with one toilet and shower in the same room, like you would find in a regular home. Just one for multiple large rooms packed with people to share. I wasn't sure if that was possible for a hostel, but I wasn't taking any chances in losing it in my contemplation either. As soon as I shut the bathroom door and picked up my toothbrush, I heard my roommate who was complaining about her towel now cursing the fact her shower had been taken right from under her. I mean, I didn't mean to, but I was disgusting and had a train to catch in one hour. I never saw her again that morning, so either she went out dirty, or found a hidden bathroom.

After my shower I enjoyed two cheap lattes in a row in the hostel's garden. I sipped my coffee and browsed the Internet while kittens batted my spoon. There were so many kittens. A woman entered the garden and started picking them up one by one to give them shots. It was nice to see that someone was taking responsibility for them. When Tim got out of the shower he called his bank to inquire about one of our credit card replacements being possibly lost in the mail, then we ran to catch our train to Cachtice.

It took three trains through Slovakian countryside to arrive in Cachtice. Why we were headed there made locals shake their heads. Either that or they had never heard of it. We were headed to castle ruins in the small town an hour and a half from Bratislava to see where the infamous Elizabeth Bathory once ruled and died. Died walled into a section of her own castle after being convicted of murder. Legend has it, she stole virgin girls from local villages to stay young by bathing in their blood. They say she was convicted of murdering eighty or more young women in the castle. Some claim the number to be over six hundred.

It turns out Bathory's story was half true. She really did murder women, but due to 18th century gender roles, it was believed a woman could not murder for sheer pleasure. There had to have been another motive. The assumption was she must have been murdering out of vanity. Eventually it was proven via first-hand accounts that she was killing for fun, but the legends of a countess who bathed in the blood of virgins was such a good story it stuck until present day. Some used the story to denounce female vanity. The myths behind Elizabeth Bathory's killings spread so far and wide, they were even thought to influence modern vampire films and literature, including *Dracula*. Admission was outrageously cheap and the rumors were creepy and intriguing, so why not check it out, whatever the truth may be?

Our last train of the three was rickety, un-air-conditioned, and for some reason honked every few minutes. It dumped us in a field at an empty barred up building next to the tracks with a big blue and white CACHTICE sign on the outside. Not only did it slip our minds to look into train times or tickets for how to get back to Bratislava, but it looked as if there was now no way to do so. And to be honest, we didn't even know how to get to the castle. All we knew is it was supposedly twenty minutes walking from the station. It was 3 PM and we had only a few hours to find the castle and explore the premises before it closed, and who knows how we would get back to Bratislava afterward.

Could the train station open again? Or maybe a bus was still running? Tim was half-jokingly pointing out places we would be sleeping that night, while I was thinking about where we could hitchhike from. Sleeping outside in Cachtice would have been fine, except for the fact I was in a skirt, we had no water, and all of our stuff was in our hostel which was paid up for the night. Who could have passed up a chance to sleep in Elizabeth Bathory's haunted torture castle though, right? Just kidding. We had no time for worrying, we had to find the castle or else our trek out of town would have been a waste. Either that or we really could be stuck sleeping in an old torture chamber.

We wandered toward the main road, well, the only road, and found a sign with a castle image and an arrow. We walked as quickly as we could past small houses, a little cemetery, a blind turn with no sidewalk, and a castle wall surrounded by rolling green forest hills. The sun was out and we were sweating. We assured ourselves there must be a gift shop with water once we made it.

Another sign pointed toward the right, down a small dirt residential road. One yard had turkeys in it, others dogs, chickens, and children playing. The road went up, so up we went. As the road got steeper there were fewer houses and more trees. We were going into the forest and the road walk became a full-on hike - in the heat with no water. It seemed to go forever and at times we wondered if we were going the right way. I was serious about hitchhiking if a car came driving up the road, but we only saw them coming down. A group of school children came down the road and I was glad to see the sight of other humans. The dark bushes had been shaking and crunching and I was worried I might come face to face with another boar like it did riding my bike out of Vienna. Up and up we went, from the trees back into the sun.

By the time we saw castle walls we were miserably sweaty. We practically crawled to the entrance, Tim with his shirt off and hung over one shoulder. We approached the ticket booth a hot mess. I was starting to question again why I had even showered. We paid the entrance fee and ignored the weird looks we were receiving and went straight for the shade. The view from the castle was absolutely amazing. Pine trees and wildflowers everywhere, and in one spot you could see down to a small remote town next to a river where children played in an above-ground pool. We were very jealous. Both of the pool, and the fact that they got to grow up in what resembled a Thomas Kinkade painting.

We found a creepy underground area of the castle to cool off in and drink our one large, warm beer we for some reason carried up the hill in our day bag. I was trying not to think of how many young virgin's skeletons were buried under the dirt I was sitting on. After somewhat composing ourselves, we went to take in the views and explore the ruins. Not much of the castle was left to explore, but there was a second story platform overlooking the small, deep tower Elizabeth Bathory spent the rest of her life sealed up in until she died there on August 21st, 1614. Four years after she was convicted. An opening in the brick wall remained where her servants could slip her food. At the bottom of the tower laid a goofy plastic Halloween skeleton to add a bit of spookiness.

Before leaving we bought some lukewarm water from the gift shop, asking first if it was carbonated. Europe loves their carbonated water (spicy water as I call it, or in Spain "agua con gas"), and for some reason I swear it's the only kind you can buy in Hungary and Slovakia. On our bike trip it felt like a never-ending cruel joke being played on us. We started the trek back down the hill and cracked open our water bottles excited to finally get hydrated. And what do you know? Carbonation.

One thing the gift shop cashier did help us with was informing us of a train coming in two hours. We raced back down the hill, past the turkeys and chickens, past the castle wall blind turn, where this time we noticed a hidden sidewalk so we wouldn't have to run from oncoming traffic. We went back through the neighborhood and to the train station to wait. It was still barred up, but I didn't care. A train was coming and I'd rather have to talk my way out of a ticket than sleep in the field. The train came and had only two cars with no connecting passenger doors between them. The first one had a train worker on it, so we took the back car.

When we stopped at a station to transfer to the bigger train (and buy tickets this time) Tim ran to a store to grab us cold water. He came back and I asked "con gas?"

"I swear I asked," he replied. It popped and sizzled with carbonation as he twisted the cap, and we laughed.

"It's the only water they have here," I came to conclude. I figured it might feel satisfying since it was cold, but as I described to Tim, "It's like drinking cold sand!"

Krakow: I Spent More Money Having a Home-less Person Teach Me Polish

We said goodbye to Bratislava for the second time, and walked a few blocks to the central station to catch a train to our sixteenth country, Poland. There was a small snack kiosk between the hostel and the train station, which a hostel worker referred to as the Blowjob Box. The nickname was given after she sent a guest there one night for snacks and he saw a little more going on inside the window than a person trying to hustle Doritos.

We passed the BJ Box and arrived at the train station confused as ever. I was feeling beyond sluggish from having a few drinks in the cave bar the night before. All I wanted was to be able to nap on the train for the rest of the day, and find both something to eat and a large bottle of non-carbonated water before doing so. Before food and water were an option, we needed to get tickets for a train.

We had missed the early train we were planning on taking by minutes, and according to Tim it was the only train of the day to Krakow. I told him that had to be wrong, trains were leaving all the time. There had to be one we could get on, even if we had to transfer. He stood in the slow-going ticket line while I used my pocket change on two giant cold bottles of water, and returned to him in the same place in line.

After waiting a few minutes longer we arrived at the front of the line and the woman told us she couldn't help us. She didn't say why, she just told us we had to move over to the next line because she couldn't get us tickets. This didn't help our frustration and feelings of helplessness. After waiting again at the following ticket window, the woman seemingly understood where Poland was and mapped out a journey for us to arrive there. The tickets were confusing, and a little pricey, but at least we had them. Tim and I split ways to buy food, then found our way onto our train to Poland.

Some trains have private rooms that can be awkward to find a spot in. People shut the doors, close the curtains, and stretch their belongings across every seat just to keep the room as their own, even though they didn't pay for a private sleeping cabin. This makes it awkward for more people to find seats as the train fills up with passengers. You either have to pull an *F you, this is my train too,* open the curtains and butt into their personal space, or split up your group to squeeze into any open seat across the train in various, friendlier-looking rooms. Tim and I boarded when the train was fairly empty so we had a room to ourselves. I tried to be accommodating to other passengers. I left the curtains open, I kept my belongings pushed to one side, but I really, really needed a nap. I took out my pillow and stretched out across three seats.

As we stopped in various other towns, new passengers would board but usually skip our cabin. As it started to fill up, a man around our age opened our door and took a seat. Waking to his presence, I scrunched my body like a caterpillar from three seats to two, making sure I didn't take up too much space, even though he took a seat across from me near Tim. I woke again to our new train-mate and Tim chatting, then sat up to join the conversation. His name was Richard and he was backpacking Europe. Richard was about my size, a fairly small guy with shaggy black hair swept over his face and a light Scottish accent.

Still groggy, I tried to be as friendly as Richard was. Most other backpackers found us odd. We were older than most of them by about ten years, covered in tattoos, dirty, long-haired weirdos in band shirts. People definitely enjoyed our company if we ended up talking, but I'm sure most didn't find us very approachable. Richard was different. Richard talked to everyone. He paid homeless men to teach him the basics of local languages, which he kept in a notebook he would pull out and study in his spare time. He talked to anyone who sat next to him, whether he spoke their language or not. We definitely hit it off with Richard. Not long after first meeting we were crying-laughing, tears streaming, joking about Australians and their lack of censorship. We talked about train cabin hoarders and Richard mentioned noticing me make room for him even though I was taking up three seats.

Our train stopped and we got out to transfer to our second train, which Richard was doing as well. He too had a hostel booked in Krakow for a few days. I grabbed a coffee in the train station that came out to sixteen dollars. My eyes widened before letting out a sigh of relief, realizing we had changed currencies again. Tim, Richard, and I boarded the next train with a shy teenage Czech girl joining us in our new train cabin. Richard of course had to talk to her, pulling out his notebook to jot down language tips.

The girl giggled as Richard tried his best to pronounce new words. In broken English she asked each of us where we were from.

"Aberdeen."

"California."

"California?!" she exclaimed, as her face lit up. Immediately she switched to a more serious tone, "Are you voting for Donald Trump?"

"No," Tim and I laughed.

Soon the Czech girl went on her way, and a girl from Australia took her place.

We arrived in Krakow and said our goodbyes, exchanging contact information before parting ways and watching Richard panic to find his wallet, which he almost lost for the third time on his Eurail trip.

Our hostel was between Krakow's Jewish district and Wawel Royal Castle. The buses seemed confusing, so we walked across town to find where we were staying on foot. The hostel had a nice front room with a nicer looking bar, which for some reason remained closed the entire time we were there. We walked up to the sixth floor and found our large, cluttered, dark room, whose beds were now at full occupancy. The one shared table in the middle of the room was filled with people's things. Chip bags, tourist maps, and a glass skull filled with green liquor.

We laid in bed for a bit to cool off from the long walk, then hit the town to explore, after confirming Tim's lost credit card would now be sent to us in Poland. While looking for punk bars online, I found a so-called socialist bar in the Jewish district and a literal underground punk bar that was hosting a show the next day. We headed out for a drink at the socialist bar, which was said to be covered in old propaganda from the communist era, and have an air-conditioned underground room. It was one of the oldest bars in the area.

We found the bar down an alley. It was dark inside and the air was thick with cigarette smoke. Men played darts by the door. The front of an old car hung on a wall, and an entire GBH album played over the stereo, making me feel right at home. We walked up to the counter which was filled with locals and asked the skinhead-looking man running the bar for a beer. Of course by asking, I mean we picked an interesting looking tap and pointed to it. We chose a dark corner away from the bar and read the walls, talking with each other while enjoying the music. I wanted to see the underground room but it was sectioned off by a velvet rope. Maybe it was used for storage? After a while men started entering the bar and going down the spiral staircase. Maybe it was open now? The rope was hanging off of its clip so I walked over and peeked down. Two groups of men sat around wooden tables, smoking cigarettes and playing poker with cash on the table. I felt it was best we remained on our couch upstairs.

The next day we did our tourist duty of wandering the old town. The weather was warm, perfect for exploring touristy trinket markets and a farmer's market down a main street. We bought large purple tomatoes and walked while eating them like apples. For lunch we stopped in for a vegan kabob that actually had fake meat on a spindle. My kabob sandwich was giant and delicious.

It was time for the show to start at the underground punk bar. I checked the Internet to get the details, but a note said the bands had canceled due to their tour van breaking down. We figured people might show up at the bar to hang out anyway, so we went to check it out.

We walked past the castle and back into the old town area. The address for the bar brought us to a small shopping center with tourist stores and offices. I was confused. There was no venue here. Where was this bar, in the post office? There was a walkway between stores so we followed it, scanning the walls for addresses. Down the alley to the right was a propped open door with nothing inside but an ancient-looking staircase leading underground. The old sloped ceiling and walls were made out of stones and covered in band posters and flyers. This must be the place.

While descending down the stone steps, the hot air immediately turned cool and wet. It had that wet-dirt smell, looking and feeling like an old castle dungeon. We were so close to the castle too, I wondered if maybe it was part of a dungeon at one time. We entered a small room and kept walking, entering a smaller room with a rounded ceiling and a bar. There was an entrance into another matching room filled with booths. A man with a mohawk sat in one of the booths, laughing with his friends. We sipped a drink or two, listening to Iron Maiden playing over the speakers, then eventually retreated back to our messy room.

One of my top European museums to visit was Auschwitz. I know it's morbid, but it's history. Sure, seeing a gas chamber in person sounded like a panic attack waiting to happen, but I still wanted to see Auschwitz. Encountering such a nightmarish moment in history that I had only read about before would of course be scary and depressing, but I still wanted to witness the memorial to these people who lived and died during the holocaust. I had read a few days before that Auschwitz was free if you weren't doing a group tour. I decided we would take advantage of that, and go at our own pace instead of with a group.

We woke up early and got ready to board our bus but I was having an issue getting the information I needed about entering. Then, last minute, I found out we still needed reservations which now were completely booked for days on end. We had to decide whether to skip eating breakfast and lunch to jump on a bus out of town and arrive knowing there was a good possibility we wouldn't be let on the waiting list, or not go at all. We ran out of the hostel door to try making our bus, arguing along the way.

Two blocks in I stopped. I was overwhelmed, and I was upset. I didn't want to make any more decisions and I felt the day was already ruined. I was sad about missing Auschwitz with it being so close, but we both knew it would be better to go eat some lunch and try to make it another day, if we ever found ourselves back in Poland again. Instead of Auschwitz we visited a few sites around the Jewish quarter and walked to Schindler's factory.

Tim received a message from Richard asking if we wanted to go out for drinks, so we met him outside of a café and went to try some of the shot bars Krakow was known for, after first dragging Richard back to the socialist propaganda bar for a beer. At the next bar, the bartender sat out a line of shot glasses, pouring different mixtures into each one. One with lemon juice, one with milk, one with red liquor, one completely clear. We shared each shot, passing and sipping, describing the tastes and which we liked best. After, we walked two blocks through a square with people everywhere and music playing. The three of us walked into another shot bar and ordered more.

"I'll have chocolate cake," "I'll have banana split." The place was packed and the sun hadn't even set yet.

We spotted a table with four seats only occupied by one, and asked the man if we could join his table. He was about our age, with dark skin, glasses, and shoulder length braids wrapped in a colorful scarf. He looked up from his book and let out a giggle, then said, "Sure, yeah no problem," with the clearest American accent I had heard in who knows how long. All three of us did a double take.

"Where are you from?" we asked simultaneously.

He giggled again, "I'm from Canada, what about you?" He put down his book and we chatted, sipping our shots. Each of us talked about where we had been and where we were going.

Tim, Richard, and I finished up and stood to leave. Our new friend Ezra remained seated, looking a little sad he was going to be left alone again with his book.

"We're gonna head to a few more bars, if you'd like to join?" I asked.

"That would be great!" he responded, shoving his book into the backpack at his side.

The four of us wandered, discussing which direction to go. We passed an Alkohole, the Polish liquor store name Tim and I found amusing, and each bought a beer to go drink along the river. The sun went down and we sat on a grassy hill over the water laughing and talking politics for over an hour. We were ready to venture on again but all of us had to pee. Bad. Tourists were everywhere so we couldn't just find a bush. Right next to us was a fancy restaurant on a ship. Nicely dressed couples would walk up the ramp, talk to the host, and continue onto the ship. Richard decided to walk on and see if he could make it to the bathroom without them noticing he wasn't a customer.

We watched from the grassy river bank as he walked up the ramp, past the host, and into the inside of the ship. After about ten minutes we still hadn't seen him, so Ezra and I decided to give it a try ourselves. We walked up, smiled at the greeter, and kept walking. Candlelit tables lined the deck with people eating expensive-looking plates of steak and fish. We walked down the stairs into the inside of the boat which was filled with more tables and waiters bustling about with plates of food. Down a small hallway near the stairs were two bathroom doors and a line of people waiting for them. Richard exited one door, waved, and continued outside as we joined the line.

The bathrooms were immaculate and adorable. I tried to pee fast, since people were waiting, and then got stuck inside the bathroom. I was trying my hardest to get the sliding wood door to roll open again as Ezra laughed at me from the outside, then tried to help. We walked back past all of the fancy dinner tables and left the ship.

Tim and I led the group back to the literal underground-underground punk bar to show them what we had found. I knew it probably wasn't their thing, but both of them definitely seemed like adventurous types, so if anything I was sure they'd be happy to try something different. We found the shopping center, followed the hall, then found the open door to the spooky ancient staircase lined with posters. We descended into the dungeon-esque room clouded in cigarette smoke and sat at a table across from the bar. We talked and laughed some more, and after a drink or two we decided to leave. I felt I had drank enough and wanted to get some sleep before we left Poland in the morning, knowing already I was going to have a rough time. Ezra seemed like he was in the same boat. We all said goodbye, as I walked back to the hostel, Ezra to his, and Tim and Richard went to try one more bar.

I woke to my phone alarm buzzing, looking around the dark room still feeling drunk. I woke Tim, who seemed to be having a rougher morning than I was, then got up to quickly pack for check out. Even though most of the roommates we started with were gone, the same chips, maps, and skull of liquor remained on the table. *Fuck it. It's obviously been abandoned.* I grabbed a bag of pizza-flavored chips, shoving a handful into my mouth and stuffing the rest of the bag into the side pocket of my backpack. Tim grabbed the mystery skull and chugged it. I gave him a dirty look.

We walked all the way back across town to the train station a literal hot mess. It was first thing in the morning, yet hot out already. We were walking fast and dripping with sweat, yelling things out at each other deliriously. For some reason even bursting into American pop songs.

"I regret chugging... whatever that was," Tim slurred. "My throat has been burning so bad ever since. I don't know what the hell I drank."

We entered the train station and I watched our bags as Tim enquired about tickets to Prague. I was trying to connect my phone to the station's free WIFI when I happened to look across the room to Tim in the long ticket line. *Is he sitting down in line?? How drunk did that damn skull get him?* He came back ten minutes later with our tickets and I asked him why he was sitting in the ticket line. He burst into laughter, "I was petting a dog." He then went on to describe how cute it was. Who knows what the owner thought about a sweaty, drunk bearded man dressed in all black, practically laying on the floor in the train station at their feet to hang out with their dog.

We had no problem finding our way on the subway or metro in any city across Europe, or the United States, but for some reason we struggled hard in non-English speaking passenger train stations. The woman told us to go to platform two but there was no train. She said we had five minutes to make it. Did it leave? We weren't given a departure time. We walked back inside to read the screen. "It must have left. We missed our train. We're screwed," Tim blew up. The words and numbers on the ticket didn't match the screen, nothing made sense. I told Tim to go talk to the lady again. After thirty minutes of getting bounced around to different information desks, we were told again to go wait on the original platform we were told to board on. The sign said the train was late. Then it said it was canceled. Then it said it was late. Two hours later we boarded our train.

The train made us backtrack a bit in order to transfer, back to the station with the coffee I thought I bought for sixteen dollars. We sat on the train platform and I pulled out my jacket to block the wind barreling down the tracks. A worker of the station came out to announce to everyone that our train was running late due to a problem with the tracks. All trains going our direction from the east would be delayed. We sighed and went back inside to buy snacks and drinks from the grocery store inside of the mall attached to the train station. The sun set, the wind tunnel grew even colder, and the mall started shutting down and locking its gates. Everyone waiting for trains sat shivering on the platform, every few minutes getting up to check the screens on the inside of the station then walk back out. Eventually trains started coming down the track but it still took over an hour for that train to be ours. In all, we waited over four hours on the platform.

A group of us cheered when the train finally arrived. We ran on and grabbed seats excited to finally make our way to Prague. I fell asleep on the train and woke up at 1 AM to the train sitting stationary for an unusually long amount of time. A voice came over the speakers and everyone on the train sighed and yelled in anger.

"What happened now?" I asked, for anyone who spoke English to answer.

"We have to get off," a passenger answered back.

Our first glance of Czech Republic was in a tiny old train station in the wee hour of the morning. "Forty-five minutes until a new train will take you," a worker announced. Some passengers wandered the small station, some sat on a bench next to a homeless man. We browsed a small convenience store in the station then sat against a dirty wall, trying to stay awake until the next train came. Out of curiosity I got up and peeked my head out of the station to see what was out on the street, but there was nothing. Just a road and darkness.

An older train with private cabins pulled up and we got on. Tim and I walked from car to car looking for an empty space, preferably one with enough room for us to curl up and sleep on. Every curtain was closed, lights off, and doors shut. We walked the entire length of the small train and found nothing accommodating. There were still plenty of people trying to board the train so we had to walk back again, this time opening all of the doors and curtains. All of us had to find seats so it was tough shit for the room hoarders. After receiving many dirty looks while popping our heads into the doors and curtains, we finally found a cabin that only had one couple stretched out in it.

"Can we sit here?" we asked, "There are no other seats," forcing them to move their bags into the designated bag area. The couple took one side and we took the other, all of us trying to awkwardly stretch out onto our significant others. We talked together for a few minutes then shut the curtains and tried to get an hour or two of sleep, being interrupted every five seconds by newly boarding passengers ripping open the curtain and sliding doors looking for a spot to sit, then moving on.

The sun came up and I hid my face in my sweatshirt hood. The train came to a stop, prompting us and the other couple to throw our things in our backpacks as fast as possible to make it off the train. We walked into Prague's central station at 7 AM, just in time for the morning rush hour. My face was puffy and I was beyond exhausted. The lights were bright and businessmen hurried past with coffee in hand. We sat against a wall by some bathrooms to get WIFI, which we hadn't had access to in about 24 hours, to get the directions to where we were staying. The WIFI was crappy and barely working. Tim thought he had a vague idea of where the hostel was, so we decided to just go try and find it. We walked the station in a circle, already lost. A homeless man stared at us and I gave him a dirty look back. I wasn't in the mood. I don't care if you think I'm some shitty tourist. I'm dirty and I haven't slept. I just want to go anywhere. Anywhere but the crowded train station.

We waited to cross a street and a man in a car honked at us which pissed us off even more. After walking about ten blocks we finally found the street we needed. We walked up and down the street, finally finding address numbers and a sign for the hostel.

In front of us at the front desk were two scrawny young men who had been on the same trains as us.

"You were on that train too?" the front desk person asked.

"Yes, it dropped us off ten hours after we were supposed to be here," I replied, obviously annoyed. They were kind enough to not charge us for the night we missed, and let us check in early to get some sleep.

Prague: I'm Allergic to Dead People

I woke up at noon and took a shower. I was excited for Prague and so happy to be in Eastern Europe again. So far I loved almost all of Europe, but Eastern Europe felt special. The sun was always shining, with weather neither too hot or too cold. The rolling green hills underneath a bright blue sky felt peaceful in a way that the bigger cities like Paris or London just didn't. The little markets felt more personable and authentic than the big tourist shops. And then there were the castles, of course. But those were everywhere in Europe.

Tim and I laced up our shoes and went to explore Prague. We were in search of a nearby ramen place, when we came across a farmer's market. I had my eye on a black onyx necklace, and Tim had his eye on solid metal dice. There were also more purple tomatoes and a man selling his family brewery's beer. We found the ramen restaurant, where I got noodles containing so much black pepper that it was hard to eat. We went back to the market to buy a few things and try the local beer, then ran errands at a neighboring mall before walking through the edge of the historic area. A man in a tourist shop was adamant about giving Tim and I plain rubber bands, telling us to wear them around our wrists and snap them if we ever need good luck. We found a well-known absinthe bar and did our tourist duties of sipping on absinthe with dry ice pouring fog out of the ice water. We wandered the cobblestone paths and drank a beer next to a Jesus statue covered in gigantic black spiders. Swans floated down the river as the sun set, with Saint Vitus Cathedral towering at the top of the hill on the other side of the water. We zigzagged down random streets across town, then went back to our hostel to sleep.

I tried to look up punk shows in Prague but didn't find much going on during the time we were there. There was a squat doing a showing of *Dirty Dancing*, but it was across town. We spent our second day traveling to the nearby town of Kutná Hora to visit another bone church. This was one of the more popular ones in Europe. Most bands traveling through Prague always stop at Kutná Hora's Sedlec Ossuary to take pictures, posing tough in front of the piles of skulls and giant hanging bone chandelier.

We rode an old rickety metal train into Kutná Hora, sitting in folding side seats since the private little rooms with real seats were full. The warm breeze whooshed through the open windows. We got off our train and walked a dirt path into the center of town. Of course we were out of cash in the currency we needed, so our first hour in Kutná Hora was viewing Sedlec Ossuary from the outside, then turning around to walk back into the sun to find an ATM to pay the 90 CZK, about $4.37, entrance fee.

Our ATM sat in the corner of a nicely air-conditioned grocery store, where we grabbed one cold beer to share and a bottle of non-carbonated water while we were there. We took a side road through a small residential street back to the bone church and stopped to sit in some grassy shade near a house about a block away from our destination to enjoy our drinks.

We successfully made it into the musty bone church and walked the few steps down into the basement area where tourists poked around in circles silently gawking at the skulls and bones of forty to seventy thousand people. Because a small amount of earth from where Jesus' crucifixion took place was scattered at the site of Sedlec Ossuary in 1278, it became a desirable burial site containing a piece of the Holy Land. The cemetery and chapel had to be enlarged after the Black Death in the mid 14th century since there were so many dead.

The Sedlec Ossuary's iconic bone chandelier had been temporarily removed for cleaning and restoration, leaving Tim and I confused. "This can't be the right place," said Tim. I knew it was, but it was definitely less impressive than we had imagined the most popular bone church in Europe, besides the Paris Catacombs, to be. The room was very small, with four large pyramids of bones, and a few skulls decorating the walls. It took about two minutes to see everything, so we went back and paid for the audio self-tour to get more history and time out of our mini adventure to Kutná Hora.

We walked in a circle, learning about the monks and the church while a tattooed band dressed in black posed for pictures with the bones across from us. Overall it was a great experience and an amazing place to visit, just a funny first impression after already visiting the more extensive bone church in Évora, Portugal.

My eyes watered and my nose sniffled as I pulled out any scraps of tissue or napkin I could find in my day bag. "I think I'm allergic to dead people," I told Tim. We left the bone church and poked around in a tourist shop filled with bone merchandise and postcards, grabbing a few to send home. A restaurant sat next door so we shared a salad and appetizer before jumping back on the train to Prague.

Our hostel bunk gained a new neighbor who had thrown his stuff all over the shared floor between our beds. I shuffled my feet to make a path through his shoes and clothes as if I was avoiding being stung by stingrays on the ocean floor. Tim and I had another night with nothing to do, so we wandered Prague in search of an interesting bar. The area we were in consisted of mostly tourists, so punk bars were something we never came across. Instead we tried our luck in a tourist trap of a bar with weird dolls and funny decorations hung in the windows. Flashing lights and music blasted from inside. It was almost half dive bar, half club. It was fairly early in the night so the bar had plenty of open stools to take a seat at.

We tried to enjoy our drinks, but an older woman with short blond hair grinding on her partner was distracting us. She was grinding all over his lap as he sat in his chair looking unamused. Tim and I giggled to each other, but went on talking about other things. The woman's grinding was moving closer and closer into our space in the fairly empty bar, becoming ever more distracting. Eventually the grinding moved right onto Tim and me. I made eye contact with the woman and laughed. We tried hard to ignore her but she wasn't picking up our clues to beat it. Tim and I were definitely picking up clues that she and her boyfriend were looking for more than just each other to grind on. We continued ignoring her and laughing to each other.

Finally I took out my phone and smiled for a selfie with the woman right next to me. She rolled her eyes, offended, and went back to her table behind us. "Aw, where'd she go?" I said while laughing. We left the bar right on time, as a bar-hopping tour group of rowdy twenty-year-olds piled in.

The rest of our time in Prague was spent drinking more absinthe, eating amazing Czech goulash at a fancy vegan restaurant, and exploring every free tourist area we could. It was now peak tourist season in Europe, so we were battling crowds, but that didn't have an affect on how beautiful Prague was from up on the hill at the Saint Vitus Cathedral.

We had come across a lot of statues in Europe that for hundreds of years people felt the need to touch, most likely for good luck or sometimes for religious purposes. The hands or feet become polished and bright from years of being touched, while the rest of the statue remained oxidized with that patina look. In Prague we came across a particular statue of a naked young man. I'll let you guess the obvious part that shined bright and polished from years of people feeling the need to touch it.

Just like our morning ritual in Athens, we developed a nightly ritual in Prague. We'd buy amazing cheese, tomatoes, and a baguette to chow down on in the hostel kitchen with a glass of wine or beer.

I woke on our last morning in town, opening my eyes to see the newcomer who had littered the floor with his belongings making direct eye contact, staring at me from only a few feet away.

"Hello!" he said, as if waiting for me to awaken.

I pulled my blanket up to my neck to make sure my clothes hadn't become disheveled in my sleep and I was giving this young stranger a show, then responded, "Um... hello?"

"Where are you from?" he asked, excited for some reason to lead me right into a casual conversation the minute I opened my eyes. I sat up and put on my glasses.

"California, you?"

"Israel. So, you guys are here for Black Sabbath?"

"What? No, we're just backpacking Europe for four months. I didn't know anything about Black Sabbath."

"Oh wow. My friends and I swore the two of you were here specifically for Black Sabbath. They played last night for only €12."

"Wow, yeah, we didn't even know about that!" I was confused and still coming to my senses. I walked out into the hostel lobby to find Tim.

"Did you hear about Black Sabbath?" he asked.

"Yes, yes I did just now."

"Damn, for only €12!" Tim shook his head.

We threw our things in our packs and checked out, ready to pass through Germany for a second time. While walking quickly to the train station we passed a young woman in her twenties and both did a double-take.

"Did you see what she was eating?" Tim asked. "A whole head of lettuce. She's just walking down the street munching on a head of lettuce like it's an apple."

Leipzig: A Punk Version of the Town from The Truman Show

The next city on our list was supposed to be Berlin, but a man Tim met at the punk festival in Vienna told us we should stop by Leipzig on the way, and that we could even stay with him while we were there. We had a full week dedicated to Berlin, so spending a day or two of that time in Leipzig wouldn't be a big deal since we had no specific plans for Berlin anyway. We arrived at Hauptbahnhof (central station) Leipzig in the evening and hadn't heard from the man we had met in Vienna, whose name escaped us. Neither us or the man we'd be staying with had consistent Internet, yet somehow we were trying to communicate strictly through email. This obviously wasn't working well.

We were in Leipzig with the sun setting, no lodging options researched, little Internet, and no one we knew who was reachable. In fact, we really didn't know anything about Leipzig at all. Or even the name of who we were staying with. We sat outside of a restaurant which mind-blowingly had an Irish Car Bomb on the menu, taking turns using the bathroom and looking things up online with our phones' battery icons quickly going into the red. We were in the nice downtown area of a small college town. Everything was overpriced, and I didn't feel comfortable sleeping in the park next to the train station with strange homeless men. I found a punk bar online that seemed like an actual real punk bar, or at least I was hoping. It was on the edge of a large forest we could possibly sleep in and was only a short two-mile ride away on the metro.

Sitting on our train looking out the window, we watched the scenery around us go from pristine downtown buildings to quaint residential neighborhoods. The closer we got to the punk bar, the more graffiti grew across the buildings. Sidewalks scattered in students and businessmen turned into couples with mohawks pushing strollers and street punks chatting in front of grocery stores. It felt like a punk version of the town from *The Truman Show*.

We got off and walked the few blocks to the bar, passing record stores, vegan restaurants, antifascist murals, and even a goth thrift store. *An entire punk neighborhood?* I thought. We found our bar at the edge of the forest and went in. I was ecstatic. Punks and metalheads everywhere. There was even a vegan taco truck in the back patio run by a Texan. We grabbed a table next to an outlet where we could charge our phones and ordered drinks. We had nothing to do and nowhere to be, so we planned on staying at the bar late into the night before wandering into the woods to sleep.

Tim approached a couple dressed in black at the bar and asked the man if he knew a small tattooed punk dude with a beard and dreads.

"That's everyone," the man replied, confused.

Tim laughed and offered to buy the couple a round of shots if he could borrow their phone to call the guy we were trying to find. They obliged, but again our call went unanswered. After staying at the bar for a few too many rounds of Pfeffi, we left at 2:30 AM and wandered into the dark neighborhood toward the forest.

Although finding a dark forest to illegally camp in was a great idea, our plan fell short by the fact we could not find an entrance into this forest. The section we found on the map was completely lined with nice houses for miles. We walked back and forth, up and down residential streets trying to find any kind of hidden nook to pass out in, and were growing frustrated. Feeling tired and desperate, we noticed a few of the houses had detached garages with flat roofs that were partially hidden by the tall trees. The first roof we found was right across the street from another house's bedroom window, making the spot not so hidden if this neighbor was to look outside. Our next option was less hidden by trees but spaced out much further from other houses. In fact, its neighbor across the street seemed to be some sort of abandoned historic mansion overgrown in vines, and its neighbor to the side was a small car dealership.

We tried to drunkenly scale the garage exterior, failing to hoist each other up or make it up the wall doing running jumps. Tim made it up and yanked me by the arm, dragging me up over the roof's edge. We walked across the roof to the far corner that was furthest from the house and road, hoping to get a bit of coverage from a large tree. We could see down into the spacious backyard, which backed right up to the forest. The yard and forest were only divided by a creek. I climbed into my sleeping bag and pulled it up to cover my eyes from the lone street lamp and fell asleep.

Early in the morning I woke to the sound of men trimming the nearby trees and doing yard maintenance down below the garage roof. It was way too early to be getting up, so I tucked my face further into my sleeping bag and continued sleeping. A few hours later the tree trimming stopped, but what started as a bit of mist turned into sprinkling rain. I was still exhausted and not going to let this ruin the minimal amount of sleep I was going to achieve.

The rain misted our things and finally Tim woke up, exclaiming, "What the hell, how is it raining?"

We tucked our shoes and valuables out of the rain's way and continued lying on the roof. Not long after we heard an angry voice.

"Great!" I said, flinging myself up out of my sleeping bag and shoving everything into my backpack as quickly as I could.

The woman who lived in the house stood on a small wall, peering over the other side of the roof to yell at us in German. I assumed she would be calling the cops, but her tone wasn't too upset. At first it was kind of a yell then turned into more of a talking or pleading tone.

"We're going, we're going!" Tim and I yelled back, still cramming our belongings into our backpacks and trying to lace our shoes. The woman looked at us, nodded, and shrugged, then went back into her house.

We jumped off the roof and limped away with half-put-on shoes and sleeping bags falling out of our unclasped backpacks, making it to the front of the abandoned mansion across from the closed car dealership to sit down and collect ourselves.

"Well she didn't seem *too* angry," I said as an awkward good morning greeting to Tim.

"Maybe she wasn't mad at all, maybe that was just German for 'It's starting to rain, come inside and have a warm cup of coffee by my fireplace!'"

"Yeah, you never know."

"What was with the rain, too? I swear I'm cursed when it comes to sleeping outside with you."

"Yeah, yeah..." I rolled my eyes and laughed.

After correctly re-packing my bag and brushing my teeth with the last few drops from my water bottle, we headed back into town. It seemed there were a lot of cafés along the metro tracks, so we walked back past the punk bar and through a graffitied alley where we found a grocery store and vegan pho restaurant next to the metro stop we departed from the night before.

We stood on the side of the road, looking up and down for different options for food and coffee, both completely out of it from such a rough night and morning. We decided on a big bowl of vegan pho to soothe our stomachs. After eating, we wandered the street peering into shop windows and searching for WIFI. We found a little coffee shop to sip cappuccinos at and check our email for any word from our friend, but again there was no response. Tim emailed him once more and I scoured the Internet for nearby hostels. There weren't many, and the ones we did find were out of our budget. Our budget at this point consisted mostly of credit card debt. Tim didn't even want a hostel at all. He figured we could find a better place in the forest, but I was longing for a shower, a nap, and somewhere to leave our backpacks.

It started to rain again, we ducked under the awning of a large grocery store, surrounded by other punks. I finally talked Tim into a hostel about a mile and a half from the punk bar towards the hauptbahnhof. It was a bit out of the way but we ended up getting our own private room for two nights, which made the price and distance more worth it. I showered, napped for half of the day, then was ready to hit the streets of Leipzig for a second time.

The night before I had missed the vegan tacos in the back of the punk bar because the taco truck was closed. This night I was determined to fill my face with them. We didn't have anything better to do than wander back to the bar anyway. We walked our way back down the main street, poking into the goth thrift store and even attempting to call our friend once more on the store's phone. No answer.

We continued a few blocks down toward tacos when a man quickly rounded the corner near a liquor store and almost right into us on the sidewalk. It was the guy we had been looking for! We greeted each other and took turns trying to explain our communication issues. We talked about ending up at the punk bar, waking up on a roof, and eventually booking a room. Our friend had someone he had to meet with, but he told us to meet him at the grocery store by the pho restaurant in two hours, at 9:30 PM, where we could then head together to a party for a squat that was on the verge of getting shut down. He begged us to cancel our room at the hostel and stay with him, but we explained that we already paid and the one hostel worker, who was also the receptionist, was only at the building for three hours a day. We told him we would definitely come stay with him after our second night though.

I was excited to find a friend and have something to do for the night, to meet more people, and for tacos. There was a free metal show going on at the bar. It was evening, but the sun was still up and the weather was perfect. I inhaled a few tacos on the back patio and sipped on cheap German beer, while Tim talked with the Texan woman running the taco truck, realizing they actually had a mutual friend. I giggled at the menu's description of refried beans, "pinto-bonen puree." By nine o'clock we left the bar and headed to the grocery store to meet our new friend.

We sat on the curb outside of the Netto Market, when eventually our friend popped out of nowhere again and led us to a park only a block from the grocery store. A few of his friends and housemates were drinking beer in the park as a housewarming party for a friend. I guess the park was more accommodating for guests than the flat the person rented, which neighbored the park.

We joined them in drinking beer and introduced ourselves to the group. Everyone was friendly and seemed to be having a good time. It was hard to tell exactly what was going on since we didn't speak German. Our host told us he rarely ever spoke English, and that he had been embarrassed by his lack of English speaking for years and purposefully tried not to speak much of it until recently. We could barely tell. Every now and then a word would come up that he didn't understand and we would explain, but that was rare. I'm sure it was also rough that us Californians speak mostly in slang or contractions, *like, yahknowwudImean?* And of course we mentioned it was way more impressive than our skills, or lack thereof, of being able to fluently speak only one language.

Our friend's roommate was very nice, talkative, and spoke very clear English. We chatted here and there as the sun started to set. A punk woman who was pregnant and a couple with a child ended up saying goodbye as the rest of us got ready to leave. After petting a few dogs, Tim and I headed over to the corner store for a road beer since everyone was almost ready to walk to the wagenplatz party. This was the name for any large squat made up of not just buildings, but a complex of abandoned trucks or trailers as well. The trailers act as separate bedrooms or houses similar to a trailer park, which is what I was told wagenplatz roughly translates to. "Not like an American trailer park though," we were told. I had figured as much.

In the corner store Tim asked for a small shot bottle of Pfeffi, which the cashier handed to him while making a funny face.

"Why drink that one? I have a better one..." he sifted through the other shot bottles on a small shelf.

"Our friends in Belgium drank this one with us in Vienna, they're crazy about it," Tim answered.

"I guess it's okay for the morning, you don't have to brush your teeth! Try this one though, it's much better," he put two shot bottles on the counter.

"Sure, how much?"

"It's free."

"Oh, thank you, cheers!" Tim said while grabbing the shots to leave.

"Oh!..." the man looked back and forth to make sure no one was watching, then cracked open a shot for himself, "Cheers!" extending the open bottle toward us.

"Oh... uh, yeah..." Tim and I cracked ours open, tapping each little bottle together before downing the minty liquor. "Cheers!" we said, expecting the original cheers to be a form of goodbye instead of meaning for us to all drink shots together. But that worked too. In fact, it was quite an amazing misunderstanding.

The large group of us walked out of the city and past a large field, staying along a road for quite a while. Eventually, we took a left down a dirt road and followed it past a warehouse that was hosting an illegal techno party, unassociated with the wagenplatz. We continued down the dirt road to a fence with a few people hanging out. We each squeezed our way through a small walkway between the fence and trailers. A few people hung out next to the trailers and talked by a small campfire, but our group kept walking. The sky was dark and we continued on the dirt road completely surrounded by overgrown plants, techno bass thumping loud in the distance and bright stars littering the sky.

We came to a small building in a dirt cul-de-sac that the trailers seemed to block the road to. There was a much larger fire pit, more people, and dogs chasing each other back and forth across the path, a small one trying to hump the others. We waved hello to the strangers, and followed our group into the building which held a small DIY bar serving beer and shots. Once more, we stayed out late into the early morning, hanging out with new friends and re-meeting a few we had seen at the festival in Vienna.

I realized it was 2:30 AM and told Tim we should try doing the semi-responsible thing of ending the night and getting our asses back "home," so that maybe we wouldn't feel like complete hell the next day. We said our good-byes, took turns peeing in the overgrown weeds beyond the campfire, and booked it back to the hostel. We had over two miles to walk in the wee hours of the morning, and somehow still had energy to burn. We passed a playground and decided to swing, singing songs and jumping all over the playground equipment like children. We played the few songs we had on our phones, which started as just swing-ing ourselves about on the random playground equipment, then turned into about a thirty-minute walk of us skipping forward and backward while flailing our arms as hard as we could, doing ballet jumps and twirls back and forth across the sidewalk. Tim tried to do parkour-like jumps off of the outer window sills of buildings while yelling "*ahh*," and do-ing full on somersaults off of benches.

We were back on the main street, jumping and twirling and yelling, with the few remaining people on the street giving us odd looks, one even asking if we were okay. We passed a closed restaurant whose picnic tables lined the sidewalk, and Tim leaped from tabletop to tabletop, then back to the sidewalk again. I've never seen all of *West Side Story*, but think of us poorly trying to recreate that while laughing so hard we couldn't breathe for two miles. I'm sure when most people think about what engaged couples in their 30's do for fun this doesn't come to mind.

After two miles of ridiculousness, we were sore and tired. We slept the next day away and felt refreshed enough by the evening to head back out again. Not until first making burritos in the same kitchen as the other few hostel guests who apparently couldn't figure out what the difference between a trash can, compost, and recycle bin were. For at least thirty minutes they continued to have a long debate with each other about what kind of trash should go in what bin. For the first time, we had purposefully prepared for it being Sunday and bought our burritos supplies before heading out the previous day, knowing we'd be foodless if we didn't. Although I would have been fine with surviving on vegan double-decker tacos for the entirety of our time in Leipzig.

Our plan for the night was to go to a low-key acoustic show in a small bar some American friends would be playing at on tour. Not just any American friends, but our last roommate of three years, Buffy, and a few other people we had met through her during the time we lived together in Oakland. We saw some familiar faces from home for the first time in months, gave hugs, and caught up. It was nice to enjoy the relaxing music and chat. Tim and I decided to head back at the responsible time of midnight, attempting to take a bus this time instead of walking the mile and a half. Our bus never came so we walked anyway. Somehow we ended up going to sleep at 2:30 again, checking out the next morning tired.

It was too early to find our friend, or feel like doing much of anything, so we spent the first few hours of the morning drinking cappuccinos and splitting a bagel at the coffee shop under the hostel. We sat outside at a table under an umbrella and I kept seeing the tiniest spiders extending themselves down on webs. I flailed my arms and hands, batting them away from me as Tim watched me like I had lost my mind.

"There are little spiders, I keep seeing them!" I tried to explain.

"*Sure* there are," Tim replied.

Every fifteen minutes or so I would violently swing my arms around again. "I think they're in my hair."

"There are not spiders in your hair," Tim reassured.

Tim then realized our bag of food was missing. Our grocery bag full of snacks and beer was still in the fridge upstairs. I buzzed the call box for the hostel, knowing a worker was actually there this time, with no answer. Finally, a businessman entered the building and I followed closely behind him to get access in, flying straight into the elevator as the man stopped to check a mailbox inside. The elevator door closed immediately behind me as I turned back to see the man heading toward it, missing his chance at entering and being left in the lobby, which oddly smelled strongly of poop. I reached my floor and pestered the hostel worker via knocking until she was kind enough to let me in to grab my forgotten belongings, consisting of mostly soy products and alcohol. Some of the best things in life, in my opinion.

We walked the mile and a half back to the hipper area of town to wander and figure out how to find our friend again. A small spider slowly lowered itself out of my hair and drifted into the wind on a single strand of web. "I told you," I said sternly.

We stopped at a pay phone to try to call our friend, who we learned was named Nils, but it ate our money and we walked on. We weren't sure how or where to run into him again, but we remembered him saying he lived close to the park we had been at two nights prior, so we decided to head that way. I laid in the grass and played with twigs as Tim read travel stories aloud from a book on his phone. We laughed at the funny parts and it helped to pass the time. We were happy we stopped in Leipzig and were having so much fun we didn't want to leave. Of course it was only the times we had no lodging when we couldn't reach Nils. Boredom and hunger were setting in so we decided to try the taco truck and bar. Between the punk bar and the park, we figured we would have a good chance at running into him.

Outside of the taco truck was an acquaintance of ours we had met in Oakland named Pablo, who we had also hung out with the previous night with our old roommate. He and his girlfriend were from Spain but were now living in Leipzig. Both of them had stayed on our couch in Oakland a few times while touring with their band. Pablo's girlfriend was actually working the taco truck while the Texan was off for the day.

We used his phone to call Nils, who this time answered and agreed to meet up with us as soon as he could. I enjoyed the sunshine and my double-decker taco while rubbing the belly of Pablo's dog, then Nils arrived, excited to bring us back to his place. We grabbed our things and walked the alleys, taking a right onto an unpaved driveway lined with trees which opened up into a big graffitied apartment complex-looking building. It was right in the center of the punk neighborhood, only a few blocks from the grocery store and park. We had even passed it while walking a few times. Nils pointed to a door that he told us was a game room and bar. He showed us a big main entrance door and showed us how to lock and unlock it, with a key he popped off of his key ring and handed to Tim.

He led us up a spiral wooden staircase and into a small three-bedroom apartment with slightly more dogs than rooms. Graffiti covered most of the walls, and a giant animal skull hung in the kitchen. The toilet flushing lever was a bike pedal and chain, stickers were stuck on windows, and there was a small windowed-in porch filled with plants.

Nils apologized to us that he had to spend the night preparing for a specific construction certification test he would be taking at 5 AM the next morning. He planned to stay at his girlfriend's house so he could go to bed early, and leave us to his room. We thanked him profusely and said our goodbyes, after first being introduced to the rest of his roommates who were mostly just as nice.

After Nils left we decided to walk the neighborhood a bit and stop into the grocery store before having an early night in as well. As we descended the staircase back to the front door, we passed Pablo and his dog coming up.

"This is where you were trying to go? I live here!" he said, and we all laughed.

We returned to the gigantic squat complex and into the apartment. We talked with the roommates while half of them and their friends prepared to go out for the evening. We were told of a Nazi rally happening in the center of town that night and how most of the squat was going to protest, as well as to back up those protesting from the other squat we had partied at a few nights prior who were at risk of Nazis potentially following them home. Most of the people left, while Tim and I sat on the couch in Nils' room to chill out and relax. Not long after, two of his roommates, a blond woman in a torn-up white shirt hanging off one shoulder and a young man with shaggy brown hair, came in and sat on the floor next to us. They asked us about ourselves and our time in Europe.

The man took out one of Nils' records from its sleeve and placed it onto the record player. The woman was nice but the man slightly annoyed me. He said he had seen us during our first morning in town, standing outside of the pho restaurant looking from side to side.

"I could tell you were confused tourists," he said.

"Yes I'm sure the backpacks made that obvious. We were also very hungover and not sure where to eat," I responded, then continued to tell him about our night on the roof. The man told us about his dislike for America, then admitted he was partially from there. A Russian refugee as a child, placed in San Francisco where he never quite fit in. His family gave up their Russian citizenship to become American, then moved to Germany when he was a young teen and had been there ever since.

"The Germans don't see me as German, the Russians don't see me as Russian, but I am *not* American," he slurred with a mixed Russian and German accent, "I belong to nowhere."

It was Fourth of July in America and a few of our friends were barbecuing just to barbecue. You know, since its typical and all for non-patriotic punk vegans to barbecue for Independence Day. Either way, we rarely had a chance to video chat with California, so we stayed up late to hang out with our temporary roommates and video chat with the party back home. We sat at a table outside in the courtyard of the building, talking and sipping on shots of some kind of liquor when I got the call and ran back upstairs to chat and wave to Americans skateboarding ramps and shot-gunning Tecaté in the sunlight, while I sat in a dark empty German squat introducing each dog. I said goodbye to California as Tim and the rest came back upstairs. Somehow, again, it was 2:30 AM. We laid our sleeping bags out on top of a stranger's bed and went to sleep.

We slept in as long as possible, then woke up to breakfast in the kitchen. The dining room table was scattered in bread, cheeses, hummus, pickles, avocados, and other vegetables. Tim and I scarfed down a few pieces of bread, trying to just take a little as to not be rude guests. Nils returned home and asked us if we wanted to go for a hike. "Nap" would have been a more appropriate word, but he was nice enough to share not only his home but his bedroom, as well as offer to show us around town, so saying "no" wasn't a valid option for us.

Sometimes you have to force yourself to say "yes" to going on an adventure when all you want to do is sleep off a rough series of nights. What initially sounds like a bad idea could end up being one of the highlights of your year. Five years before arriving in Leipzig, Tim and I found ourselves pulling our backpacks out of the back of a stranger's truck in Dunsmuir, California, where we then wandered through the small town down to the train tracks surrounded by pine trees and waterfalls.

We sat on a log next to a creek to soak our feet and cool off in the shade before heading back up to the one small grocery store for water and snacks in the summer heat. We hadn't eaten or drank much since leaving Portland, Oregon that morning. Tim got up to run to the store while I sat with our things, and the minute he walked toward the clearing in the trees by the train tracks a freight train rumbled past and stopped directly in front of our spot. To make things even more convenient it was the steps up to a very rideable car, a Canadian grainer, right at the end of our dirt path.

Tim looked back at me, "Should we get on?"

I ran over with my backpack and jumped up onto the porch and poked inside the grainer hole. "It's hot in there. How hot do you think it is? Hmm I really don't know what we should do." I took out a small plastic keychain I had with a thermometer on it and left it in the hole for a few minutes. I ignored my flip-phone buzzing in my pocket. "It says 90 degrees."

Time was ticking and we needed to make a decision. Do we go eight hours in a hot metal hole with no water, or risk losing our train and not even making it out until late at night or even the next day? "How about this," I proposed, "I'll stay here with our things and you run to the store. If the train starts to leave while you're gone I'll throw our stuff off and we'll wait."

"Okay," Tim said, simultaneously with the train airing up to leave. "Well, fuck it."

We climbed in our hole, trying to relax against our hot, dirty, metal seat to Roseville.

I pulled out my phone to see why it was buzzing. "Huh, I guess Amy Winehouse died." I said after reading a text from a friend.

The ride was hot, and to make things worse almost the entire beautiful ride followed the glistening, blue Sacramento River. I found a snack pack in my things of veggies and Ranch dip, sharing them with Tim then spilling the dip all over my hands, which then became coated in dirt and dust from the bottom of the grainer. I was a hot mess. Toward the end of the ride the sun set and the sky grew dark not long before pulling into Roseville.

The train came to a quick stop just outside of the train yard, then aired up to go again. Tim was concerned this meant it might keep going through without stopping. Either that or it was going to stop again in the middle of the train yard, making it harder for us to get off without being spotted.

"We need to go *now*," he said, throwing his backpack off of the train and climbing down the ladder.

After a graceful exit of me launching myself backward off of the ladder because I didn't know what to do, we somehow made it safely to the outskirts of Roseville next to a gas station where we could drink Gatorade and water to our heart's content, then fell soundly asleep on an expensive mattress left outside of a mattress store.

We woke the next morning early and groggy, pushing our sleeping bags back into our backpacks while passersby did double takes. Before we could lift our butts off of the mattress to figure out where the hell we were and how to leave, Tim received a call from our friend Austin in Sacramento wondering if he could pick us up to go speed boating on the Sacramento River. Less than an hour later a car pulls up to a new spot we found under a tree, and Austin jumps out to throw our backpacks into his car.

We first stopped by his house in Sacramento to throw our backpacks down and brush our teeth, then headed to a store for beer, with me *begging* for pizza. I am rarely a grumpy person, but man I was grumpy and trying my hardest to hide it. I was filthy. Remnants of Ranch dip and train dust were still caked under my nails. I was hungry. I was sleep deprived. Spending a whole day under the hot sun on a boat with Austin's lawyer sounded hellish. And I *love* boats. The guys let me run into Little Caesars which at least temporarily helped my mood. For some reason stuffing my face with as much cheap, greasy cheese pizza as possible felt like winning the lottery.

We arrived at the dock and introduced ourselves to Austin's lawyer, who was a close friend of his. She immediately helped us onto the boat, handed us beer, and turned up the

music. I felt relieved. I thought I was going to be half naked, dirty, tattooed, and hairy around a stuffy professional
I had to make small talk with for an entire day. Instead
she was cool and fun to be around. We partied and swam
and intertubed, gliding across the same glistening waters
we would have given anything to be in the day before. I
kicked back with my sunglasses on and took in the sun
and wind, drying my river-soaked tank top and underwear
I was wearing as a bathing suit. Something about beer and
sun feels exhaustingly euphoric. I watched the riverside
houses each with their own private dock and envied them.
After a great day out on the water we went to sleep early,
feeling thankful for saying "yes" to more adventure.

Our jaunt through the forest in Leipzig wasn't quite as
impressive as our day out on the Sacramento river years
prior, but it definitely added to my ever-growing love for
Germany just the same. We grabbed our day bag, Nils
grabbed his dog, and we hit the street followed by a few
other housemates who were planning on walking with us
partway to the forest.

The group kept asking us why we were going to Berlin.
"Leipzig is better," they would say, "stay here instead." Every time we met a new person who found out Berlin was
our next stop they would say the same. We were trying
to find a ride there, but the only person heading that way
wasn't leaving for a few more days, and we were running
out of time. The group of us walked through the neighborhood's muraled alleyways, through a park, and to an actual
opening to the edge of the forest. We said goodbye to the
roommates, who had other things to do, and introduced

ourselves to Nils' girlfriend and her dog, who came to join us.

We followed trails through the dark trees, with the dogs far ahead of us, knowing exactly where to go. We passed a small river which the dogs instantly jumped into, swimming against the current with large branches they tried to tow ashore. We left the shelter of the trees and walked through a large open field in the sun. The field turned back into a neighborhood and the streets led us back to our Leipzig punk Truman Show neighborhood. We said goodbye to Nils' girlfriend and sat with him outside of a grocery store, sipping ice cold water we had bought inside.

"I'm in a bad mood today," he said. "I received some bad news."

"Oh?" we asked.

"I checked my mail and I had a ticket for three hundred euros. I was really hoping that wasn't going to happen." Nils went on to tell us about how a few weeks back he and a friend of his got drunk at a bar then wandered the streets past rows of makeshift beer gardens outside of restaurants for a soccer game being broadcasted. We had seen these beer gardens. They line the streets and had rows of banners with the German flag in support of their team.

"We took a flag and started cutting it. We cut the yellow stripe off so that it was just red and black. We were just messing around, but looked behind us and a cop was right there. It is illegal in Germany to destroy the flag. I thought he might let us off with a warning but I guess not."

Nils had some errands to run before staying at his girlfriend's house again, so we headed back to the apartment and I finally got my nap. The complex we were staying at was having a ping pong and foosball game night later in the evening, so once the time came Tim and I headed alone to the game room where we knew nobody. We ordered drinks at the bar and sat at a dark table watching the games, until getting up to play a few rounds of ping pong ourselves. We finally got our quiet night in and packed our things to catch a bus to Berlin the next morning.

When we woke no one else was up. We wrote a note saying goodbye and thank you to Nils and his roommates, then jumped on the metro back to the central train station where we would board our bus. The metro passed through the neighborhood, the graffiti dwindled, appearing less and less, and the buildings grew taller. *Whoever thinks punk is dead has definitely never been to Germany*, I thought. I was sad to be leaving Leipzig. It was a bittersweet goodbye. Saying goodbye to one of my favorite cities so far, yet still getting to experience new ones.

We sat in the grass waiting for the bus' doors to open and let us on, doing our familiar dance of me taking the backpacks to load them under the bus simultaneously as Tim waited in line to show our tickets. Then we would fly up the stairs in a race to get the best possible seats. Before I could make my mad dash, the woman told us our tickets weren't valid.

"How so??" Tim demanded.

"These tickets are for this time tomorrow."

"Shit!" Tim sat back down in the grass, connected to the bus' WIFI, and quickly bought us the correct tickets while the woman let the rest of the passengers board.

"Here!" he ran back up to her sweating, me behind him dragging both backpacks.

"Thank you, have a good bus ride," she waved us on. We ended up still getting decent seats, and Tim was able to get a full refund for the wrong tickets he purchased.

I sat in my seat with headphones on, listening to sappy folk punk travel songs, and caught myself becoming teary-eyed. I'm usually not much of an emotional person, but all of a sudden the realization that we only had one month left in Europe almost became unbearable to me. It seems most who vacation in Europe only come for a few weeks, at most, yet having only that amount of time left felt heart-breaking. This fast-paced, sleepless, sunburnt, dirty, broke, unplanned routine, where I never knew where I was going to sleep, or what the ingredients on a package say, was my life now. It was my life every day for the last three months, and even the year before that when I was hiking the Pacific Crest Trail. It was my life, and it was so incredibly uncomfortable.

I longed so hard for my own bed. I mean, not my *literal* own bed, which was in a dark storage unit near Oakland, but any comfortable, private, permanent space that was mine. Where I could sleep in as long as I liked. I knew though, that the minute I went back to California and obtained that, there would be a piece of me missing. I thought about how drastically San Diego and Oakland had both changed since we had lived in either of them, and now neither really felt like home. I had heard about the feeling of being homesick for a place that doesn't exist and I guess exploring fifty cities in five months was filling that void. I was too busy and too tired to be homesick. But once I got that bed to lie in and wake up in every morning to go to work, boy would I be.

> *And what if when we get back to this town*
> *everything is different*
> *All those familiar places we once loved no longer exist*
> *Well at least I'll still have you and you'll have me*
> *That's all we need*

The song sang in my headphones. *Berlin*, I thought. *Berlin will be fun.*

Berlin: How's God? She's Black

Not long into our ride, our bus pulled into a vacant lot in the middle of nowhere, where all passengers were escorted off the bus. Apparently there was an issue with the bathroom, which meant all of us were to be stranded for an unannounced amount of time while the, for some reason, unmarked bus with our belongings on board, left to fix the problem. We sat on a curb in the sun, picking at weeds and chatting with other passengers about whether the bus was going to come back or not. Fifteen minutes later, it circled back around and let us back into our seats.

We had a hostel booked in Berlin, and for some reason the fact my throat hurt from second-hand cigarette exposure made me feel like I needed a shower. Our room had four bunks, two of which were sectioned off with their own

private door. We took the private room and collected ourselves before exploring the city. There wasn't much time
left in the day so we wandered the neighborhood looking
for food and groceries, laughing at funny German words
with "ASS" in them, then returned to the hostel to see the
widely-advertised rooftop bar. Which was of course closed
indefinitely, despite the pictures in the hostel's windows
and lobby.

The one full day we had in Berlin was spent covering
the city by bike, cycling our way around tourist attractions,
exploring a farmer's market, and finding a punk café for
WIFI and beer.

Our room gained a roommate, which was apparent
when we came home to a B.O. smell and puddles of shower
water drenching every surface of the bathroom. Even the
top of the toilet was wet.

Toward the end of the day we rode our rented bikes
across town to a show in a large squat, planning to see the
Berlin Wall on our way there. We locked our bikes up to a
bike rack at a metro station near the wall, when we heard
the sound of live music. Peering over the railing, we could
see a band playing a show by generator on the metro platform below. A crowd gathered both around the band and
around the railing we leaned against. It was a very cool
sight, but we continued across the street to see the Berlin
Wall as planned.

This part of the wall was called the East Side Gallery,
and was decorated by artists and photographers. Part of it
went on for at least a block in large, detailed images of war
scenes in Syria, including pictures of children with ampu-

tated limbs from bombings. One section of the wall read, "How's God? She's black."

The show was a short bike ride down the road, and we arrived there early, before the sun was even down. We locked our bikes outside and wandered the tree-lined neighborhood, which was a mix of residential and commercial. We walked a few blocks to explore, stopping into a corner store just to kill time. Even after wasting time we still showed up hours before the music started, since we were early and the bands ended up being late. We each bought a beer in the squat's bar, which was also a small venue, then went outside to drink them in the courtyard while people watching.

Painted murals and green vines scaled the tall brick walls spanning five stories. It seemed like an amazing place, similar to where we had stayed in Vienna. We didn't explore inside except for the venue and bar, but I had heard there was also a theater for movie nights, an indoor climbing gym, a café, a recording studio, a library, and a silkscreen shop. Dogs chased each other across the courtyard, and new people entering the space would excitedly greet small circles of talking friends, being enveloped by the group. I wished we could do the same. The time we spent waiting would have been more fun with some new friends or people to hang out with. Yet we didn't know anyone, and didn't want to interrupt strangers.

It got late and eventually we moved inside to watch the bands who were on tour from Israel and Russia. I stood in a back corner of the venue to sip my beer without being pushed around, and spotted a band sticker belonging to friends of ours in San Diego. Things like this made the world feel small. In between sets, we would follow the crowd back out into the courtyard for air. Eventually we did find a few people to briefly chat with. It was after midnight when the show ended, and was time for us to bike back to the hostel were we had to check out fairly early the next morning. We jumped back on our bikes and rode over the river, past the Berlin Wall, through the tourist area with museums, old buildings, and a large Holocaust memorial, through a tree-lined park, back to our beds. It was so late no one was out, and we had the city to ourselves.

The next morning we woke up groggy, arguing our way to the train station where we ran into a German acquaintance, Max, who we had met in San Diego. He was out of town for the entirety of our short stay in Berlin, or else we would have had a friend to show us around. Berlin was fun, but our time there was definitely too short. I still had no regrets about spending the time we did in Leipzig. Someday, far into the future, we would have to make another trip to see more of Berlin. For now it was time to board a train to Hamburg.

Hamburg: Unicorns, Rainbows, and Penises

I was exhausted getting off of the bus in Hamburg. I stepped out of the small station to grey skies, empty streets, and plain buildings. I wasn't sure what part of town we were in, but by first impression Hamburg wasn't a very fun or lively place. I just figured the last-minute area we chose to stay in was further from the cool parts of town, and I was correct.

The hostel was enormous and slightly awkward. An eight floor, tan building in an industrial and business neighborhood. It looked more like a giant hospital converted into a hostel. Maybe it was? This was another hostel packed to the brim with children and families. Possibly even a family reunion. But because of the enormous size, we were given a smaller room out of the way of the screaming young'uns. Our room had a full bed in one corner, a couple of bunks, and a small bathroom to share with the other bunkmates. We had first choice and took the full bed.

We spent the evening napping, eating out, exploring the hostel, and planning our next day in Hamburg. After getting dinner at a vegan food chain we have in California called Loving Hut, whose menu I was excited to read in German, I arrived back to the hostel with an unexpected upset stomach.

Wanting some privacy, I attempted to walk the maze-like halls looking for a single bathroom where I wouldn't have to relieve myself alongside strangers. I followed signs for a lounge, which took me down into a basement. The stairs ended at a door, so I entered. There was a big empty room, one I assumed they had plans to turn into the lounge the signs mentioned. It looked partially under construction. *There has to be a bathroom down here*, I thought. I continued through the large carpeted basement down another hall. *Aha! Bathroom sign.* I opened the door which led to another hall, lit by a motion sensor light that flickered on when I entered. I followed the signs until I had, in total, made it through five different doors in the basement. It was definitely creepy, but if I wanted privacy, I sure as hell found it.

The large tiled bathroom had at least ten stalls, like a bathroom you would find in a mall or a movie theater. I entered a stall toward the middle then sat down simultaneously while the light shut off. I swung the door open, waved my arms over my head in pitch-black darkness, and the light flickered back on again. I sat on the toilet by myself, in the creepy basement maze, waving my hands above my head the entire time I used my private toilet so that I wouldn't be stuck in complete darkness.

I made my way back to the lobby bar and fought for a seat between children and parents for a drink, then went to bed. I repeated this the next morning for a five euro miniature cappuccino. Tim and I walked back to the metro station for a ride into the city center to see what Hamburg had to offer.

Out of the metro window we passed docked ships along the harbor. We wandered from downtown along the lake into the St. Pauli neighborhood, which is known for its "sinful mile," containing bars, clubs, theaters, and an iconic red light district, once an entertainment stop for passing sailors. In the 17th century St. Pauli was a neighborhood called Hamburger Berg, which sounds pretty adorable to me as an immature American imagining a land of cheeseburgers. Especially if it was called Hamburger Berg, Hamburg.

It was apparently "hen party" day in Hamburg. A hen party is what they call a bachelorette party in British English, and Tim and I were referring to them as such since the term was funny and new to us. Every corner we turned, around every part of town, was a giggling group of women in pink, with one wearing a white veil. They ran down the main streets cheering, flirting with bar security guards, darting in and out of bars and restaurants. I couldn't even count how many groups there were. Maybe it was Germany's national bachelorette party day.

We continued to tour Hamburg on foot, from St. Pauli to the closed Fish Market, through residential neighborhoods and into a park with a small festival taking place. We got pizza and wandered aimlessly back to St. Pauli, then back to the lake again. Couples laughed on paddle boats, and Tim convinced me we should join them in paddling around the lake. We paid a few euros for a paddle boat, yet were warned of a coming storm. The sky was growing darker, but we took our chance. The woman let us borrow a large umbrella just in case. We paddled out over the dark blue water, surrounded by trees, old bridges, and an ancient cathedral. We passed a group of tourists and I decided to try putting the few German words I knew to work.

"Ahoy there, land lubbers! Guten tag to swab the poop deck! *Prost!*" extending my coffee to the sky to cheers.

Tim shook his head and tried to hide his face out of embarrassment. It started to sprinkle so I flung open the umbrella as we dodged large groups of swans and headed back to shore.

This was our last evening in Hamburg, but the city center seemed expensive and not quite our scene. Figuring we might as well just head back to the hostel and veg out, we started walking toward the metro station. We walked past a row of stores and poked our heads into each one looking for shots of Pfeffi. It was the last chance we would have to see Pfeffi again, so we wanted a few airplane bottles to bring back to the states as gifts to friends who were familiar with its hangover from touring Europe years prior.

The sun was setting and the streets were flooding with tourists pouring out of the train station and into the bars. We shoved two double shot bottles of Pfeffi into our day bag and started walking toward the crowd, when we heard music in the distance. This wasn't just any music, this sounded like an outdoor live punk band. We followed the sound of the fast guitar and screaming vocals down a street, until we found a half-open door on an unmarked red building with punk kids sitting on the sidewalk smoking cigarettes. A man sat on a stool inside the door taking donations for the band. We handed him a few euros and he pointed us to the bar, and where the bands would alternate playing between the alley outside and the stage inside.

The bar was pay-what-you-want, so we paid one euro each for a bottle of beer, then went outside to watch the band we had heard echoing through the alleys. Outside of the back door was a little smoking patio surrounded by green plants. We continued following the music past the patio and down a short dirt path opening up into a dirt lot in the alley. A female-fronted band played on a wooden stage with a small crowd gathered round, some of them leaning against a school bus painted black. When the band stopped we moved inside where another band immediately started up. I sipped my beer from the back of the room, reading stickers on the wall and the vest patches of a big bearded man in front of me, towering over most of the crowd. This big burly man had a backpatch of unicorns, rainbows, and penises.

When the band started, the singer started to take his clothes off piece by piece while singing. The large man in front of me blocked most of my view, which I wasn't too disappointed about, but I could still see what was going on from a mirror that ran along where the wall and ceiling met. The singer had scribbles tattooed all over his body, including his face. I heard buzzing and noticed another man on stage sitting next to him with a small table of tattoo equipment. The buzzing started again and the man started tattooing more scribbles across the singer as he screamed into the microphone naked.

We stayed for the rest of the bands then jumped on a metro train back to our hospital-hostel in the industrial area, planning on checking out before 9 AM to catch the only available bus we could find to Copenhagen.

Copenhagen: A Lovely Morning of Trying Not to Get Shit On

It only took eleven countries of buses to realize the bus company we usually went with offered free streaming media when you connect with your phone. Tim was excited about this and started blasting Queen in his headphones, flailing around in his seat. I plugged my headphones in and started to watch *Little Miss Sunshine* in German. As our bus got closer to our destination, we were driven onto a ferry, then let off to enjoy the deck, ten-dollar oatmeal, and other cramped, overpriced ferry amenities.

Seagulls swarmed relentlessly overhead as a family let their children throw entire whole hot dogs into the air for the birds to eat. A lovely morning of trying not to get shit on while watching people throw away food the price of the hostels we normally stayed at.

I could see swarms of jellyfish in the water, and a bit of the Denmark landscape off in the distance. I went inside to blow some money on a cup of coffee and a muffin, which I ate sitting on the floor of a walkway since all seats were completely packed with tourists and elderly folk. People walked past me, giving me weird looks and bumping into my elbows as I took bites of my muffin even though they had plenty of room to go around. A voice came over the intercom telling the crowds of walking dead to waddle back onto their buses for departure. Another two-hour bus ride later, we arrived in Copenhagen's main station.

We threw on our backpacks and followed a central street downtown, past the town's permanent fair, which is said to be the second oldest in the world. Our hostel was in a great location right in the city center. Outside of the front door was a large fountain and sidewalk cafés which sometimes had live music. The bedroom we were led to was tight and cramped. It was dark and stuffy. People's belongings covered so much of the floor and communal counter spaces that you could barely see them. I threw my backpack in a rickety wood locker then went with Tim to run errands across town.

We needed groceries and cash, but both were hard to find. Slow moving tourist crowds lined the streets, and all of the stores were fancy and far out of our budget. I knew Denmark was expensive but it was still a shock, especially with it being one of the last cities we would visit, meaning our funds were becoming scarce. We grabbed a bag of potatoes, bread and hummus, and an oven lasagna from a grocery store that looked more like an Abercrombie and Fitch, then headed back to the hostel to snack and catch happy hour.

The happy hour special was a liter of Tuborg beer in a huge stein for the equivalent of seven dollars. This was around the same price they were charging for a single twelve-ounce bottle of beer at the grocery store, so we took advantage of the deal. A French man started playing acoustic covers on the hostel bar's small stage. He belted out Johnny Cash's *Folsom Prison* with a thick French accent, which sounded a bit odd. We talked with the bartender and he gave us free shots of some sort of Danish liquor

that reminded me of an elderly person's perfume or co-
logne. A soccer game was starting on TV and people piled
in to watch. It was France versus Portugal. We cheered for
Portugal with the bartender, only because we liked visiting
Portugal better than France, and they ended up winning
the game.

I went back to the room to climb into my rickety wood-
en bunk and fell asleep. We both slept in, then hit the town
ready to really see Copenhagen. We bought vegan hotdogs
from a street vendor then ended up in a small, quirky bar,
where some friendly locals who sat down at our table to
chat quickly made it apparent they were full blown con-
spiracy theorists. One told us the only way we could eat
food that is pure would be to grow it far underground,
thinking it would be out of reach from Earth's man-made
toxins.

"Ah, so besides grow-lights, would you pump city air
in from the outside, or use some other carbon dioxide
source?" Tim asked.

"Um, I didn't know the plants would need that," one of
the men said, scratching his head.

We wandered back toward the hostel and sat near
the fountain outside. Another local, who looked possibly
homeless, came up to tell us his life story and ask about
ours. We chatted for a while before he randomly handed
us colorful bracelets and some hash, then left. It started to
rain so we went inside the bar, which was the only place to
hang out in the hostel besides the kitchen. The bartender
told us that while we were out, one of the guests, a young
man just out of high school, had ventured to the popular

tourist area of Freetown Christiania - a small peninsula squatted since 1971 by hippies who are known for having a large marijuana black market. He tried smoking weed for the first time and ended up so high he was standing in the street in the rain, taking his clothes off while asking for an ambulance. I felt bad for the kid, but I couldn't stop myself from laughing with the hostel worker either.

People crowded into the bar every few minutes, many of them with backpacks, banging me or Tim in the arms and shoulders as they walked by. A worker was trying to get whoever they could to sign up to participate in their pie eating contest, at a fee. Tim and I joked that the pies would be $100 each. We each drank one large happy hour Tuborg then decided to escape the loud, young bumper car backpackers to relax in our cluttered wooden nooks instead. Tim's bunk was across from mine, and under me was a young woman who I swear never left her bed. The whole time we were there I only saw her under her blankets, with the contents of her belongings scattered across the entirety of her mattress on all sides of her body. Maybe she experienced some of the weed the other guy had.

We had only booked the hostel for two nights, leaving our options open for the rest of our time in Copenhagen, but the hostel booked up so fast we had no choice but to check out the next morning even though we had nowhere else to go. I started packing my things for check-out, when I received a message from a woman offering us a spare room in her apartment. Tim and I jumped on it. It was further out of town, but near city bikes which made getting back and forth quick and easy. Having a private room to chill out in for about the same price as the hostel was especially worth the trek.

Tim glued his disintegrating shoes back together as construction next door rocked the large windows, dust and debris drifting into an open crack. It left everything near the window covered in a light layer of wood dust, including the hair of a man lying on his bed while video chatting a lady friend. I threw my things in my backpack and headed to the bar for a coffee as we figured out what to do in between home bases, and I felt a pain in my throat. I tried my best to ignore the irritation, but next came fatigue and a never-ending runny nose.

I had bought a few packets of latte flavored instant coffee, which I dumped into boiling water in the kitchen and stirred into a colorful mug. No matter how much I stirred, I could not get the consistency any smoother than watered down chunky gravy. If you've ever made country gravy out of a packet, this is exactly what it looked like. The white liquid swirled in circles followed by big white chunks of powder turned into moist globs. I stirred for so long, trying to mash the lumps into the side of the mug to disintegrate them, that eventually I gave up and tried to pick the clumps out with my fork and fling them into the sink. I sipped on my chunky gravy "coffee," every now and then getting a booger-like glob in my mouth, eventually dumping the entire thing into the sink out of frustration and disgust.

We attempted to venture to our new home via the main station, but no metro trains seemed to go in the direction we needed, so we decided to suck it up and walk. I spent money on a real coffee in the station, and grabbed a handful of napkins to stuff in every pocket for my nose. We walked the two miles with heavy backpacks, as I traded off between sipping my coffee and patting a napkin to my nose. We were halfway to our destination when it started to rain. It went from zero to pouring in less than a minute. We ran as fast as we could to shelter, the only thing in sight being an awning over a bike rack. Another woman ran with us, all three of us panting as we squeezed up against the bikes. After a few minutes the rain died down, we said goodbye to the woman, and booked it to our new room.

The woman, Rikke, let us in and showed us around the small but spotless modern apartment. We rested for a few minutes then packed the day bag to wander our way over to Christiania, which wasn't far from our new place. Christiania is an eighty-four-acre peninsula which was once used for military barracks and protective city walls dating back to 1617. One of the old walls, which still exists today, was used as an execution site from 1946 to 1950. The wooden shed that held these executions is gone, but the concrete foundation containing a drain for the blood still remains. The peninsula and barracks were abandoned between 1967 and 1971, when it was broken into, then squatted and proclaimed an autonomous anarchist district by families and homeless people protesting the lack of affordable housing in Copenhagen.

In 1971 a journalist named Jacob Ludvigsen published an article about Christiania titled *The Forbidden City of the Military*, in which he described Christiania as "the land of the settlers. It is the so far biggest opportunity to build up a society from scratch - while nevertheless still incorporating the remaining constructions. Own electricity plant, a bath-house, a giant athletics building, where all the seekers of peace could have their grand meditation - and yoga center. Halls where theater groups can feel at home. Buildings for the stoners who are too paranoid and weak to participate in the race... Yes for those who feel the beating of the pioneer heart there can be no doubt as to the purpose of Christiania. It is the part of the city which has been kept secret to us - but no more."

Ludvigsen also helped to write Freetown Christiania's mission statement, stating "The objective of Christiania is to create a self-governing society whereby each and every individual holds themselves responsible over the wellbeing of the entire community. Our society is to be economically self-sustaining and, as such, our aspiration is to be steadfast in our conviction that psychological and physical destitution can be averted."

Close to one thousand residents now live in Freetown Christiania, and it is considered the fourth largest tourist attraction in Copenhagen, hosting half a million visitors each year. Pusher Street is Christiania's main attraction, even though marijuana is illegal in Denmark and technically also illegal in Christiania. Everything about Christiania is, or at one time was, illegal. For years residents and activists rioted against police and government workers trying to enter the space or close down Pusher Street. Criminal circles and gangs also fought against residents, trying to take over Pusher Street for themselves. This even led to a shooting in 2005, killing one resident and injuring three others. Over the years new common laws were passed by the citizens of Christiania, stating the nine rules. They barricaded the streets in to forbid cars, also banning weapons, hard drugs, violence, bulletproof jackets, biker colors, fireworks, and the selling of stolen goods. Christiania has its own flag, red with three yellow dots, the colors of the paint cans found by original squatters who painted the first flag. It also has its own anthem, titled *You Cannot Kill Us*. A portion of the song, translated to English goes:

> *You can put us in prison*
> *Bereave us of the world*
>
> *You can spy on everyone*
> *Always know what they've done*
>
> *Wreak havoc with your bombs*
> *Leave the world a land of waste*
>
> *It is us, or is it yourself*
> *You are terrified to face?!*
>
> *You cannot kill us!*
> *You cannot kill us!*
> *We're a part of yourself!*

We trotted up the hill toward downtown, over a bridge crossing a river, turned a corner at an old cathedral, then walked under a graffitied arch on a dirt path. We were surrounded by greenery, with old muraled military buildings turned into restaurants and stores on either side. Tourists, hippies, and people of all kinds funneled in and out of the arched pathway. We followed the dirt paths past more fascinating repurposed buildings and beautiful green trees.

People sipped beer on picnic benches outside of small bars and windows selling snacks and drinks. A small flea market of tents sold t-shirts, jewelry, and clothes.

Next to this flea market was another opening into Pusher Street, the weed market. Its entrance lined in large signs scrawled with rules for entering: "No pictures, No running." We walked down Pusher Street to continue our path and get a look at what Christiania was famous for. Both sides of the path were lined with more tents and tables, run by men dressed in black with black masks over their faces and sunglasses covering their eyes. This market stretched across to another area with food and beer windows. Young people smoked and drank on amphitheater style seating lining a wall of gardens. On the other side was the river and trails through the trees where more people chatted together on logs circling un-lit fire pits on the water's edge.

We walked back to the first beer window we saw and conversed with a friendly man who sold us two beers. The man in the window asked me about my tattoos and I answered in short responses, focusing my attention on reaching down to pet his French bulldog. Tim and I enjoyed our beer in the garden with the young people sitting on the amphitheater steps, then wandered the trails around the small peninsula Christiania encompassed.

The water's edge was scattered with makeshift houses – small cabins made out of wood and full walls of glass windows. Some had swings and sitting logs with fire pits. These were some of the most beautiful, modest little houses I had seen in my life. Surrounded by green trees, with private docks that stuck out over the river's edge, and they were all free. No mortgage, no realtors, these houses were only owned through seniority and being a part of the squatted land since the 70's. And I guess after an agreement with the city of Copenhagen, they now pay utilities and taxes to the city, as well as making payments to eventually buy the land from the military. I wandered the quiet trails along the river in awe. Freetown Christiania was mind-blowing, but not in the psychedelic way some experienced after spending time on Pusher Street.

Eventually the sun started to set and the weather grew cold, so we wandered back to our room to make dinner since we were now in the land of regular, although still pricey, grocery stores. We bought ourselves ingredients for breakfast burritos, some instant ramen, beer, wine, and palatable coffee. I also needed soap. I'm so allergic to perfume I had to carry special soap with me to wash my clothes and use on my body. In Antwerp I ran out of my travel size bottle of hippie soap from the states and had to buy another bigger bottle I then dispersed into small, flight-friendly, bottles. I bought the soap from a "bio," or natural foods, store. By now, that had run out and I was left with no choice but to buy liquid baby soap to use until I could make it back home.

I went back and laid in my comfortable bed and felt sicker than ever. I was definitely getting a cold. The possibility of sitting on a bus the next day for a day trip to Malmö, Sweden was starting to sound like a bad idea, if it meant getting up early and bustling around instead of taking advantage of a comfy bed to relax in. I pulled out my tablet and put on a movie while lying in bed. Tim pulled out weed Sour Patch Kids we completely forgot we had been carrying since Denver. Normally I didn't partake in getting stoned, but I was sick, and I was in Copenhagen, so why not have some pre-bedtime relaxation and entertainment with the movie we were watching, which was *Willow*. The candies we had smuggled through nine international and domestic airports were so old they ended up not working anyway.

By this time I felt so sick I tossed and turned the entire night instead of getting any sleep. I felt so rough the next morning, getting out of bed didn't feel like an option. Tim didn't mind laying around all day, watching movies, napping, and doing laundry. Once it was evening I felt okay enough to leave the bedroom, just to make it to the market for ice cream. The pints weren't too outrageously priced, and all of the prices were labeled except for the one I wanted most, Ben and Jerry's. I should have known better, that this imported ice cream from the homeland would have been more expensive, but in my fogginess I threw it in the basket anyway thinking it couldn't cost much more. And that is the tale of the day I bought an eight-dollar pint of Ben and Jerry's. We stayed in with our ice cream and movies, preparing for one last day in Copenhagen in the morning.

I woke up and tried my best to pull myself together for another day exploring Copenhagen, this time by city bike share. The city bikes were heavy, thick metal, more along the lines of small mopeds than bikes. They had electric assist for those who want to ride a bike without having to do any of the work, I guess. At first I figured I would turn it off and just pedal, but the bikes were so incredibly heavy there was no way I was in any shape to do such a thing. They even had moped kickstands, since a normal bike kickstand would be smashed into oblivion under the pressure of one of these massive bikes. I got on my big metal bike, trying my best to keep the heavy thing balanced as to not topple me or any of the other bike riding tourists over with its weight.

The bike seat was slightly too tall and wouldn't go down, so I had to be extra careful riding through crowds of people. It was easy for the bike to lunge into traffic by barely tapping the pedal, and since I could barely reach the ground it would have been easy to just completely lose control and eat shit into other cyclists. I put my foot on the pedal, which lunged me forward with a whiplash-inducing jolt, and I was off to see Copenhagen's downtown by bike, including visiting Freetown Christiania once more.

Off we went through downtown on bike lanes with our own traffic signals, across town to see the iconic little mermaid statue, then through more wooded trails of Christiania. We rode as far as we could to the end of Christiania's peninsula when my bike started warning it was about to run out of battery. We had to get it back to a docking station as fast as possible.

Earlier on our ride we had seen a warehouse filled with food trucks which the people at our hostel raved about. We saw there was a docking station outside of the warehouse and planned on visiting it for lunch at some point anyway. We turned around and made it to the station without being stranded with a powerless electric dump truck of a bike. We now had the opportunity to eat street food and switch our bikes out to new ones when we were done. Hopefully one where the seat would go down.

The warehouse was right on the water, and had a patio of tables and chairs to sit at outside to watch the boats go by. Inside were rows of pop up shops selling food, clothes, and housewares. I found some vegetable chowmein and scarfed it down while Tim decided to wander, grabbing freshly ditched meat entrées from the tops of the trash cans.

In most big cities we visited, in both Europe and the US, I was often forced off the sidewalk and into the street by pushy sidewalk hogs with no manners. I *always* gave other people room, but it was often not reciprocated by men and wealthy-looking women. Early into the trip, I started purposefully not budging when someone was pretending I was invisible on the sidewalk. Instead of jumping into the street or bike lane last minute, I started playing sidewalk chicken while staring them right in the eyes. Men would always give in, choosing to jump off the sidewalk or make room for us both over creaming into a small woman. The wealthy-looking women would not. They would almost always choose to run into me, continuing to ignore my presence the entire time. I was walking through the street food market when another one of these women appeared, taking up the entire aisle as if she had a parade of servants trailing behind her to satisfy her every whim. I looked her dead in the face and continued on my path as she looked past me, avoiding eye contact. We both continued walking as she elbow-checked herself on me *HARD*, right in the boob. *BLAM*. Or maybe she titty slapped my elbow. Either way it had to hurt. After she passed I glanced back and she was still completely unphased, as if I wasn't there and we never collided. No "sorry," no dirty look. She just kept on her path. I had elbow-checked quite a few women but that was my grand achievement. I'm not sure if that's something I should be proud of.

For our last day in town, we packed our things and threw our backpacks on the city bikes for one last breakfast of 7-11 donuts and Tuborg, which we consumed on the colorful 17th century harbor of Copenhagen called Nyhavn. Buskers on the dock covered Michael Jackson songs while we enjoyed our breakfast. Before leaving we had two bags of hash to get rid of that were given to us and we didn't touch. It didn't take long to find someone interested in free weed.

We rode the city bikes to the closest bike dock to the airport as we could, planning to take the metro from there. On our way, we stopped to rest on a beach where we could see Sweden across the water, and the second largest bridge in Europe connecting Copenhagen to Malmö. It was cold and gloomy out, but still Tim decided to strip down to his underwear and jump in the water, just to experience a new sea. The gloominess made it feel like my little hint of summer was gone already. A family down the beach gave us funny looks since Tim was the only person swimming in the cold water. We made it to the last city bike station, which was only three metro stops from the airport yet for some reason cost us as much as a long-distance bus.

Edinburgh: Backpacking for Two Weeks with a Large Hobo Clown Painting

Our plane left Copenhagen at 10 PM, after our flight kept getting delayed. We arrived in Edinburgh so late we had not much of a choice but to sleep at the airport. The only area to do so was a tiny little nook outside of security, filled with waiting family members and other people sleeping across multiple hard, connected plastic seats.

The dark corner toward the back was occupied by sleeping travelers, so I took up a few of the only empty seats under a bright light next to a vending machine, dozing off for a few minutes at a time with the help of my ear plugs and a bandana tied over my eyes. Tim tried the same, from a spot on the floor leaning upright against a wall. I woke up repeatedly, freezing cold and worried a stranger was coming too close to me or a worker would kick us out of our sleeping spots. I also heard constant delays over the intercom due to the possibility of a coup happening in Turkey, where the government had without warning stopped all incoming and outgoing flights to the country. An organized faction within the Turkish Armed Forces were attempting to seize control of a few key places in Istanbul and other cities. First riot cops physically stopping a trans pride parade in Istanbul at the time we were in Athens, and now this. I was glad we changed our plans to go to Istanbul, but felt for the people caught up in the violence.

Every now and then I lifted my bandana to peer around the brightly lit seating area, then tried to doze off again. Throughout the little sleep I got, song lyrics kept playing through my head, *"May your songs never get stuck out of my head."* I peeked out from my bandana again after a few hours of barely sleeping under the spotlights and noticed the back rows of seats in the dark corner had emptied. I shook Tim awake and we moved to the better spot and pulled out our sleeping bags, where we could fully stretch out for the rest of the night.

I woke up early, still sleep deprived. News of Turkey was still being announced over the intercom. I brushed my teeth in a nearby bathroom and wandered the airport looking to see what there was to eat or drink. We moved our bags to a nice little airport coffee shop with crappy WIFI, but comfortable seats to wait in as we charged our phones and sipped lattes. I was feeling better than I did in Copenhagen, but still blowing chunky green snot into any napkin I could find.

We had no idea where we were or how to get to wherever we should go in Edinburgh. To be honest I had no idea what Edinburgh was like, nor had even seen a picture of it as far as I knew. Enough people told us it was nice, and we were near it on the map. Our planning and research had gone as far as "what the hell, we'll go to Scotland."

Last minute we were offered a random room we could stay in for the night, but it was still too early to be showing up. The man wouldn't be there to let us in until evening. There was a mall between the suburb outside of downtown we would be staying in and the airport, so we decided to take a bus there to waste a few hours.

We wandered the mall, which was filled with screaming children everywhere and for some reason live owls you could pay to take pictures with. This was the first time I had been back to an English-speaking country in three and a half months. I looked around the bland mall in awe, because I was no longer illiterate for the first time in so long. We were back in the land of too-sweet food, toilet paper that comes in individual squares, breakfast fry-ups, and accidentally vegetarian liquor store Cup-O-Noodle style microwave meals. Yes, Pot Noodles.

I was still incredibly groggy; the mall was fairly boring and irritating, so I sat on a bench to lounge and use WIFI. An elderly woman sat right next to me, engulfing me in her bad perfume, which ruined that idea. Tim and I took advantage of the crowded food court then headed out on a city bus to the suburbs.

The spare room we were occupying was actually our host's bedroom. He offered it to us for the night for a small fee while he slept on the couch. He was a nice man from Romania named Lulian, living in Edinburgh for college. I felt bad kicking this man out of his own bedroom, but falling backward into the soft bed felt so nice. I just needed a quick nap before heading out on the town. It felt so good in fact, I didn't want to get up. I forced myself, still groggy, to get ready to leave. At least we would be leaving the man and his roommate to use their own apartment in peace, since we would be gone until it was time to sleep again.

Our friend Mhairi we had met in Amsterdam was from Edinburgh, and told us about a good punk show in an underground labyrinth bar. The show would be our first experience of Edinburgh, besides the mall, airport, and a stranger's bedroom. The show started at 10 PM, but we left just before sunset to buy snacks and wander downtown. We waited at a bus stop in the suburban neighborhood, where a very obviously drunk man waited with us.

After a quick ride through residential neighborhoods then into a downtown shopping district, the bus dropped us right next to a big green park with a ferris wheel. Looking out across downtown and the castle district from the park next to the bus station was jaw dropping.

"Where *are* we??" I asked Tim in disbelief. Somehow after all of the places we had been, we were just now stumbling upon the largest protected medieval city we had ever seen. As far as the eye could see were cobblestone roads that wound through dark stone walls that towered over old bridges, and above it all was a castle built on the remnants of an extinct volcano.

The sun was disappearing, leaving the sky a cloudy dark blue, and all of the ancient buildings, bridges, and streets a darker blue and grey. Tight 16th to 18th century alleyways, called closes, could be seen around every corner. They once homed tens of thousands of poor families ravaged by the plague. To me it looked practically untouched, like a movie set. "New" parts of the city during medieval times were built on top of poor neighborhoods circling the castle, leaving some of the 7th century houses literally untouched, besides for use as military bunkers at one time.

Mhairi told us about places in the bridges the poor lived and died in, called the Edinburgh Vaults, where you can still sneak into today. In 1786 the massive bridges were constructed to connect parts of Edinburgh. The bridges are called North Bridge and South Bridge. South Bridge was a nineteen-arch viaduct, where eighteen of the arches were enclosed to be used as a part of a commercial district. The arches were constructed with multiple floors and rooms inside, making up 120 rooms used for storage, workshops, and other businesses, yet eventually became damaged by water and were abandoned by 1795.

Some of the city's poor moved into the empty vaults, which then became part of the slums. These slums became a renowned red-light district, with brothels and pubs opening up within empty vaults. Families living in the vaults crowded in, sometimes ten people to one room. There was no sunlight, fresh air, sanitation, or running water. Supposedly a team of serial killers murdered people in this area then temporarily hid their bodies in the vaults before selling them to medical schools, but it is likely that this story is just a myth. The labyrinth bar we were going to was actually built inside of the Edinburgh South Bridge vaults, and considers itself "Scotland's most haunted pub." They claimed drinks have been thrown across rooms, smashing into walls, and screams have been heard by workers throughout the vaults.

We walked toward the venue wide-eyed. Taking spiraling steps in a stone bridge tower from a lower part of downtown to a higher street, I saw a man with a blue mohawk turn a corner, so I knew we were getting close. We arrived at the venue, which looked on the outside like a normal little bar in a very ancient neighborhood. Inside sat a restaurant surrounded by cave-like walls. "Haunted" tunnels lead from the large room to different nightclubs and bars, like a tunneling ant farm.

Its seven rooms included bars, a billiard room, a small venue, and a fifty-seat cinema. We drifted underground, following signs for the show. A man took our money in a small, dark cave room with a stage. People stood around chatting and clinking beers together. I couldn't help but eavesdrop just because I could actually understand the language. Punks and metalheads were walking in and out of another dark tunnel, so I followed figuring it went to the bar. In another little ant farm cave was a nice bar with Guinness flags, people talking together on bar stools, and a large flat-screen TV displaying what was happening on stage in the other room. I was smitten.

Men roughhoused and laughed with each other, sitting on the ground pretending to row a boat during songs by a band playing music themed after the movie *The Goonies*. A woman thrashed around, bumping into people, mistakenly holding up the sign for "I Love You" in American Sign Language instead of the metal horns. A nice man talked to us for a while and invited us to stay at his place since we had nowhere planned to stay for the rest of the week. I went back to the bar to sit down for a bit and next to me were a few women with familiar American accents, awkwardly asking locals what they thought of Brexit.

Tim and I were having a wonderful night out filled with great music and drinks at the creepy cave bar, but as the last band ended their set we knew we had better wander back into the night to find our bus. We barely recognized where we were dropped off at. We wandered in circles through the neighborhood until finding a field to pee in then eventually finding the apartment. We went to sleep late, and woke up early to leave Lulian to his bedroom, after he first made us coffee and we conversed more. We thought about contacting the man we met at the show about staying at his place, but he seemed a little odd and drunk the night before, so we settled on a cheap hostel across the street from the castle on the edge of the Grassmarket.

The bus dropped us off about a mile away, where we walked through what once was another red-light district, then right up to the base of a hill seating the ancient castle. Edinburgh couldn't stop impressing me. We paid eight pounds each to stay in a clean, empty, ten-bedroom dorm under the castle, surrounded by buildings from the 1500's. We spent the evening walking the steep hill to the castle, exploring the Royal Mile, and looking for more punk bars, then settled on playing ping pong in the hostel bar to horrible dubstep music. This is where Tim got into Scotch. Not in an old Scottish pub alongside bagpipe players, but in the hostel's bar listening to dubstep. The bartender nerded out with Tim about different kinds of Scotch and poured him samples. After this he usually ended each night in Edinburgh with a glass of Scotch.

When we went back into our room to sleep, our empty ten-bedroom dorm had gained one more person, who of course, felt the need to sleep in a bed directly next to our bunk. Instead of a regular light switch, this hostel had window light during the day, and what we called the "thirty second fuck light" for night time. As to not wake your fellow hostelers, the light switch turned on a red light that only stayed on for thirty seconds at a time. Tim and I, of course, had to make a dirty joke out of it. Figuratively speaking, it was like Edinburgh's third red light district. I did appreciate that little amenity from the hostel though, being a light sleeper. The shared bathroom was also nice and clean, with private stalls that were full-on toilet rooms like a half-bath you would have in a house. The privacy was nice but, like in Hamburg, the motion sensor light only stayed on for about three seconds, unless you did a gyrating dance or had a shirt to swing over your head while using the commode to keep the light on.

Since we booked late, we had to check out the next morning to move rooms, stashing our stuff in a baggage room until the normal check in time. Our new room was a much smaller room, with one private bathroom and only five bunks, but each bed was occupied, making the room feel cramped. We grabbed some horrible coffee from the hostel's coffee shop then went out again to explore.

I found a little breakfast joint with house-made veggie sausage, veggie haggis, bangers and mash, and some of the best cider I'd ever had. I decided to skip out on the vegetarian blood pudding. They also had a British flag toilet seat in their bathroom, which I jokingly asked Tim if I could add one to our wedding registry someday. We left what became our daily breakfast place to continue being tourists and to look for thrift stores. In one I found a Top Shop dress that I liked. I'm not one for dresses or fancy brands, but it stood out to me. Honestly, I only knew what Top Shop was because of the British TV show *The Mighty Boosh*. And to think of it, the dress was "creamy beige," too. I tried it on and it made me look like a frumpy marshmallow, so I left it and went on to the next thrift store.

While perusing the dusty shelves, a large painting stood shining and sparkling to me from the corner of the store. I walked over and picked it up, knocked the dust off, and held it up in all its glory, attracting the attention of a little old lady who was telling her life story to the cashier.

"Look at 'im!" she let out, approaching the painting closer, "Tucking into a hotdog and bottle of wine. With a dog at 'is feet. My kind of guy!"

She was right. The large 20X28 inch print of a painting mounted on wood showed a sad hobo clown with a sleeping dog at his feet and a half drank bottle of wine sticking out of his coat pocket. In one hand he held a hotdog up to his mouth, while concentrating hard at the café menu he held in his other hand, reading it as if it was a good book. It was so damn American. I had no idea how or why it ended up here, but I was in love with it. I sat it back down, disappointed I would be leaving such treasure, when both Tim and the old lady surrounded me, giving me ideas of how we could continue traveling with the picture. We had two weeks left before returning back to the states, and then another week before returning to California. That meant two flights where we could possibly check the painting as a bag since we never checked bags. I was convinced I could keep traveling on with this clown, so I handed the cashier

£5 and headed back across downtown Edinburgh with my new friend.

After relaxing in the room for a bit with a clown that now lived next to our bunk, Tim and I started a new daily Edinburgh tradition, apart from our new breakfast spot. We grabbed a local beer from the store and headed to the lawn under the castle to enjoy the sunset. Other people picnicked and drank beer around us as well. The sun set over the ancient dark grey buildings and I was so content I could barely notice the midgies sucking my blood.

The next day we walked the city finding packing material to wrap the clown in, then went to a free photography exhibit. The gallery was showing current work from photojournalists around the world, much of it depicting war torn Syria and other unfortunate current events. One image showed a man sitting in a chair looking down at his lifeless little girl in his arms, with her throat slit open. Nicely printed and matted gore and suffering. This definitely didn't leave us in the best mood, but I felt a strong sense of importance in these photographers' works, getting strangers' stories out there to the world. Showing what is really happening and what we all continue to turn our heads from.

We walked from the exhibit up to Arthur's Seat, a plateau you can hike up to overlooking the entire city. The hike was hot, and my knee was bugging me, but the view from the top was breathtaking. The sun was shining and all of the dark ancient buildings sparkled, surrounded by green fields and trees. A few fluffy white clouds hung over the city surrounded by bright blue sky. After descending the mountain, we grabbed ice cream cones from an ice cream truck and walked back toward the castle to drink cider on the street.

"How is your knee?" Tim asked.

"Why, did you fart?"

"What? I asked about your knee!"

"Oh, I thought you said 'it wasn't me.'"

From the curb we sat on I could see a short, colorfully-dressed woman with so many piercings I couldn't see her face. She looked so familiar to me.

"I think she is in the *Guinness Book of World Records*," I said to Tim.

The woman had a little table and was selling things to tourists or charging them to take pictures with her. Most would try to take pictures with her without paying or without her permission and she would tell them off. We drank our beer and wandered the streets, eating chips. I decided I wanted a picture with the woman and noticed I had a few £1 coins in my pocket. I went back to where she had just finished packing up her station and I tried to introduce myself.

"I'm closed! Time for me to go home." she said, without even looking in my direction.

"I was just wondering if I could get a picture with you?" I asked while outstretching my hand with the £1 coins. She looked at me then looked at my hand, and her face lit up.

"I love you!" she exclaimed, hugging me then introducing herself. "I can't believe you are going to give me money," she said with a big smile.

"I wouldn't ask to take your picture and not give you money!" I said back.

Tim took a quick picture of us sticking our tongues out, then we went back to wandering the streets.

We finished our drinks and browsed a tourist shop where we looked up Tim's last name and found information on its Scottish origin. The last name was claimed to originally come from vikings who settled in Scotland. We joked about how much this explained. Mostly due to his beard and his way of cussing. For the first time in his life, Tim had stopped shaving altogether, from the time we started our hike on the Pacific Crest Trail to this point in Europe. So by now it had been over a year. His hair was light brown, but his big beard grew out dark red. If he had a hat or a hood on he looked like Yukon Cornelius from *Rudolph the Red-Nosed Reindeer*.

Around the time we were in Scotland, Donald Trump unfortunately made a trip there as well. The Internet was full of viral insults the Scottish virtually hurled at the man. Things like "toupeed fucktrumpet," "mangled apricot hellbeast," or even "tiny fingered, Cheeto-faced, ferret wearing shitgibbon." These insults were uncannily and hilariously similar to how Tim hurled obscenities at people or things which attracted his ire. If something wasn't going his way, random sentences such as "son of a ninja's dick-knuckle" would fly out of his mouth. Ah, the Scottish blood must run strong through this one.

Tim and I exited the store and decided on taking our first and only paid tour in Europe. It was already three and a half months in, with two weeks left, so why not. We wan-

dered a musty, flashlight-lit underground close and its preserved houses, standing in bedrooms children died from
the plague in, hearing their stories from a guide dressed
of the era. After our tour we went back to our sunset spot
under the castle, watching people below us step in dog poo
and having a stranger ask us if we had weed.

We booked an extra night at our hostel and welcomed
a new girl to our room. She was young and from Los Angeles, and even though she had just gotten to Edinburgh,
was complaining she had to return back to Los Angeles
for important medication. She stayed up what seemed like
all night long packing her bags, using the bathroom light
with the door propped open to light the entire small room
instead of courteously using the thirty second fuck light. I
fell asleep listening to the sound of rain and thunder, until
another roommate's alarm went off throughout the entire
morning without them seeming to notice. My knee was
also throbbing throughout the night.

We woke up late for bangers and mash with caramelized
onion gravy and bad coffee. Then some whiskey-casked local thistle cider in fancy Celt glasses. While sipping our cider, Tim told me the girl who had been packing until six in
the morning had a bag of medication sitting on the ground
all night that was labeled for organ transplant patients. I
guess she wasn't kidding about needing to get back.

Our last night was spent writing postcards we had collected all over Europe, packing our things, then getting another night of bad sleep. We had one more morning of bad
coffee before walking the city with my clown to catch a bus
out of the main station.

When the bus pulled up I got my first pick of seats up on the second story, grabbing the first two I saw right over the bathroom near the stairs so no one could sit behind us and we'd have some extra space. The bus smelled of fish, and once we started going I think the movement kicked up something in the bathroom. As the fish smell dissipated, a diarrhea smell took its place. Eventually we got up and moved to an area less vomit-inducing and stared out the windows at passing fields, listening to music in our headphones, rolling away from Scotland.

Leeds/ Hebden Bridge/ Heptonstall: You Know when Someone Has a Urinal Tattoo Everything's Gonna be Cool

We arrived at the Leeds bus station and walked through town with our backpacks on, dragging the large clown painting wrapped in packing paper. The plan was to either explore Leeds for a few hours or book it straight to Tim's old friend Star's house, which was about an hour outside of town on the train. Star used to own a venue and record store in the late 90's in San Diego, and lived in a punk house only a few blocks over from it; which is how Tim came to be friends with her and her partner at the time. We sat in a shopping area and people-watched while trying to make our decision. Tim texted a friend of ours from home who was also in Leeds, seeing if they wanted to meet up, while I eavesdropped on a woman's phone conversation about Pokemon.

The people of Leeds were very fashionable, yet many seemed a little too into spray tan. Young twenty-some-things walked by in their retro hipster fashion, designer brands, platform shoes, and orange skin, giggling or talking on their cell phones as they walked the shopping center. I felt like I was in a futuristic British version of *Clueless*.

With no response from the nearby friend, we left Leeds for Hebden Bridge. Star was busy for part of the day and told us we could wander the small town of Hebden Bridge or Heptonstall, about a mile further down the road, which is where she actually lived.

Since we were heading out of the city, I imagined Star's neighborhood as a cookie-cutter suburb. A beige colored sea of matching houses all of the Leeds shopping district hipsters would live in with their parents. Instead we departed the train to a misty little medieval town. If you could even call it a town. More like a neighborhood.

"Which way do we go?" I asked Tim.

"I don't know, but it looks like there's only one street," he replied.

We walked through thick trees over a small bridge, then a few blocks along a river speckled with adorable vintage-looking house boats in all different colors. We walked through a grassy park with a hillside of dark green trees on one side and rows of medieval-looking grey brick buildings on the other. A hidden side of a building over the water had "I Love Crack" spray painted in large black lettering. "Hmm," we said, critiquing the graffiti with hands on our chin as if at a museum, then laughing. Besides someone's public expression of love for crack, the town was spotless. Everyone moved around with somewhere to go, saying hello to their neighbors as they passed.

We found the old town center and sat on a bench to decide what to do. Tim texted Star letting her know we found the center of old town and she, confused, wrote back "that is *the* town." We connected to the WIFI of a nearby restaurant and checked our maps to see what else was nearby.

A drunk man sat down at an outside table of a restaurant and started to chat with the customers. Tim asked me if I was hungry, but our conversation was loudly interrupted by a restaurant guest becoming offended by the drunken man and then screaming at him to leave. Her table of friends stood up as support, as her and another man tried to drag the drunk man away from their table. He stumbled and fell while slurring cuss words at the top of his lungs, his hat flinging off his head after being pushed by the woman. The restaurant staff came out and announced the police would be called if he didn't leave, so he stumbled across the street toward us, magically pulled a tall-can of beer from his things as a magician would with a rabbit, then struggled to pop open the beer and take a sip without tipping over. He continued to cuss under his breath until an acquaintance of his walked up calling him by name, then grabbing him by the neck of his shirt.

"What are you doing, man?!" he yelled in the drunk's face. "These people are trying to eat, you're embarrassing yourself, go home!" The drunk man listened and then sloppily struggled to ride his bike down the empty road.

Now that our entertainment was over, we decided to take Star's advice of trying a local beer at the Fox and Goose Inn which was just up the street. There Star and her boyfriend would meet us and show us to her house up the hill another mile or so.

In the United States a lot of small towns consist of unfriendly rednecks and poor folk. This town surprisingly seemed very middle class, hippie, was called the lesbian capital of the UK, and even had a big punk venue in a neighboring town. Even the punk band Doom had a member or two living nearby. Some houses were also government funded housing for low income or disabled families and you would never know which ones were and which were owned by more upper class families.

We walked past hippie stores and a grocery co-op until we saw the pub on our right-hand side. The Fox and Goose was originally just a traditional neighborhood local's pub with an extensive specialized beer selection, but after the owner became ill and decided to close the pub the locals decided to all pitch in to keep it alive, turning the pub into a co-op. We walked in and took a seat. The locals eyed us, being tourists with backpacks in an un-touristy town always got us looks. Three men greeted us with thick British accents, introducing themselves from their bar stools as the bartender stood up to pour us a drink. Realizing we didn't have cash, Tim ran to the ATM at the grocery co-op while I waited with our things for Star. The men at the bar asked where we were from, then nicely offered me a beer on their tab while I wait. I graciously denied it, since he would be back soon, then tried a tasty local beverage once Tim returned.

Halfway through our beers, Star and her boyfriend Tom appeared. Star was in her early 40's, tattooed up to her neck, and wearing a low-cut black dress. Her long hair with bangs was half black and half bright teal, she had a small heart tattooed under her eye, and always had a big smile. After catching up for a bit, Star recommended an open mic night going on soon at another pub. For the rest of our stay her daughter would be with us so our adventures would have to stay somewhat kid-friendly, but this night Millie was staying with a friend so our options were open. We went to Star's house to drop off our backpacks then headed to the open mic.

The locals' acts consisted of mostly acoustic covers. People kept coming up to ask Star why she wasn't on stage, but due to a cut finger she wasn't feeling up to playing her songs, which were mostly originals. On our way out a man with face tattoos was frustratedly trying to defend himself to a man asking too many questions. As we walked past he stopped his sentence and turned to Star.

"Ask her... Why would someone tattoo their face?" he demandingly pleaded out of frustration.

"Why not?" Star replied without missing a beat while walking. "Why not..."

The next morning we went out for veggie dogs and "Vanilla Ice Coffee" at a nearby cafe owned by friends of Star's. The three of us then stopped by the grocery co-op for taco supplies and arrived back at the house in time for Millie to be dropped off by the school bus. Millie was an excitable twelve-year-old, always ready to tell you about her favorite TV shows or share unusual facts about anything from types of metal to our solar system. Millie took me and Tim to a park a block from the house where you could see amazing views of nearby fields and forest.

Tom and Star met up with us and we walked the opposite direction to an old cemetery and abandoned cathedral ruins. On the walk home we found an alley archway inscribed with the year 1578, and even found an old stockade against the wall of an auto shop. We walked back to the house and I sat in the backyard petting the cat until Tim and Star were done making tacos.

Since Millie is autistic, tacos were a big milestone and cause for excitement for her and Star. It was the first meal Millie would eat with different types of food ingredients all mixed together. Millie held her tacos, singing out the ingredients from a taco song she had showed us online. Eventually we were all singing about tacos and going back for seconds in the form of taco bowls, a mixture of the leftover ingredients plopped into a bowl and topped with fresh salsa.

During dinner Star grabbed my arm to look at the urinal I have tattooed on it (no, I'm not even joking, I have a urinal tattooed on my arm), "Is this *Fountain*?!" she yelled out.

"Yep," I responded. The urinal signed with a fake name was one of Marcel Duchamp's readymade art pieces from the Dada "anti-art" art movement, which formed during World War I in Zürich. Dada artwork was mostly nonsensical and a form of protest against the war. It also led the way to Surrealism. The ridiculousness of it as a movement both politically and artistically holds a place in my heart. Which is why I decided to tattoo a few of its iconic pieces across my shoulder under the quote by Max Ernst, "Art has nothing to do with taste, art is not there to be tasted." We were in Europe during Zürich's celebration of one hundred years of Dada, but unfortunately we never made it to Switzerland.

Star continued to check out my Dada tattoos, excited as a fellow artist and art history nerd. "You know when you meet someone and they have a Dada tattoo including Duchamp's *Fountain* that everything is gonna be cool!"

The next day Millie was taken swimming by a friend while the rest of us went hiking. We hiked an hour of green forest next to a rushing river. We passed large stump-like ant hills that, out of an unfortunate personal experience, Star informed us were *not* seats. We finished the hike with ice cream and met Millie at the house for pizza and salad.

In the morning we talked over tea and caramelized onion hummus before catching a ride back to the train station. After finding a stockade and ancient archway in such a small neighborhood without any real tourism, I decided to look up the town's history while snacking on my breakfast. As it turned out, Sylvia Plath's grave was roughly two blocks from where I was sitting in Star's kitchen drinking my tea. Before heading out we decided to go see it in the old cemetery near the cathedral ruins.

Star, Tom, and Millie gave us a ride to the train station where we said our goodbyes and thanked them for their hospitality. The train took us to Leeds where we walked back through the shopping district to the bus station. On our way, we stopped into a store for snacks and cider for the bus trip to London. Tim paid for our things as I stood off to one side, yet for some reason the cashier wanted to card both of us. It was pretty obvious we were both well over eighteen (thanks, though). It also caught us off guard since this was the first and only time we had been carded anywhere in Europe. Of course it had to happen now, on our second to last day, with my wallet shoved deep into a pocket in the backpack I was wearing and my arms were occupied juggling a massive hobo clown painting.

"Um, okay, but this is going to take me a minute," I said, pulling everything down one at a time. After a successful transaction, we were back at the Leeds main bus station awaiting our Megabus.

The Megabus line spanned across the station. There was only one sign for Megabus patrons to line up at, so ticket holders for multiple destinations were all lined up together in anticipation for the first come first serve seating. When a bus came, half of the line would leave and the rest would stay and move forward. It really didn't make any sense. While waiting in this unorganized line, we watched a couple who didn't know the drill, or lack thereof, not notice their bus until it was pulling away. They ran outside yelling "wait!" swinging their bags over their heads to catch the attention of the driver. Without even giving them a second glance, the driver pulled away and out of the station. "*Oooohhh*," the line chanted in unison while wincing.

We boarded our bus and I tried my best to work through the crowd to get the perfect seats. Not too close to the bathroom, not too close to fussy babies. Then somehow, I ended up getting top row front seats. These you normally have to pay to reserve in America. But here we were, getting best seat in the house, or, bus. One woman situated her things in the two seats on the right side of the front row while her husband loaded their bags below. Since she was blocking the aisle I waited about a foot behind her, making it clear I was headed for the other two empty seats. She seemed to be blocking the aisle so no one else could even try to get them. The woman took her time, looking at the seats I wanted then looking back at the two she had already claimed. It was obvious I was ruining her plan to take the front four for herself. Not only did she want the best seats, but she wanted *all* of the best seats. There was no way I was going to let her and her husband be that selfish. I was preparing myself to sit on a lap if needed be. Thankfully after a few minutes she sighed and let me through. I settled into my seat, followed by Tim, and the bus pulled away - right as two young women ran out of the door waving their hands for the bus to stop. But off we went.

London: Like I Owned the Place

We were back in London for the first time in four months. We jumped on the Tube to the Camden neighborhood and arrived to the town dark and asleep. We walked the wrong way to our hostel, admiring the graffiti and wondering how we had not ventured out to this part of

London before. After realizing we were going the wrong way, we spun ourselves around and eventually made it to the correct address. We then found ourselves trying multiple wrong doors before finding the correct door into the building. I walked up to the check in counter while swinging my backpack onto a couch. Check in was at the bar, which was fairly empty.

"Have you been here before?" the man at the counter inquired.

"Nope." I responded casually.

"You walked in like you owned the place so I figured you might know your way around."

"Nah, this is just our twentieth country in four months... I don't even know how many hostels that would be? So I guess you could say I'm familiar with the routine."

We ordered drinks while the man tried to get the credit card machine to work. We only had this night and the next to see Camden, yet we planned for this night to be spent doing laundry.

Many countries in Europe have a fast setting and an extremely slow regular setting on their washers. Hostel workers are usually very adamant about pointing this out, especially on washers whose instructions are not in English. Even though the hostel made sure to inform us of the short versus long settings, the information didn't seem to stick to the person using the washer ahead of us. They chose the multiple hour wash setting. We were going to have to stay up most of the night to get our one load of laundry done.

Our small room was hot and stuffy with rickety, squeaky bunks. Not the nicest hostel we had stayed in, but the location was good and the bar was an actual, hip, large pub open to the public, not just for the guests. This was nice yet it was also a bit awkward having to sit on the pristine leather stools, at the perfectly polished wood bar, in the dim blue lights with bumping jukebox, surrounded by dressed up bar hoppers in our pajamas sipping on a beer while our laundry was being done. After a late night up, we woke to roommates banging around at 7 AM, then got ready to explore Camden Market.

The neighborhood Camden Market was in looked amazing, the murals, the art, the stalls of junk. But in reality it was kind of a tourist trap, and every stall sold almost the same thing. The market went on forever. Crowds flooded the aisles, food carts lined the walkways. Tim ate some free chicken out of the trash. After a few hours of watching hipsters eat from a cereal bar, wandering into goth stores, and eating British Mexican food, we grabbed a bottle of smoked cherrywood beer to split along a small restaurant-lined river in the center of another small crowd. We chatted with a man who had a white pit bull named Casper. Tim instantly fell in love with Casper, letting him lick all over his face. A friend of the man came up with a bar of chocolate, asking if he could feed it to Casper.

"Hell no man, what are you thinking?" he responded.

"Oh. Damn, I don't know what dogs eat," he replied back.

It was our last night in Europe. We went to a grocery store to grab candy bars and Pot Noodles to bring back to the US with us, with our smuggled absinthe from Prague and Pfeffi from Germany. There in the cooler sat something Tim and I had been avoiding for four months: tequila flavored beer. It was everywhere. In almost every country. It was cheap. And it sounded disgusting.

"We should just try it," Tim laughed. "Just one."

"Why not, it's our last night!" I responded, cringing already. We took a seat against the wall outside of our hostel and each tasted the beer.

"Wow!" I said, my eyes widening. "It's actually not bad. It doesn't taste like tequila at all though. It tastes more like Bud Lime."

Tim took a sip of the beer then looked at me. "We could have been drinking this the whole time!"

"It's not *that* good." I laughed.

We finished our tequila beer which didn't taste like tequila, then went back to the store for another. Our hostel's bar sold them, but it was much cheaper to buy them from the market then drink them against the wall outside, where we could still get a bit of WIFI. After, we went inside to sleep in our bunks for the last time in Europe.

We woke up on our last morning in Europe exhausted. I threw everything into my backpack, put on comfortable clothes for spending the day on a plane, and headed downstairs to wait for Tim as I snacked on the continental breakfast options and charged my phone at the bar. I was feeling a little rough. A hostel employee gave us directions to the Tube, and we took off with the clown painting under one arm and headed for Heathrow airport.

We were making decent time, but while waiting to transfer from one train to another I went to check the time and realized my phone was nowhere to be found. I frantically checked my pockets and backpack pockets. I had forgotten it charging at the hostel. The thought of just ditching it ran through my head, but I had no money to buy another smartphone, plus all of my information and pictures were on it. I really needed my phone. Tim waited in the station with our things while I hopped on a train heading back to Camden. I speed walked and jogged the few blocks right into the door, where the hostel employees handed me my forgotten phone. I ran back to the station and was let in by a security guard I explained my situation to so I didn't have to pay twice, then made my way back to Tim.

We jumped on a train to the airport, now running quite a bit behind on time. It was a long, stressful ride to the airport, where we then realized our airline was listed on two different terminals. We figured the international terminal must be the correct one, but were informed the opposite after arriving there. Tim and I ran back to the airport shuttle and out onto terminal four, hoping it was the correct terminal. Not only was it correct, but thankfully our flight was also delayed. If it wasn't, there would have been no way we would have made our flight on time. We were still panicked, thinking that our flight wasn't going to have free food and drinks like our arriving flight to Europe, yet we were in luck. We sat down in our seats, pulled out the free blanket and pillow, put in headphones, and relaxed enjoying the free drinks and movies.

I was too exhausted to have any real feelings about our trip to Europe officially being done. In fact, it hadn't actually set in. I blindly followed the familiar routine of moving from one place to another, focusing only on being comfortable in the present moment. At this point we had no plans for landing in Philly, no plans for the next part of our lives. I was disappointed we were so close to ending up back in California with just our backpacks and no money, expecting to be thrown full force into the soul-sucking daily grind of scrubbing toilets and paying bills. That time would come when it did, but at this point I would occupy myself by basking in the high of the life we'd been living. Enjoying the last remaining feelings of sweat-caked tan skin, dreaming of vegan cheesesteak.

Back to America: You Can't Go Home Again

We arrived to a 90-degree Philadelphia. Quite a shock compared to London. America! Good ol' 90-degree America! Of course we're flying into Philly at the same time as the Democratic National Convention. We had no clue until we reached the airport, scrambling to find a place to stay. We reactivated our phones and spent hours searching for any type of lodging. Even a shitty motel on the edge of town was either fully booked or $500 a night. We sluggishly started to drag ourselves and our backpacks across town in the sun, when Tim received a message from Mary, an acquaintance of his, saying we could stay with her in South Philly for a few days. We felt bad imposing, especially jet lagged, but couldn't say no.

While walking to Mary's house, we passed two young women having a conversation. "That dude is money, his whole family is money," one of them said.

Oh yeah, slang! I thought. I don't have to watch my slang anymore in order for people to understand me. In fact, I could say dollar without having to correct myself too. All of these things that were part of me for my entire life were now novelties. I could use my cell phone however I wanted. I could search the web and pull up a map if we got lost. Everything was back to normal, yet it felt there was still a transition process we were going through.

We arrived to Mary's two story apartment where she introduced us to her dogs and her roommate. The minute my butt hit the couch I was struggling with all of my being to keep my eyelids from closing.

"I'm guessing you guys want to go out to bars or museums or something?" Mary said.

Hell no, I thought. "We're pretty jet lagged, honestly just hanging out here and having a beer then going to sleep kind of early sounds amazing." I said instead.

It occurred to me as it did on the Pacific Crest Trail that people haven't comprehended all that we'd been through, and there is no way I could or would expect them to. And it wasn't just that our friends had to host us, but we felt we had to be active guests in return. Mary was nice enough to let us stay, so we were trying our bests to pep ourselves up to seem lively and gracious of her hospitality instead of rude, brain dead zombies.

Thankfully after a night's rest Tim and I were feeling refreshed and ready to explore Philly. We jumped in Mary's car and drove around town, stopping to visit an empty lot where once sat the abandoned house Tim lived in in the early 2000's.

"I need to run into this store real quick, if you don't mind," Tim said as we passed a liquor store. He ran in and came out with a Philly cheesesteak and a tall can, for old time's sake.

Mary took us to a park her dogs could run around in as the sun started to set. We each cracked open a cold beer from a six-pack we bought to split and watched the fireflies start to appear. We talked and laughed until it started getting late, then returned to her place to sleep.

The next day Tim and I decided to wander downtown and South Street on our own before spending a few days in New York and catching our flight back to California. As we were walking, we stumbled on a large museum with signs for a free exhibit called *Truth to Power*. Tim and I entered and were awe struck by the pieces on display. Inside of the entrance sat nearly a hundred fake guns strung up with clear string, as if they were floating. Their shape created an outline of the United States. As we walked the side profile changed to the outline of one large handgun. On one wall was an American flag created from pieces of colorful Mexican blankets. There were pieces displaying rape statistics and a lifelike painting of Kim Kardashian wearing a punk jacket. One painting showed a cop stopping another from beating a handcuffed black man with his nightstick. There were pieces about student debt and homelessness. There was so much meaning and power behind each piece it engulfed the room in heaviness, hopelessness, inspiration, and ambition for change. We left the museum feeling grateful we were able to experience such a meaningful and beautiful exhibit.

Even though we would be flying out of Philadelphia airport and had already spent a week in Brooklyn before departing for Europe, I wanted to spend a few more days in New York before taking off. Lodging was still pricey and hard to come by in Philly, and we didn't want to wear out our welcome with Mary and her roommate. Also the Museum of Modern Art was having an exhibit on Dada, which was fitting since we missed seeing the exhibit in Zürich. We took a bus to Brooklyn, where we would be staying with a few women from the area who had a spare bedroom.

We wandered Brooklyn, hanging out with bodega cats and stopping for Little Caesars, then made our way to Times Square and the museum. We rented city bikes and decided to ride them from Central Park to Tompkins Square Park just for the hell of it. It was kind of a big deal for me, since just before our trip I was afraid to ride a bike near car traffic. Within just a few months I went from being afraid to ride around cars to riding from Vienna to Budapest, across Berlin and Copenhagen, and now across Manhattan at rush hour.

Our time on the East Coast had been fun, but it was coming to an end. We had to get on a bus back to Philly for our flight. Of course we did the same thing when traveling to London. Staying with a friend in Brooklyn then taking a bus to sleep in the Philadelphia airport. The funny thing about it was both flights had an immediate layover in New

York. It's funny to think of all the backwards things we did to save a few hundred bucks.

Tim and I were greeted in San Diego by California sunshine, burritos, beach days with friends, and even a generator punk show in a sewer. The clown painting safely made it to the attic of a family member's house until we could find our own place to hang it in. We immediately went back to hustling to make ends meet. The magical dreamlike mentality of floating across continents however we wanted quickly faded and we went back to working and hanging out as if it had never happened at all.

Two years after returning from Europe, as Tim and I were successfully settled in El Cajon, I visited Oakland after four years of leaving it and two years since moving our things out of our storage unit in Hayward. I was by myself, traveling for work, yet spending my free time having drinks with old friends. Oakland felt like a different place. I felt I was in a dream, where I knew where I was but nothing looked the same. The people, the buildings, everything was different. The trees and buildings had grown taller. The Berkeley hippies and homeless had been replaced with food-delivering robots roaming the sidewalks, and my favorite punk dive bar had a new look featuring "Edison" light bulbs. I used to go there by myself after working rough, soul-crushing retail shifts, continuing to subconsciously nod and smile at everyone around me as if I was still on the clock, coming to my senses to realize I was awkwardly silently greeting people with face tattoos in dark corners of the bar who stared back confused. Where had home gone? We had left San Diego for just as long, even longer if you combine the years we'd left in our early twenties, and it too had gone through similar changes. An area which was once littered in record stores and hole-in-the-wall punk venues was now flooded with seas of club-goers drunkenly tripping over their high heels. Although I still considered these physical places home, because they were all that I knew, home had taken on a different meaning all together. Home wasn't a destination anymore, but a spontaneous and fleeting motion. Oakland and San Diego were familiar and comfortable, yet foreign and ever changing places. They had the sunshine and smells and people we longed to be with, yet there was an empty space making us feel like we never quite fit back in. Our true home had become an uncomfortable routine of spontaneity and exhausting adventure. Our home was longing for whatever was next. The anticipation of whatever miles were left to walk, whichever bus was left to take. My home is my backpack, and I have everything I need.

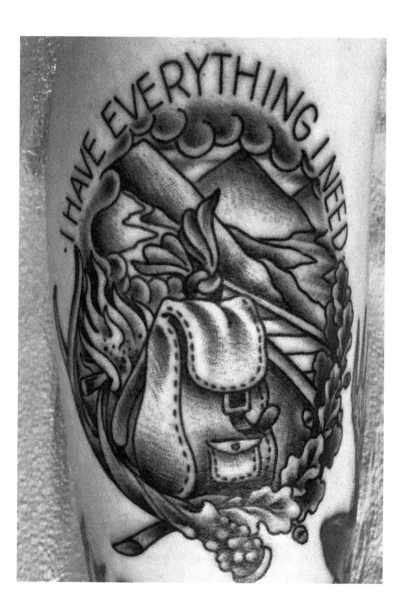

Where are They Now?

After returning to San Diego, Tim and Bridget got married on top of a jacuzzi in the forest of Idyllwild, where Bridget spent her first day as a married woman watching her husband sing to Taylor Swift karaoke while high on mushrooms. As of this book being published, they are both working legit full-time jobs while sneaking away every long weekend and holiday to travel more. Tim spends his weekends waking up before 5 AM to hike, while Bridget spends quite a bit of time writing. She finally got a job with her degree as a full-time remote field photographer, and gets to travel the country taking pictures of buildings. Tim decided to go to college part-time, taking his first class since 1999. Their plans for the future are up in the air, since they are constantly dreaming of what possible new adventures could be had. You can find more of Bridget's work and stories at www.roamsandwrites.com.

Acknowledgments

The dedication of this book mentions thanks to all who have helped Tim and me, or who we've had in our thoughts, but I would like one last chance to give thanks to Stephen Courtney for helping me edit *I Have Everything I Need*. I would also like to honor the memory of his brother James Courtney. Of course I couldn't have done it all without my husband and best travel partner, Tim Houchins! Thanks for being there to pick cactus thorns out of my butt.

I would also like to give credit to those whose works have been quoted throughout the book, including song lyrics from *Alternative Ulster* by Stiff Little Fingers (Inflammable Material, Rough Trade Records, 1979) on page 119, *I'll Be There For You* by The Rembrandts (East West, Atlantic, 1995) on page 150, *DBS Out* by Days n Daze (Rogue Taxidermy, 2013) on page 389, *You Cannot Kill Us* by Tom Lunden (1976) on page 405, and *Departure Arrival* by Mischief Brew (Smash the Windows, Fistolo Records, 2005) on page 413. Passages from written works include a quote from *The Letters of Jack London* (Jack London, Stanford University Press, 1988) on page 107, Jon Krakauer's *Into The Wild* (Anchor Books, 1996) on page 82, *Yogi's PCT Handbook* (Jackie McDonnell, 2014) on page 34, and from Bill Bryson's *A Walk in the Woods* (Broadway Books, Penguin Random House, 1997) on page 79. The chapter title "You Can't Go Home Again" was inspired by the quote "...there are three things you just can't do in life. You can't beat the phone company, you can't make a waiter see you until he's ready to see you, and you can't go home again." by Bill Bryson's *The Lost Continent: Travels in Small Town America* (HarperCollins Publishers 1989, William Morrow Paperbacks 1990). As you can tell I like his books, so go buy them. Tattoo on page 451 by Samuel Townsley @samhain_grim.

Thank you so much for supporting me by purchasing, borrowing, or stealing this book (just kidding?). This is my first attempt at professional writing and self-publishing, so if you would like to support me further, feel free to leave a review on Goodreads or Amazon, subscribe to my blog at roamsandwrites.com, and find me on Instagram @roamsandwrites.

What I Brought: *Pacific Crest Trail*

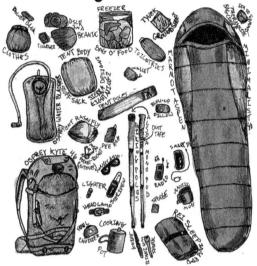

Check my blog to see how my hiking gear has changed. Some items carried by Tim

- Backpack: Osprey Kyte 46

- Tent: Sierra Designs Lightning 2

- Sleeping: Marmot Aspen Minimalist 40 sleeping bag with Sea to Summit Thermolite liner, REI Trekker sleeping pad, blow up pillow, Tyvek groundsheet

- Eating/Drinking: Cooking pot, MSR pocket rocket stove and fuel canister, lighter, tinfoil DIY wind blocker, titanium spork, plastic mug (which was also used as a bowl), knife, 1 gallon Ziploc bag of food, mini sponge, Steripen, Osprey water bladder 2.5 liter

- Electronics: Canon SL1 dSLR, iPhone, power bank, chargers, head lamp, small radio

- Clothes (Worn or in Stuff Sack): 2 Exofficio underwear, puffy jacket, sports bra, 2 Injinji socks, 1 pair thick sleep socks, fleece leggings, running pants, trail runners, sun hat, running shorts, tank top, long sleeve sun shirt, beanie (doubled as camera bag)

- Toiletries in Mini Ultralight Bag: Toilet paper, baby wipes, tooth brush & paste, sunscreen, chapstick, hand sanitizer, floss, nail clippers, hair ties, mini deodorant, soap (for in town)

- First Aid (in Same Bag as Toiletries): Headache meds, Pepto chews, Benadryl, Technu, period stuff, inhaler, bandages, electrolyte pills, water purifying tabs, other wound closures/gauze pads, moleskin (duct tape does the same thing), antibiotic ointment, waterproof matches
- Misc: Hiking poles, sewing needle, permits & maps, duct tape (wrapped on hiking poles), clean bandana, pee rag, glasses & sun glasses, cuben fiber wallet, compass, ear plugs, sun umbrella

What I Brought: *Europe*

- Backpack: Osprey Kyte 46
- Sleeping: Marmot Aspen Minimalist 40 sleeping bag with Sea to Summit Thermolite liner, blow up pillow, ultralight tarp
- Electronics: Canon SL1 dSLR, iPhone, power bank, chargers, iPad, outlet adaptor, headphones
- Clothes (Worn or in Stuff Sack): 3 Exofficio underwear, sports bra, 4 socks, 1 pair of jeans, denim skirt, trail runners, running shorts, 2 tank tops, t shirt, long sleeve shirt, flannel long sleeve shirt, sweatshirt, ultralight rain jacket, beanie (doubled as camera bag)
- Toiletries in Mini Ultralight Bag: tooth brush & paste, sunscreen, chapstick, floss, nail clippers, hair ties, mini deodorant, soap, reusable makeup removing cloth, q-tips
- First Aid (in Same Bag as Toiletries): Headache meds, Pepto chews, Benadryl, period stuff, inhaler, bandages, water purifying tabs, other wound closures/gauze pads, moleskin, antibiotic ointment, nasal spray
- Misc: Sewing needle, clean bandana, pee rag, glasses & sun glasses, wallet & passport, ear plugs, titanium spork, pencil and small notebook, padlock and key, cheap jewelry, sometimes scissors, a very small beach towel I carried for a few countries, a mini mascara and liquid eyeliner, snacks, a few knickknacks bought, lightweight packable day bag (REI Stuff Travel Pack)

Vallela Vallela in Nice

Found NAPOLI ANTIFASCISTA

CAFE "MUST" BE BLUE

Brussels

Found HOMOPHOBIE NEIN DANKE

Creepy ass sheets

DEVILS SLIDE TRAIL

Wiener Pumpe

Krakow bar in shopping center

RIP Chris Upham